DEATH BEFORE DISMOUNT

DEATH BEFORE DISMOUNT

U.S. Army Tanks in Iraq

DR. ANDREW ERIC WRIGHT SR.

CASEMATE
Pennsylvania & Yorkshire

Published in the United States of America and Great Britain in 2025 by
CASEMATE PUBLISHERS
1950 Lawrence Road, Havertown, PA 19083, USA
and
47 Church Street, Barnsley, S70 2AS, UK

Hardcover Edition: ISBN 978-1-63624-475-4
Digital Edition: ISBN 978-1-63624-476-1

A CIP record for this book is available from the British Library

Printed and bound in the United Kingdom by CPI Group (UK) Ltd, Croydon, CR0 4YY
Typeset in India by DiTech Publishing Services

For a complete list of Casemate titles, please contact:

CASEMATE PUBLISHERS (US)
Telephone (610) 853-9131
Fax (610) 853-9146
Email: casemate@casematepublishers.com
www.casematepublishers.com

CASEMATE PUBLISHERS (UK)
Telephone (0)1226 734350
Email: casemate@casemateuk.com
www.casemateuk.com

Front cover image: Alpha Company, 2nd Battalion, 116th Cavalry Regiment, conducts table six tank crew qualification Feb. 4, 2019, Orchard Combat Training Center. (U.S. Army/Sgt. Mason Cutrer)

The Publisher's authorised representative in the EU for product safety is Authorised Rep Compliance Ltd., Ground Floor, 71 Lower Baggot Street, Dublin D02 P593, Ireland.
http://www.arccompliance.com

Contents

Acknowledgements

There are several people that I would like to thank for their help with this book. I want to first thank my God, for the strength that he has given me which allowed me to endure the lulls and emotional stress that writing a project of this magnitude can present. I want to thank my dissertation director at Liberty University, Dr. Martin Cantino, for his continued support, guidance, and constant availability during this process. I would also like to thank my two children Kaitlyn and Andrew Wright II. These two have supported me and allowed me to work. During this process, my daughter was a big help in making sure the house continued to run smoothly even as I spent late nights and early mornings in front of my laptop writing and researching. Without them, there would truly be a void in my life that would be impossible to fill. The veterans of the armored corps are the ones who gave this dissertation life. Every armor officer or NCO that was interviewed took time out of their life to talk about the armored corps and give their opinions about the army in general.

This work would truly not exist if it were not for the brave men of the army's armored corps. I also want to thank the 1st Infantry Division in Ft. Riley, KS, the 3rd Infantry Division in Ft. Stewart, GA, the 4th Infantry Division in Ft. Carson, CO, and the 1st Cavalry Division in Ft. Hood, TX. All of these duty stations allowed their senior leaders at the brigade and battalion levels to speak with me about tanks and their role during Operation *Iraqi Freedom*. This information was vital as it was able to illuminate the culture of the armor for many of the units today and allowed me to compare them to the units that took part in several key battles during OIF. For those I did not mention, please charge it to my head and not my heart. I truly appreciate every ounce of encouragement and direction I received during this process.

ARMORED BRIGADE COMBAT TEAM (ABCT)

TANK PLATOONS

Platoon Leader
First Lieutenant
19A00

Gunner
Sergeant
19K2O K4

Tank Driver
Specialist
19K1O K4

Tank Loader
Private First Class
19K1O K4

Platoon Sergeant
Sergeant First Class
19K4O K4

Gunner
Sergeant
19K2O K4

Tank Driver
Specialist
19K1O K4

Tank Loader
Private First Class
19K1O K4

Tank Commander
Staff Sergeant
19K3O K4

Gunner
Sergeant
19K2O K4

Tank Driver
Specialist
19K1O K4

Tank Loader
Private First Class
19K1O K4

Tank Commander
Staff Sergeant
19K3O K4

Gunner
Sergeant
19K2O K4

Tank Driver
Specialist
19K1O K4

Tank Loader
Private First Class
19K1O K4

ABCT ABRAMS TANK PLATOONS COMBINED ARMS BATTALIONS (CAB) & CAVALRY SQUADRONS				
	AR CAB1	AR CAB2	IN CAB	CAV SQDN	AC / NG // TOTAL
Platoons	6	6	3	3	198 / 90 // 288

288 Tank Platoon Leaders for Active and Guard Components

ARMORED BRIGADE COMBAT TEAM (ABCT) CAVALRY SQUADRON SCOUT PLATOONS

ABCT CAVALRY SQUADRON SCOUT PLATOONS			
	TRP	SQDN	AC / NG // TOTAL
Platoons	2	6	66 / 30 // 96
96 Cavalry Squadron Scout Platoon Leaders for Active and Guard Components			

Armored brigade combat team (ABCT) company, tank platoon formations.

BDU-era tanker boots. (Wikimedia Commons / Pretzelpaws)

Glossary

240	Machine gun used by loader.
.50-cal	.50-caliber machine gun used by tank commander.
IBCT	Infantry Brigade Combat Team.
1SG	First sergeant. Senior enlisted NCO at the company level.
ABOLC	Armor Basic Officers Leader Course.
ABCT	Armored Brigade Combat Team.
Battery	Artillery company.
BCO	Brigade Commanding Officer.
Can–round	Canister round. Tank main gun round used primarily for enemy-dismounted troops. Acts as a shotgun shell.
Captain/ CO (O-3)	Commanding officer at the company level.
COIN	Counter Insurgency Operations.
CLC	Cavalry Leaders Course.
CSM	Command sergeant major. Senior enlisted NCO at battalion level and above.
DCO	Deputy commanding officer. At the brigade/regiment level, the XO is not second in command but focuses on supplies, maintenance, and officer-related issues. The DCO is second in command and has the same authority as the commander.
HBCT	Heavy Brigade Combat Team.
HEAT	High Explosive Antitank. Tank main gun rounds used primarily for bunkers and other enemy positions.
Lt.	Lieutenant (O-1/2).
LTC	Lieutenant colonel (O-5). Rank of battalion commander.

MBT	Main Battle Tank.
MOUT	Military Operation in Urban Terrain.
NCO	Non-commissioned officer. Enlisted soldier equal to or above the rank of corporal. Specialist/corporal (E-4), note: A corporal is an NCO while a specialist is not.
PSG	Platoon sergeant. Senior enlisted NCO at platoon level.
Sabot	Tank main gun round, used primarily for other tanks or armored vehicles.
SFC	Sergeant first class (E-7).
Sgt.	Sergeant (E-5).
SSG	Staff sergeant (E-6).
Stryker	Medium Armored Vehicle Variant created for IBCT.
Troop	Cavalry company.
XO	Executive officer. In charge of maintenance and supplies at the company, battalion, brigade/regiment level. Second in command at company and battalion level.

Introduction

Tanks are a part of the history of our nation and the Abrams tank is one of the world's most powerful and destructive combat tanks. It has served as the main combat battle tank (MBT) throughout Operations *Iraqi Freedom* and *Enduring Freedom*. During Operation *Iraqi Freedom* (OIF), armor (tank) units were asked to confront the enemies of the United States and were placed in extremely hostile and dangerous areas. These units were asked to spearhead the nation's battle against Al-Qaeda and insurgents in Iraq (AQI). The United States Army's armor units had the highest kill rate of any American armor units.[1] They were such a powerful force that the insurgents had to completely change their tactics to account for the Abrams that they were facing.

Operation *Iraqi Freedom* shared similarities with the situation faced by the 1st Air Mobile Cavalry Division in Vietnam, namely the unfamiliar terrain and the determination of the enemy to fight. The key difference was that American forces did not have armor superiority in Vietnam, hence the different outcomes in strategic effectiveness. Tanks changed the game in OIF.[2] For the infantry to truly be effective and dominant, they need to have the backing of tanks so they may continue dismounted operations while having the firepower of a tank to overwatch their positions.

The army has become reliant on armor units over the years. This work explores why the armor units of the army were so successful, and what made them so much more effective at killing the enemy than other armor units in the U.S. military, by examining how the army used the Abrams tank strategically to effect success in five major battles during OIF: the "Thunder Run" raids into Baghdad (2003), the second battle of Fallujah (2004),

Ramadi (2006), Baqubah (2007), and Sadr City (2008). These battles were vital to victory in Iraq, and in them tank-heavy task forces were put together to lay siege on or attack enemy forces.[3] Each of them was either completely changed or significantly aided by the presence and efficiency of U.S. Army armor units in the area. Well trained and well equipped, they provided armored support and devastating firepower that the enemy could not counter.

The army's armor units were one of the primary tools of success and efficiency in these key battles. The notion that American tanks are powerful and without equal during this "golden age of tankers" can certainly be argued,[4] and many modern military works discuss how tanks are used—making them seem invincible and without equal on the battlefield—but not all consider the valuable role of tankers. For example, a 2019 article by Maj. Amos C. Fox, "On the Employment of Armor," discusses how the tanks of the U.S. Army should be deployed in combat situations in Iraq. He argues that tanks were vital to combat operations in Iraq. He also discusses how conditions meant that the need for the leadership of an experienced or competent armor officer was even greater; someone who knows how to deploy their tanks in a manner that can be an asset to ground forces as well as achieve the mission—tanks need to be put in the right position to be able to be as combat effective as possible. Having tanks in too small an area is just as problematic as having them in a space that is too large without enough friendly armor to cover your rear. Fox discusses the armor almost as a group of machines that need to be placed properly. This book aims to dismiss that ideology by placing the focus on the men who operate the machines—it argues that armor units were so dominant due to the training and ability of the men who were inside the turret: men who, trained to the high standard maintained since the early 1990s and Operation *Desert Storm/Desert Shield*, were able to seamlessly transition into combat during the beginning of OIF. Without that connection between the human element and the amazing marvel that is the Abrams tank, the historiography of armor during this conflict will not be complete or whole. Both mounted and dismounted combat will be explored for their differences in combat and garrison.

The history of tanks in American warfighting is a rich one. From the time General Patton instituted an armor training center for tankers after World War II, tankers have benefited from the style of soldiering that could only be found in armor units.[5] This work will decipher what made the army's tankers unique and how they were able to function as a cohesive unit inside the turret of a 70-ton machine and fight the enemies of America during the Invasion of Iraq.

The first two chapters of the book focus on the anatomy of the tanker—how they are trained, the differences between tankers and other combat jobs in the military (MOS, or military operational specialties), and the individual specs and capabilities of the MA1/A2 Sep battle tanks. Subsequent chapters will focus on the five major battles, covering the importance of each battle and the events leading up to the actual fighting, along with how tanks played a significant role in the outcome of each battle. The conclusion will then focus on why tanks are important; what makes them different to the infantry, cavalry, or field artillery; why they were needed during major fighting in Iraq and what combat might have looked like without them there. The whole book is built upon interviews with enlisted tankers (19K/Z) and armor officers (19A) who predominantly served between 2003 and 2009. Mainly undertaken remotely, these interviews feature veterans and active-duty soldiers from 1st, 3rd, and 4th Infantry Divisions, and the 1st Cavalry Division. (The U.S. Army has 22 armor or "tank" battalions, of which 14 lie within these four divisions.)

The history and battle techniques of the army's armored core in other military conflicts have been discussed in depth. But the role and usefulness of the tanks in Iraq have not yet been fully explored and studied, and the story of the tankers has been under-taught and under-studied. The stories of tankers have not been told in depth throughout the history of OIF. Most of the books about OIF have been written from the perspective of enlisted infantrymen or infantry officers. One of the reasons for this is the fact that the infantry was the closest to battle. Many military historians have stayed away from telling the story of the army's armored corps, but to leave this area of combat undiscussed or improperly studied is an insult to the tankers who fought and died during this conflict. It is also important that military historians examine every aspect of combat and relay that information back to researchers and students. This work will shine a light on the mounted side of combat and show why the tank and those who fought inside it were the best America had to offer during this portion of military history,[6] enabling the coalition forces to achieve victories or, at a minimum, to push the enemy away from these five major cities, thus permitting the population to grow and flourish again.

CHAPTER I

Basic Training and the Golden BDU Era

In a 2013 article, McKinney, Elfendahl, and McMaster—all armor or mechanized infantry-experienced officers—stated that the key contributor to the armored core of the army is the tankers. Without the training and capability of the men using the Abrams, the tank would simply be a 70-ton piece of equipment. These tankers found success because of their training.[1]

Through the years the armored core has become a breeding ground for disciplined armor crewmen. General George Patton had a profound effect on the armored core of the army. In 1940 he and Adna Chaffee Jr. (Chaffee is known in military history as the "father of the armored force") helped create a blueprint for how the army needed to transform into an armor-heavy force. This led to the creation of the 1st and 2nd Armored Divisions as well as training doctrine for the armored corps. Patton saw how difficult it was to defeat a determined enemy that had armored capability throughout their military. He knew that something had to be done to make the U.S. military more of a mechanized force that would have the capabilities to stand up to those who would choose to engage in a military conflict with this country in the future.[2] This type of thinking led to the formation of an Armor School which would allow both enlisted men and officers to go and train specifically on aspects of mounted warfare and tank battle: something that had not happened previously. During the inception of armor into the U.S. forces, men were simply picked and told that they would be operating tanks.

This type of involuntary admission into the armored core was adequate during the two World Wars. However, things needed to change if the armored core was going to stand at the forefront of the world's armor. Patton knew that the armored core needed a tradition of training men to ensure the brotherhood would take hold in the way that some of the other combat specialties had enjoyed up to that point. Fighting inside of a tank is simply different from other combat jobs—armor officers and enlisted men are different from other members of the military, both in garrison and in combat.[3]

While the structure of NCO-led men is prevalent in every combat aspect of the army, the actual training, discipline, and teamwork are different in a tank than in other jobs within the military. Every military training instructor across the services has the responsibility of turning civilians into entry-level service members. But, for those in the army who choose a combat MOS, their basic training is called OSUT or one-station unit training. Most non-combat, entry-level recruits go to basic training for 12 weeks, get some leave, and then are sent to their assigned duty station.[4]

For decades, men who wanted to be tankers for the army have been sent to Fort Knox, KY. This would come to be known as the home of the armor. Upon the recommendation of Lieutenant Colonel Adna R. Chaffee Jr. and Colonel Daniel Van Voorhis, Camp Knox was chosen to be the new headquarters for the mechanized cavalry in 1931, just a year after the mechanized force's creation. The size and terrain of Camp Knox made it a suitable area for such training.[5] So on January 1, 1932, Camp Knox was renamed Ft. Knox. From this point until their mass exodus to Ft. Benning (today known as Ft. Moore) in May of 2011, Ft. Knox became home to armor training. The unique culture for tankers started here.[6]

The mechanized cavalry was the staging point for things to come at Ft. Knox. The training of the cavalry was something of a test run for the army when it needed to make sure that the land and terrain were suitable for armored vehicles and their training. The cavalry by nature has always been the eyes of the armored force. It is their job to alert the commanders on the ground to the enemy's disposition and numbers.

This allows the armored force the capability to send troops in to counter the enemy in a manner that would achieve success.

It was important that Fort Knox immediately begin to conduct armored operations. Doctrine and training for cavalry officers were quickly set up, creating a standard that all officers followed.[7] That doctrine was important for both cavalry and armor. The armor and cavalry are the only military occupational specialties that have the same officers, meaning that armor and cavalry officers are trained the same way and have been since the armor training center came to Ft. Knox. After armor officers leave their entry-level basic course, they have been trained to operate on tanks in armor units, in a Bradley in armored cavalry units, and in Humvees in light cavalry units. By the time these young officers get to be battalion, brigade, or regiment commanders, they have the experience to lead all levels of combat. This gives armor officers (19A) the flexibility and knowledge to fight from within the mounted armored corps as a tank commander and from the ground as a reconnaissance unit leader in a light cavalry platoon.

With the outbreak of World War II in Europe, the American Army prepared with the creation of the armored force and headquartered it at Ft. Knox in the summer of 1940.[8] From that point forward, tank training was the cornerstone of Ft. Knox. Training shifted from giving those already in the army education about tanks and how they function, to training entry-level soldiers (privates) to be tankers in the armored corps.

The training of soldiers at Ft. Knox has evolved over time from a simple basic training area where soldiers were sent to indoctrinate themselves in the army values, to the Armor Training Center: a rite of passage that all tankers who served during Operation *Iraqi Freedom* would pass through. Basic training for tankers is different from that of many other basic training centers during this time.

Once someone went to an OSUT basic training, they had 10 weeks of training, a "family weekend," and then six more weeks of MOS-related training. Drill sergeants (U.S. Army basic training instructors) were tasked to do much more in an OSUT setting of the army than in any other setting in the U.S. military. They were asked not only to train civilians to be entry-level soldiers, but also to train them to be entry-level tankers, artillerymen, cavalry scouts, or infantrymen. These are the basic training areas that offer OSUT training.[9] From the very first time that they were brought into the military, tankers were taught the importance of teamwork, maintenance, and attention to detail. These are the cornerstone of all armor units, and how the young privates reacted and converted to that new way of life and teaching was one of the factors determining if those young men would be an asset to their tanker brothers once they got to their line units.[10]

Senior drill sergeants (senior enlisted instructors in a basic training platoon) implemented the training given to them by the commander.[11] Tankers who left basic training were expected to have the knowledge to enter their line unit as either a loader or driver.[12] Although these positions are entry-level, they are two of the most important aspects of a tank. The driver must know the limits and controls of the tank to make sure that it functions properly while being driven. The loader must know how to properly load the main gun, work the radios inside of the tank, and use them for communication; as well as operate and function the 240 machine gun located on top of the tank in the hatch (the circular area where the loader can function standing upright during combat situations). The drill sergeants from the illustrious BDU era—when most tankers and soldiers, in general, have said that discipline was at the highest level[13]—were given freer rein than today to train soldiers and often this training was very rough and rugged. The army and military wanted to make sure that soldiers who served during this time were disciplined and physically fit, and a tad more rugged than the soldiers that are produced today. One of the other issues was the fact that these were all-male basic training companies. Male NCOs can treat male soldiers differently than they can female soldiers (which is the model today as women have been allowed to join combat units).[14]

Armor drill sergeants were selected from the armored force within the U.S. Army. They either volunteered or were given written notice that they must report to drill sergeant school. These men were usually either staff sergeants (E-6) or sergeants first class (E-7). This means that these men had served in every area of the armored force and therefore were perfect candidates to train young tankers to join the armored force as well.

The Armor Center's basic training started with receiving. This was the moment that civilian men were ushered into military life. They were funneled into a classroom where they would observe a drill sergeant for the first time. During this time the drill sergeant let it be known that he was not your basic training drill sergeant, but rather your receiving drill sergeant.[15] This statement was important for young privates as the goal was not to have them be lulled into a sense of peace and tranquility. The hounds of Ft. Knox would be unleashed on them once they got to their training platoon, but they must be walked into that portion of basic training lest they be overwhelmed and discouraged early in the process. The drill sergeant went on to explain what the next few days would be like for young privates while they were in the receiving company. This included a young tanker's indoctrination to military paperwork and the medical process.[16]

It likely seemed during the first few days at receiving that soldiers would never get to experience life as a tanker. The 0600 wake-up on the first full day of receiving was followed by a formation led by the leadership of the receiving company including the commander, executive officer, and first sergeant. The roles of the leadership at the company and battalion level shall be discussed later. At Ft. Knox, the normal receiving time for a young private was from Monday through Thursday.[17] This meant that all the necessary paperwork and medical procedures must be completed by then. The first day consisted of more lectures and verbal indoctrination from the staff at receiving, including proper hygiene, hydration, and a small snippet of what life would transform into over the next few days. Then soldiers were then herded into a room where they were fitted with their initial issue of clothing. For soldiers that came into the army before 2005, this clothing was known as BDU (battle dress uniform). For those that came between 2005 and 2009, it was called ACU (army combat uniform). This was the first taste of soldiering that privates at Ft. Knox would experience. After the initial clothing issue (including tops, bottoms, boots, t-shirts, and covers or hats) privates were then moved into the medical phase of receiving.[18] The first portion was the vaccination stage, then dental screening.[19]

Over the next few days, the new privates would have found themselves engulfed in a series of routine receiving customs: the formation, meal, and then more briefings. This would go on until Friday morning. After morning formation on Friday, soldiers were told to gather their gear and stage it (orderly storing in an assigned area) and then the barracks had to be cleaned. This cleaning was rigorous and time-consuming, as the receiving barracks had to be pristinely clean for the next cycle of privates. After the cleaning of the barracks, privates were directed to their equipment and awaited further instructions.[20]

For most privates at Ft. Knox, the staging area was either outside near the same area where morning formations were held or in a classroom. Either way, this next phase was called "pickup day":[21] the day when the drill sergeants relocated the privates from receiving to their company area in 2-81 AR (2nd Battalion 81st Armor Regiment). First Sergeant Marshall Yuen had this to say about the pickup of entry-level soldiers: "This day is important to both the soldiers and to the drill sergeants as it allows us to imprint on them how things will be from now until they graduate."[22]

The first few hours, that turned into the first few days, were spent learning the way that things were done in the military and in the armor community. While most new soldiers go through remarkably similar training those first few days, there are always different nuances between the combat jobs in the military. Some universal aspects are how to make their bed, proper uniform wear, and how to address NCOs (noncommissioned officers) and officers. Another important training aspect during this "crawl phase,"[23] is formation and drill. Although simply lining up properly may seem trivial, it is the cornerstone of discipline for tankers. Knowing where you need to be and how to be there is vital to combat training, and drill and formation are how drill sergeants teach that.

Basic training at 2-81 (2003–2009) was divided into four phases: red, white, blue, and gold. These were important to the privates as each phase allowed them to garner more privileges and military knowledge.

Red Phase

The first few days of red phase were low on intensity and corrective training or "smoking."[24] This changed on the Monday following the pickup day. The soldiers were given three full days of training and instruction on the ways of the army and Ft. Knox. From this day forward, all mistakes were met with intensity, loud voices, and corrective training (smoking). This made the red phase the most arduous and demanding of the new privates. Basic training lasted approximately 16 weeks. The first four weeks were the period where most soldiers failed or were removed from the basic training setting.[25] First Sergeant Bryan Greenlee (19Z U.S. Army retired) had this to say about the red phase of basic training at Ft. Knox: "Red phase is where you have strangers yelling and screaming at you and pushing your body to limits they have never gone to before, and this is difficult for many of the soldiers to conform to."[26] During the red phase, soldiers were taught the basic skills that entry-level soldiers needed to be functional in the army. For many, this was their first introduction to military weapons.

Soldiers learned to handle the M9 Beretta and the M4 carbine rifle. Tankers were trained with the M4 as opposed to the commonly used M-16 because it had a retractable buttstock and could more easily fit into a tank. Many of the new privates had managed weapons in the past and for them, the introductory weapons training was a bit monotonous. But the for the rest of the new soldiers, this crash course in military weaponry included proper stance, trigger firing, target acquisition, placement, breathing, and weapons maintenance.[27] This was also the phase when new tankers would be shown the motor pool[28] and be given a rundown of the rules and regulations around it. As was the case with the M-4 carbine, this was the first time that new soldiers would have seen a motor pool. This was also the first time that new tankers viewed their primary battlefield weapon, the M1A1/2 Main Battle Tank (MBT).

During their time at Ft. Knox, new soldiers would only be taught the loader's and driver's station in depth. The gunner's and tank commander's stations were viewed but not examined in detail as new tankers were only expected to have a semi-mastery of the driver's and loader's station when they entered their first duty station. One of the things that the first day in the motor pool was meant to indoctrinate, was the idea of vehicle maintenance. Maintenance has always been the cornerstone of tanking. Every active-duty armor unit in the army devoted at least two or three days a week to maintenance (mainly Monday and Tuesday).[29] During the red phase, entry-level soldiers were immersed in PMCS (preventive maintenance checks and services). This entails soldiers doing a complete check on the tank. Every level of the tank was checked, and any deficiencies were written down and given to the leadership of the platoon to make sure that the tank mechanics assigned to the company had an opportunity to fix this tank.[30]

This initial introduction was short-lived as the goal of the red phase was to give the soldiers a basic level of understanding of tank maintenance. Many of the tasks that soldiers went through during this phase were commonly called "infantry tasks."[31] Young tankers first learned to master dismounted fighting before they were allowed to enter their tanks. These tasks included dismounted patrols, the M-4/M-9 rifle range, the grenade range, room clearing, sniper reaction course, casualty evacuation, and reacting to fire: all important if tankers were asked to dismount and become infantry soldiers (as was the case on many occasions during OIF).[32] Red phase was the time that the young tankers were tested physically. The drill sergeants had to get the soldiers physically fit to take on the rigors of both their first duty station and combat in Iraq.

This was accomplished through both formal morning physical training (PT) and improvised platoon-level PT. The first few weeks of morning physical fitness were meant to test the soldiers' fitness level. On the very first training day, soldiers would conduct an initial physical fitness test called the Army PFT.[33] This consisted of a 2-mile run, timed push-ups, and sit-ups. The initial scores were expected to be low, but it gave the drill sergeants an idea of what needed to be worked on before the next PFT which took place during the white phase.

White Phase

The white phase began after four weeks of training. A formation was held and the company's first sergeant alerted the soldiers to the new phase along with the expectations of that phase. The biggest events that would take place during this phase were the record PFT, rifle range qualification, and the first field training exercise.[34]

It was also during this phase that the soldiers became more familiar with the motor pool and were allowed to enter the tanks for more in-depth and hands-on training within the driver's station.[35] White phase also brought with it a series of briefings that were meant to indoctrinate the soldiers in the history of the armored force and what tanks bring to the battlefield. These were important as they were meant to instill a sense of pride into the tankers and show them the remarkable things that the armored core has done for the army. The history briefings were reinforced with a trip to the Patton Museum;[36] truly a unique time for soldiers because, firstly, they got away from the drill sergeants for a few hours, but also they were able to see the history of the armor and cavalry in warfare. Although there is a healthy rivalry with cavalry as enlisted men, tankers must know what the cavalry do in battle and what they did historically as well.[37]

In this phase the soldiers also had their first encounter with the radio communication system used on a tank. This portion of training served as a rite of passage as the loader of the tank was the one responsible for the radio and its functions in an armor unit.[38] The radio system used on the tank was called a Joint Tactical Radio System (JTRS).[39] There were several functions of this radio that the loader must master before they left basic training and entered their line units. They must have the ability to do what is called a "comms check." This was simply the radio operator communicating with the other tanks, and company radiomen, to check the functionality of the radio as well as to alert them of their position. They also must be able to do what is called a "fill," when the radio operator fed the radio information that it would need to communicate with the company and battalion leadership. In most cases, certain individuals were charged with filling all the tank's radios in the company so as not to overburden the loader with an additional task.[40]

The goal of this training—which took several days to complete—was to make the move to an armor unit seamless for the new tankers. The training consisted of army instructors giving a full breakdown of the radio and showing the privates how to operate them. The training culminated with soldiers being assessed on the functionality of the radio and how to properly communicate with others. Like all tests at basic training, this was graded with a go/no-go format: Either the soldiers completely passed the test, or they failed.[41]

Another aspect of white phase was the rifle range. During white phase, the soldiers were introduced to several methods of training and practice regarding their M-4 rifles. One of the rifle training days was spent at the rifle simulator. This allowed the soldiers to engage electronic targets and learn how to load and unload their rifles without the dangers of real rounds (bullets) being fired,[42] and gave the soldiers the initial training necessary to go "down range," and qualify their weapons at the range. After approximately two days at the simulator, the soldiers completed this training by doing what is called "dry drills," when the drill sergeant would show the soldiers the basic mechanics of the rifle including loading, unloading, firing stances, functions check, and how to properly fix a malfunctioned weapon.[43]

The last rifle training event would be going to a rifle range and firing their weapons. This training event consumed an entire day, and thousands of rounds would be fired to prepare the soldiers to qualify. It was supervised by the drill sergeants and each private would have the opportunity to observe the range that they would use for their qualifications. After a chance to refit and retrain, the soldiers would then attempt to qualify their rifles. Each soldier attempted to fire and hit a pop-up target from 100, 200, and 300 yards. They were scored on the number of times they hit the target.[44] Those that failed were given a second chance to qualify that day. If the soldier failed to qualify after the second try, they could attempt to qualify with another basic training company. If they failed to qualify with that company, a report was written stating that the soldier had failed to meet the standards as laid out by the 2nd Battalion 81st Armor Training Regiment, and Fort Knox. That written report was given to the first sergeant and the fate of that soldier would be decided by the company leadership. There were several things that the leadership could do to attempt to fix this problem. These included allowing the soldier another opportunity to qualify, removing the soldier from his current company and relocating him to another training company and allowing them to retrain and requalify with them, or discharging him from the army as he had failed to adapt and meet the standards needed to become a soldier.[45]

The other major function of white phase was to administer a record PFT. This physical fitness test was the first time that the soldiers had their scores recorded and put into the military system, and it was the second major obstacle that the soldiers had to encounter after the rifle range. The test consisted of the same events as they completed in red phase (push-ups, sit-ups, and a 2-mile run). This was the last major event of the white phase, coming on the heels of soldiers conducting military-style physical fitness for 8 weeks.[46]

The final event of white phase was the soldiers' first field training exercise or FTX. The armor routinely participated in field training and the goal of any FTX during basic training was to indoctrinate the soldiers into what life would be like in the field during their military careers. For basic training, the company of tankers marched up and down two legendary hills at Ft. Knox passionately named "Agony and Misery."[47] This was also the first time that the privates were introduced to ruck marching. The rucksack is the military version of an all-inclusive camping bag. When soldiers went to the field, they were given a packing list and those items went inside of the rucksack.[48] During basic training, ruck marching was used to assess the physical endurance of the soldiers.[49] During this first ruck march, the soldiers marched approximately five miles to the FTX site.

This site was a training ground that consisted of an old, abandoned house, living quarters for soldiers during the 1970s to 1980s. Soldiers arrived at the site, built military tents, and set up a guard schedule. This guard schedule was meant to simulate being on guard during combat operations where you must be the eyes of a military outpost in a combat situation. The soldiers spent three days there and learned some of the basics of "infantry" or dismounted tactics. Some of these tactics included room clearing, medical evacuation, sniper reactions, combat signaling, and radio communication. The first iteration of training was meant to be a precursor to the final FTX that took place during the final stages of the gold phase.[50] After the three days had passed, the soldiers marched back to their company area and began the next phase of training.

Blue Phase

Blue phase training was something that most new soldiers at Ft. Knox looked forward to. Much of this phase was spent in the motor pool and on the M1A1/2 battle tanks. This was also the phase that led to a family weekend and a break from training. The Marine Corps recruit training only lasted 12 weeks and they got to go home for two weeks, whereas OSUT training lasted for a minimum of 16 weeks and it was for this reason that a break in training was granted to soldiers who earned it after week 12.[51] There was also a ceremony held at the end of week 12 to commemorate the soldiers completing the standard 12 weeks of basic training. In many of the basic training installations, soldiers did not have combat military occupations, and training lasted for only 12 weeks. But, for those that had combat jobs, it was deemed necessary to give the soldiers an additional four weeks of nothing but their specific combat training.

During the blue phase, the soldiers were given a bit more freedom. The drill sergeants shifted in tone from hard-nosed yelling and screaming to becoming more of a mentor that guided their decisions. It is important to note that this does not mean that the drill sergeants took it "easier" on soldiers or allowed them to be lax during the blue phase; it simply means that the soldiers were being pushed to graduation. At their next unit they would encounter mentors and "normal" leadership, and the drill sergeants wanted to make sure that the soldiers were ready for that transition.[52]

Some of the transitions may seem small or trivial from the outside looking in. Things like private-led morning wake-up, or the drill sergeants allowing the platoon guide (a soldier selected by the senior drill sergeant) to be the bearer of the platoon's identification flag; this soldier is also the leader of the platoon amongst the privates during basic training. These subtle changes were not only a pseudo rite of passage for the company, but also showed other basic training companies what phase the company was in.[53] The tank training was also a rite of passage for the soldiers during the blue phase.

The soldiers were then introduced to the more intricate functions of the driver's and loader's station. They were taught every single button, switch, warning light, and sound that the tanks made. This was important not only for the soldier but also to help the army brothers of the drill sergeants that would take the reins from them once basic training was complete. One of the most important aspects of this training was the function of the loader's weapon. The loader has three main jobs that he is responsible for in a combat/garrison setting. He is the primary handler of the radio, the loader of the main gun, and the operator of the loader's station M240 machine gun.[54] This weapon is the responsibility of the loader to not only operate in combat situations but to maintain during garrison. The loader is responsible for cleaning this weapon and maintaining its functionality.[55] During combat, when the commander of the vehicle has ordered that the main gun be used, the loader has the responsibility of making sure the proper round is uploaded and prepared to fire. When the main gun is not being used and a "routine" combat patrol or training is being completed, the loader must man the 240.[56] During this in-depth training in blue phase, the types of main gun rounds that will commonly be used on the Abrams tank are also taught to the future tankers. Although there are several tank rounds that tankers have historically used, most of the tank rounds used in Iraq can be boiled down to three main rounds.[57] These were all 120 mm rounds that were fired from the gunner's station of the tank: sabot, HEAT, and canister rounds.

Sabot rounds are primarily used against other tanks or armored vehicles. They can also be used for enemy technicals (civilian vehicles with mounted or unmounted weapons used to attack military personnel during combat). A "combat load" is when a soldier or military vehicle packs ammunition for a mission and the load is the amount and type of ammunition that is used. During the initial invasion of Iraq in 2003, most of the tanks used a substantial portion of sabot rounds in their combat load in preparation for enemy armor.[58] The combat load for army tanks during this conflict was 40 main gun rounds. The HEAT round (high explosive antitank) is also a round that can be used against enemy armor and technicals but it also was used for bunkers and enemy positions during OIF/OEF. The canister round is an anti-personnel round. It works very similarly to a shotgun: once it explodes, small round pellets explode out, spraying those around it. This round is excellent when encountering a group of enemy dismounted troops that are bunched together.[59]

It was vital that loaders know and understood the differences between the tank rounds and when to utilize them. As LTC Nathan Davis explains: "Loaders are not simply inside the tank to be mindless sheep. They need to recognize the situation that they are in whether it be gunnery or combat. For instance, if they are in combat and they know they are encountering enemy tanks, they need to set their gaze on where they stored the sabot round in the ammunition rack."[60] Loaders were taught to have a system for where they needed to place each round. When they arrived at their duty station, they would be educated on how that unit wanted to load rounds for gunnery. In general, they simply needed to have a method for remembering and identifying where each round was, to ensure the proper ammunition type was readily available. The loader's station was intense for basic training soldiers as it cannot be understated how important each station is: the tank simply cannot kill the enemy with an untrained or incompetent loader. Therefore, the initial training of the tankers was important so that they had a base of knowledge to draw from as they moved on to their first unit.[61]

The blue phase also offered a change in the physical fitness regimen that privates had become accustomed to. During the initial phases of basic training, the soldiers were divided into three groups based on their physical fitness abilities and in particular, their run time in the PFT.[62] During the red and white phases, the company divided itself into three running groups, Alpha, Bravo, and Charlie; Alpha group being the soldiers that ran the fastest, and Charlie, consisting of soldiers that had the slowest run times. During the blue phase, these groups were cut down to simply Alpha and Bravo. The goal was that those soldiers who had slower run times were put into a group that forced them to push their bodies to bring down that run time.[63] This change was important as the soldiers took another PFT at the end of the blue phase. The stakes were highest during this phase as the soldiers that did not pass the blue phase PFT were not permitted to have a family day weekend.[64] If a soldier failed the PFT, the decision of allowing the soldier to participate in family day activities is up to the company commander. After the family day and weekend festivities were completed, the soldiers who returned for the gold phase would will focus entirely on tank training and the final FTX.

Gold Phase

Gold phase was often called "auto-private" by many of the drill sergeants.[65] This is the phase where the soldiers took full control of their military lives.

Guides would march the soldiers to nearly every event (with the drill sergeants in more of a monitoring role); the basic training life that soldiers had become accustomed to now was more routine and the mistakes that were made early on were often corrected by other soldiers.[66] During this phase, the routine for soldiers shifted as well. The mornings still consisted of physical fitness, breakfast (chow), hygiene (changing into your uniform, shaving, brushing your teeth, etc.). But now, after that was complete, most of the day was spent in the motor pool. The training in the motor pool focused on the maintenance details that needed to be done on the tank: checking the oil and fuel levels, breaking down the breech and cleaning it, cleaning the inside of the tank, changing track, changing trackpads, and other issues that may arise.[67] This training culminated in an evaluation called ACT (armor crewman test).

This evaluation tested all the skills that had been learned that were unique to tankers. Some of these skills were: assembling and dissembling the 240 and M9 Beretta, gas mask timed donning, timed loading and unloading of the main gun round, ammunition and vehicle identification. These tests were vital for tankers as they would need these skills to function in the armor community. This phase also brought the final FTX. The biggest difference between this FTX and others was the ruck march to the site and back. During this era of basic training, the march to the site was 10 miles in length including the trek up Agony and down Misery.[68] This FTX again focused on dismounted training and how to use dismounted tactics to destroy the enemy. During this period in Iraq, tankers were often heavily involved in the clearing of rooms, dismounted patrols, and many other aspects of combat that have been described as "infantry" tasks.

This was due in part to the lack of troops in certain areas. Many times, an infantry unit was paired with a tank platoon to present the enemy with more obstacles in terms of firepower. However, what happened in many cases was that although tanks were at their disposal, dismounted patrols were still important and necessary to bring down the violence and secure certain areas.[69] This idea was not lost on the drill sergeants and dismounted training was heavily incorporated into the overall training schedule for new soldiers during this time.[70] This phase also introduced soldiers to a pseudo gunnery. To be brief, gunnery is where tankers show their competency in identifying targets, choosing the right ammunition to destroy targets, engaging and destroying those targets promptly, and the overall cohesion of the tank crew.[71] The soon-to-be tankers would be exposed to a small portion of this event. Privates were allowed to man the driver's and loader's station. The gunner's station would be manned by soldiers selected by the company leadership and senior drill sergeant. As 1SG Greenlee explained, "During basic training, when we allow the young privates to use the gunner's station, it is a privilege. Therefore, only certain soldiers that have shown the ability to perform at the highest levels during basic training will get to sit in that seat during our mock gunnery."[72]

Firing from the tank would commence through the night to allow soldiers to use the night optics of the tank and to show how these could be used against an enemy. At the end of this mock gunnery, the soldiers would be exposed to the first maintenance and cleaning of the tanks after they had been fired and used. First Sergeant Greenlee spoke about the maintenance after gunnery: "This is vital to the soldiers as they will be able to see how essential maintenance is to tanks after they have been fired and driven. Up to that point, the new soldiers had conducted maintenance on tanks that have sat in the motor pool."[73] After the tank maintenance and clean up, the soldiers spent the next several days conducting a cleaning of the company area to which they were assigned. This cleaning detail was extremely meticulous and time-consuming. Every aspect of the company was cleaned to welcome the parents of the soldiers that would arrive for graduation. This cleaning was also in preparation for the final inspection that would be conducted by the battalion CSM (command sergeant major).

For most of the new privates, this would be the first up close and personal interaction that they would have had with the CSM. Several weeks prior, the soldiers took their "dress greens" (military dress uniform for special occasions or inspections) to get pressed, and once they were done, the drill sergeants guided them on how to properly wear the uniform.[74] The inspection itself was not a stressful situation on the part of the CSM. He simply inspected the barracks, and the soldiers' uniforms, and asked each soldier some questions about military or tank knowledge.

The CSM inspected an entire armor basic training company which consisted of over 120 soldiers, so he was not interested in spending a lot of time with one individual soldier.[75] Once the soldiers had completed the inspection and the cleaning of the barracks, the last event of meaning was the final PFT.

For most soldiers, the final PFT was less daunting or arduous than any of the ones before it. The last one should be stress-free for the soldiers: they had been conducting an extremely strenuous physical fitness regimen for over 15 weeks and their bodies were better equipped to manage the test than in the red phase.[76] After the PFT, graduation was next for the future tankers. It was a straightforward event. The soldiers would be called one by one (by platoon) across a stage and afterwards they were free to go home with their parents. Before graduation, the soldiers were told by their senior drill sergeants where their first duty station would be.[77] Once they left with their family, they would be granted a minimum of 10 days' leave (vacation) before being required to report to their duty station. Once at their duty station, they would go through receiving, and processing, and then be assigned to their unit.

Armor Basic Officer Leader Course/Cavalry Leaders Course

Officers had the same intense tank training that new privates endured; they merely took a different path to get there. The most common path for armor officers was to get their commission as an officer through a college ROTC (reserve officer training corps) program that taught them many of the leadership skills they would need to be officers. The other popular option was to be accepted and graduate from the prestigious West Point Military Academy.[78] For either path, officers could choose two or three service jobs that they would like. They would then be assigned based on their choices as well as the needs of the army. The second lieutenants that were chosen to be armor officers would go through the armor officer leadership course and cavalry leaders course. In total, these courses would have the new officers training for nearly five months as they learned how to lead the armored force. Armor officers were different from other officers because they were asked to be both tank and cavalry leaders. An armor officer could be in command of a tank unit where they fought on tanks much of the time, then be sent to a light cavalry unit where they were conducting dismounted operations.[79]

During the BDU era, this training course took place at Ft. Knox, KY. During their training, the new officers would be prepared for both types of warfare that they may face in their future duty station. On the armor side, they learned the basics of tanking. Maintenance and familiarization with the tank were paramount and were taught to the new officers by other senior officers and enlisted men.[80] Officers were taught every aspect of the tank, just as the new enlisted privates were. They would, however, never be loaders, gunners, or drivers except in training. Officers who graduated from this course would be immediately thrust into the tank commander's position. That meant that they must learn on the fly and make every day count in training as they would not have the opportunity to "grow up" in the armor. The officers would conclude their training with gunnery as well. This ensured the officer knew exactly how to function as the commander of the tank. This course was described as a "gentleman course." Officers were not subject to the same type of rigorous verbal attacks by drill sergeants; however, they were required to report to the armor training course in top physical condition.[81] This was because the officers' training during the tank portion was designed to get the young officers caught up on tank tasks, not get them into physical shape. They would of course conduct physical training while they were at Ft. Knox, to be able to lead their troops once they arrived at their duty station.

Garrison Life

During oral interviews with veteran tankers, the idea that life changed for tankers after the end of the BDU era became a common theme. A retired anonymous army MSG had this to say about the BDU era for tankers:

> Life was simply different during the old BDU age. We were held to a much higher standard as tankers. Do not misunderstand, we had fun, and we enjoyed every day of tanking. I'd argue the one bad day of being a tanker was on Mondays. Holy shit! Mondays were just awful. We had to sit in the motor pool all day doing

maintenance. And it wasn't just a once over, we had to go step by step from the FM [field manual]. This took hours. Usually, we had PT in the morning, would go back and have some chow, shower, and change into our BDUs. Morning formation was almost always held at the motor pool. After the platoon sergeants gave an up to the top,[82] we started maintenance.[83]

This golden era seems to have started after Operation *Desert Storm*.[84] The discipline that was born and maintained after this conflict directly led to much of the success that tank units were able to have during OIF. One of the main things that separated tankers from other units during this time was morning inspections, as noted by 1SG Greenlee: "Morning inspections was a tool that we as NCOs used to instill discipline and military knowledge to the younger tankers."[85] Morning inspections consisted of a uniform review (inspecting the soldiers' top, bottom, and boots), along with asking several questions that pertained to the army or the armor. For many soldiers, this was the most stressful portion of the week. For soldiers fresh out of basic training, it was something that they were used to, but not to this extent. Soldiers in the armor were often told to have four uniforms: two that they kept in pristine condition, meaning they kept the uniform pressed and the boots mirror-shined, and two uniforms that they would use for the field or motor pool.[86] In an armor unit, the first sergeant was the one that routinely conducted the inspection or at least stood in front and supervised as it took place. This was also something that brought added pressure, to have the senior enlisted man watching and noting who did not take pride in their appearance or had forgotten their military knowledge.[87]

First Sergeant Marshall Yuen explained why inspections were more common in armor than other combat MOS:

> Yes, we would see armor guys conducting inspections with their companies because it's a lot easier when the company is floating between 60 and 65 soldiers. It was a lot easier for me as 1st Sgt. to supervise that and maintain that inspection integrity. For an infantry 1st Sgt., his company is around 120 to 140 soldiers. It was simply a lot easier for us to do that. That does not mean that it was not happening on the infantry side, it just means we didn't see as much. The infantry 1st Sgt. has to delegate a lot more information down to his platoon sergeants to make the same things happen in terms of the discipline of the company. A good 1st Sgt. regardless of the MOS is not going to want an undisciplined unit.[88]

During the BDU era, inspections were simply a way of life and a way of discipline. Soldiers could routinely be seen walking around in pristine uniforms and it was a compliment to the unit and their MOS. Tankers could often be easily identified by their unique footwear known as "tanker boots." Designed in 1937 by George Patton, the boots had straps instead of shoestrings to prevent entanglement with the tank and its many parts. These boots were awarded to the soldier after they qualified on their tanks during gunnery. It could be seen as another rite of passage for tankers.

Armor officers also would wear tanker boots to show that they had been through tank gunnery and met the standards as well. This would be important to the enlisted men to know that their officers had gone through the same hardships as them.[89] This era was also different for officers. Before the change to ACUs, an officer's MOS insignia could be found on their collar. This was also a sense of pride for those that had a combat MOS. "One of the main reasons the army took the logos off the collar is because you had officers that were butt-hurt because people would see them and not give them the same respect as those who had a combat job.[90]

Garrison training also played a key role in the discipline of an armor unit. The day-to-day training and lifestyle engrained in the minds of the tankers are what allowed what they did in combat to become second nature.[91] Physical fitness in the morning was the bedrock of every armor unit during this time. Tank units were occupied with vehicle matters throughout the day; therefore, they did not have the opportunity most days to have physical training in the afternoons as the infantry did.[92] This has often been a source of the rivalry between the armor and the infantry. Many infantrymen felt that tankers were lazy or "gearheads" because they spent most of their time on tanks and not doing some of the extra physical activity that they did. This would often lead to resentment by the infantry. Mondays for tankers would consist of PT in the morning from 0630 to 0745, then morning formation (usually in the motor pool) at 0930. From there, the soldiers conducted "by the book" PMCS.[93]

PMCS on the tank consists of doing checks on every part of the tank and checking its functionality. Just as in basic training, each tank crew had to conduct checks and annotate all issues with the tank. After physical training, Tuesdays and Wednesdays were remarkably similar: morning inspections, followed by trips to the motor pool. Those days in the motor were spent fixing significant issues that arose from Monday's PMCS. Thursdays and Fridays were meant for any additional company training or administration issues with the soldiers such as dental, medical, and weapons training. Thursdays also allowed platoon sergeants to be able to "free-lance" train their tank crews. This was important because it allowed the platoon to better familiarize themselves with each other, as the goal was for the crew to become a cohesive unit.[94] Fridays had several minor events going on. Many of the tank crews took their vehicles out for a "forced march." In an armor unit, this is merely where the tanks were driven in a designated area and assessed to make sure that everything worked. This allowed the tank crews the opportunity to work as a unit on the tank, and the command staff to practice having control over the tanks and their men. The command staff could also ensure that maintenance was being carried out on the vehicles and get the deficiencies fixed.[95] Fridays were also when the enlisted soldiers who lived in the barracks had their rooms inspected, usually by the first sergeant.[96] These inspections helped the armor company maintain the cleanliness and discipline that had to be part of every tanker's life to be successful on the tank.

The company was where most tankers spent their time. They were a part of the company and the company was a part of them. The makeup of the leadership structure in an armor unit is something that needs to be addressed as well as the tank and its capabilities. The platoon is the first level where the tanker leaving basic training would enter. A tank platoon comprised 16 tankers, who were divided into two sections, Alpha and Bravo.[97] Each section consisted of four tanks, and each tank had a driver, loader, gunner, and tank commander.

The Alpha section was manned by the platoon leader's tank and the section sergeants' tank. The platoon leader was generally a first or second lieutenant, while the section sergeant, in general, was a staff sergeant (SSG E-6) or a sergeant (Sgt. E-5) promotable.[98] The Bravo section consisted of the platoon sergeants' and Bravo section sergeant's tank. The platoon sergeant is in general a sergeant first class (SFC E-7). In some cases, that position is manned by a staff sergeant.[99] In garrison, the role of the section sergeants was to ensure the tank crews are professionally trained, and that discipline and order were maintained throughout their section. It was important to have these section sergeants be in charge as often the platoon sergeant and leader were busy doing administrative things.

The platoon leader was rarely on the tank with the crew for maintenance and PMCS. Therefore, a well-rounded gunner must lead that tank.[100] The gunner of the tank was known as the "first-line supervisor."[101] They were given this name because they oversaw the tank crew. The section sergeant oversaw one section of the platoon (Alpha or Bravo) but the gunner oversaw what went on in the tank. SFC Johann of the 1st Infantry Division said of tank gunners: "A squared-away gunner is worth his weight in gold. A good gunner will make sure that all the comms [communications, or radio checks] are done, all the weapons systems have been tested and are Red Con 1, PMCIs are complete, and all the TC [tank commander] must do is hop on the tank and say move out."[102]

The gunner was responsible for firing the main gun and the coaxial machine gun (coax), a version of the 240 that the loader used. He was also responsible for the maintenance of those two weapons and the care of the BII (basic issue items). These were items attached to the tank that were used daily or in case of emergencies, such as tools or maintenance equipment. The rank that the gunner had often depended on the unit. Many units were okay with a gunner being a specialist (E-4). During an interview with SFC Timothy Williams Sr., he had this to say about the matter: "The gunner on the tank is supposed to be the one in charge. In my experience, I have thought it to be an innovative idea to fight to make the gunner at least a corporal. This allows him to stand apart from the other soldiers on the tank even if they are E-4s as well. Over time, the gunner should have a good grasp on tanking and how to lead if the TC does his job."[103]

The rank of a platoon sergeant (PSG) was reserved for either an SSG (E-6) or most commonly, an SFC (E-7).[104] The platoon sergeant was the senior enlisted NCO in a platoon. Their job was to advise, train, and work with the platoon leader to meet the commander's intent.

The platoon sergeant had perhaps the most unique relationship with an officer in charge of his organization. In many cases, the PL (platoon leader) was a brand-new second lieutenant straight out of armor school. This meant that although they had some experience on the tank, they had limited experience overseeing a tank platoon. Therefore it was vital to have a platoon sergeant with knowledge of every aspect of the tank at their side. They relied on the PSG to be the disciplinarian and the backbone of the platoon to have a disciplined and capable unit. The PSG was also there to help the PL grow into an eventual company commander.[105] The lessons that the PSG taught the PL, about both the men and the tank, would help him as he went on to lead a tank company. The PSG was responsible for every aspect of the men in his platoon. Although the officers were the ones in command, the senior NCOs were the ones that made the unit run at a high level. The PL was responsible in general for everything the platoon accomplished or failed to accomplish.[106] They had their tank and crew and met regularly with the company commander to relay his intent to their respective platoons.

The first sergeant was the most important piece of the company. Although the company commander was responsible, without a good first sergeant, the company would be doomed to fail.[107] The first sergeant's responsibility is the discipline, welfare, and training of the enlisted soldiers in their company.[108] First Sergeant Yuen recalled being a first sergeant in an armor unit:

> I think a lot of the role of a 19K, or any 1st Sgt., has to do with discipline. I'm not there to be the soldier's friend, I'm there to ensure that they are taken care of and well-trained. A lot of my job was to advise the company commander on the best route to take to maintain a disciplined unit. It was also my job to supervise every aspect of enlisted soldier training from PT to weapons training, to drill. I also had to maintain all the human resource actions that came across my desk. This would include promotions, awards, UCMJ (Uniform Code of Military Justice), housing issues, and the overall welfare of the unit.[109]

The army did something unique when it comes to its enlisted senior NCOs. Once armor enlisted men reached the rank of first sergeant or higher, they were then considered 19Z instead of 19K (this went for tankers and for cavalry scouts 19D). This meant that just like their officer counterparts, once they reached that rank, they could potentially be sent to a cavalry troop instead of an armor unit. The numbers in a cavalry troop matched closely the numbers of an infantry unit. In a tank or armor unit, the number of tankers was roughly 65 soldiers. Each platoon had four tanks and 16 soldiers. A tank company (during the time examined) had three platoons. Some companies would have either a mortar or scout platoon (infantry or cavalry) to make a fourth line platoon.[110] This also gave the company a dismounted element.

After 2005, the army shifted from having "pure" battalions (battalions with just tanks or just infantry) to the combined arms battalion model. The first sergeant no longer has a tank as the senior enlisted NCO. His new vehicle is known as an APC (Armored Personnel Carrier) or a Humvee (High Mobility Multipurpose Wheeled Vehicle). The XO (executive officer) at the company level has the job of being second in command and the overseer of maintenance and supplies of the company.

In garrison, his job is to make sure that the company has the supplies and resources that they need to function and train for the upcoming mission.[111] The XO works with the company master gunner (MG or Mike Golf) when it comes time for gunnery to ensure that the ammunition that the tank crews need is readily accessible. The XO is normally a first lieutenant. The master gunner is the subject matter expert for all things tank-related.[112] His job becomes vital during gunnery or anytime the company goes to the field. During gunnery or field training, he is responsible for setting up targets and ranges for the tank crews. He advises the XO on what ammunition is needed and makes sure that the ammunition is there to assist the tank crews with their training. The CO (company commander) is the senior officer and the man in charge of the company. He is responsible for everything that the company does or fails to do.[113] He is advised by the company's first sergeant on what is needed to properly train and look after the enlisted men. The commander sets goals and makes his intentions known to the first sergeant who then acts on those intentions and relays the commander's intent to the platoon sergeants.

The commander of an armor unit has the added duty of being a tank commander, but the commander's gunner is the one that is truly in charge of the tank. The company commander simply does not have the time to train and interact with a tank crew so the commander's gunner must be an NCO or a well-trained junior soldier that is seasoned and a capable leader. The battalion staff, in an armor unit, is very similar to the company staff in terms of their responsibility. It is just on a much bigger scale. The XO is still in charge of maintenance and supplies. The difference is that now, instead of overseeing one company, he oversees four to five company-sized units. The senior enlisted adviser in a battalion is the command sergeant major (CSM, E-9).[114] He holds the same responsibilities as any senior enlisted NCO as his duties are the discipline, training, and welfare of the enlisted soldiers in his battalion. As is the case with the first sergeant, he does not have a tank at this level. He also does not directly interact with soldiers daily as he disseminates information and instructions down to the company first sergeants.[115] The battalion commander (BCO) holds the rank of lieutenant colonel (O-5). He is the commander of the entire battalion and responsible for everything that goes on in it. Armor officers who have achieved this rank have gone through ABOLC as well as a captain's course that focuses on leadership from the company commander's perspective.[116]

It is important for any armor officer who has reached this rank to have tactical or educational experience in both mounted and dismounted warfare as they could be in command of a combined arms unit that has both armor and infantry, and the commander must have the ability to deploy both types of units effectively.[117] The battalion commander is the only commander at the battalion level who still has his branch's weapon as his main vehicle. Colonel Jonathan Bender explained why BCOs still have tanks: "The battalion commander is still part of the fight in an armor battalion. During some of the major conflicts in Iraq, it was not uncommon to see the commander put a main gun round down range. No officer in a combat MOS has that. It gives the commander great firepower, and a fast vehicle to reach the objective."[118] The command staff in an armor or combined arms unit have a different perspective on logistics than perhaps the command group in a light infantry or airborne battalion has. They not only have the task of taking care of the soldiers, but they also must deal with the vehicle aspect of combat. Providing the fuel, equipment, and maintenance equipment needed to make an armor unit function properly is essential. During the time period covered by this book, the army was making the transition from pure units to a mixed CAB (combined arms battalion) model.

This was new for the army and the tankers. Tankers were accustomed to having leadership that was "armor pure" as well. That is to say that the BCO, XO, and CSM at one point were all tankers in an armor battalion. This changed after the shift in the battalion makeup. For a time during the inception of the combined arms model, you would often see a light infantry battalion commander with an armor CSM, or vice versa. The effect that an infantry CSM has on an armor or combined arms battalion is often felt more than perhaps an infantry officer's presence. This is because the CSM is the leader of the enlisted men. It is his job to be the voice of the enlisted men and to help guide the commander's decisions regarding their welfare.[119] Often, if the CSM was a career light infantryman coming into an armor battalion this would be something of a challenge when it came to leading the men and allowing them to do certain things that were MOS-specific. One example of this was illuminated by another oral interview:

> I think the army made a huge mistake by mismatching the command staff. Even though the battalion is combined arms and no longer pure, the reality is what does a sergeant major from the 82nd or the Rangers know about tanks or mechanized infantry fighting for that matter?
>
> They come in the battalion and try to implement rules and policy that worked in a light infantry battalion on a tank battalion, and it just doesn't work.[120]

This switch was made to give armor units the ability to deploy dismounted troops, and for the infantry to have the speed and firepower of an Abrams tank. The move during that timeframe was still in its infancy and several CAB units had to work out the kinks while they were being engaged by the enemy. Gunnery is one of the most important and exciting aspects of garrison life for a tanker. Gunnery is the tool the command uses to judge the tank crews' proficiency and effectiveness. During the time before 2003 when units were still pure, gunnery was a different experience for armor units.[121] For most armor units, record gunnery happens twice a year. For units such as the 1st Infantry Division, which experiences extreme weather changes in winter and summer, the gunnery is divided into cold and warm weather gunnery.

This is also a natural way to relieve stress on tankers and to see how they perform during the weather change. During winter gunnery, the weather could be 10 degrees outside. It makes the tank crew focus on the targets and come together as a unit better. On the other side, during the summer gunnery, the weather could be extremely hot and muggy inside the turret of a tank. An anonymous source said this about the summer gunnery: "I've been at Stewart [Ft. Stewart, GA] where it was 105 outside and it was like a sauna inside the tank."[122] "Going to the field" is what translated to gunnery for most tankers. Nearly all active-duty combat units go to do field training (like the FTX that was discussed earlier) three or four times a year.[123] For armor units during this time, field training could last up to 60 days. Gunnery lasted at least 30 days. For the duration of that time, armor units conducted what was called MOUT training (military operations on urbanized terrain).

This training was meant to get soldiers accustomed to fighting in urban terrain. For tankers, this meant allowing them to be able to learn to fight alongside infantry, and cavalry scouts, in an urban environment.[124] During the first few days of "being in the field," armor units drove their tanks to the training site and staged them in an assigned area. They then did a check of all "sensitive items."[125] Once the items were accounted for, the platoon gave an up to the first sergeant. The next day was spent setting up tents and living areas for the platoons. Field training could be a company event, but normally the battalion went all at once. This meant that large areas must be set up, and food and water supplied for the duration of the training. This was where the XO must be organized and educated on the details.[126] The battalion XO must organize and coordinate with the support battalions to ensure that cooks, mechanics, and medics are all present and accessible to the battalion. Once the living areas were set up, and the men and equipment all accounted for, the platoon and company leadership met with the battalion command staff. This meeting was to give the companies a rundown of what training they will be conducting over the next few weeks[127] and also gave the CSM a chance to set some boundaries and guidelines for the enlisted soldiers.

An anonymous master sergeant (Army Retired, E–8) had this to say about the briefings given before field training:

> The battalion commander tells you exactly what you will be doing for the next two months in the field. As tankers, we knew that the first portion of field training is going to be gunnery. After the commander does his spiel, the XO talks about some maintenance things and some of the things that we need to be doing with the vehicles. The sergeant major then takes the NCOs aside and lets them know the dos and don'ts while they are in the field. This changes depending on the sergeant major. A tanker sergeant major is going to have different expectations than an infantry one will.[128]

The platoon sergeants then went and gave the information back to their platoons. The first day of gunnery for the tank crews consisted of bore sighting their tanks and zeroing all the weapons on the tank.[129] Bore sighting required a calibration device known as an M27A1 MBD. This device allowed the sights on the main gun (120 mm) to be aligned with the sights of the tank gunner. This was done before every gunnery or field training to ensure that the sights that the gunner used were aligned with the main gun and, in essence, allowed the gunner to hit what he fired at.[130] After the sights had been calibrated, and the tank crews zeroed their weapons, the next several weeks would be spent on the actual gunnery. During the time examined, gunnery consisted of 12 tables with Table 8 being the qualifying table. Each table consisted of certain weapons engagements that the crews must master. Every single weapons system that the tank had would be used and mastered.

The one position on the tank that has not been discussed regarding the weapon that they are responsible for is the tank commander (TC). The tank commander (BC, CO, XO, PL, PSG, and two-section sergeants) was responsible for a .50-caliber machine gun. The ".50-cal" (.50 BMG, 12.7 × 99 mm Browning machine gun) was used for lightly armored vehicles, enemy positions, and cover fire.[131] The commander had to qualify on this weapon like the rest of the crew. This weapon must be mastered because the M1A1 and A2 versions were not remote and thus if the main gun was not operational for some reason, the .50-cal could still function.[132] Gunnery was scored from 0–1,000 and the tank crew scored higher for hitting the target promptly. Every table had different targets that must be engaged within the allotted time. The time restraints depended on the target.[133] First Sergeant Crandall discussed gunnery scores during his oral interview:

> Gunnery has changed significantly from the time I joined the army in 2007 until now. We as senior NCOs have to change with it. There was a time when if you got in the 700s, you would get laughed off the range. But we have just started to get back into the groove of doing "tank stuff." For so long we were focused on dismounted operations. It will take the armored core a while to get back to the standards that it once had.[134]

Before the war in Iraq, the "armored core" focused solely on their tank. As stated earlier, everything that tankers did revolved around mastering their vehicles and building a cohesive unit. Gunnery was the point where units showed off that mastery. During the initial stages of Operation *Iraqi Freedom*, those gunnery scores were high across the board according to oral interviews. It was after the rise of CABs, and the mixture of leadership and combat philosophies, that the focus shifted.[135] Any score under 700 is a failure. However, the command staff has the authority to make a crew with "lower" passing scores reshoot a certain table to ensure their proficiency.[136]

After gunnery had been completed at the platoon level, the company would complete a live fire exercise. This was an evaluation for the battalion commander to ensure that the COs could coordinate and maneuver tanks with live rounds and in a combat-simulated situation.[137] If he saw something that was out of place or needed to be worked on, he would then discuss the matter with the CO to make sure that the company was on the same page. Once the company had completed its live fire exercise it was then time to move on with the battalion live fire. The battalion live fire was a bit more complex. At that time in the armor, a battalion live fire did not simply consist of Abrams tanks, but Bradleys as well. The battalion commander coordinated a live exercise from the turret of his tank.[138] This consisted of targets and an area that mimicked urban operations in Iraq.[139] Targets comprised both mounted and dismounted troops, and the company commanders throughout the battalion needed to coordinate with the BC on the fly. This allowed units to learn to communicate and destroy the enemy while on the move and under duress. At the end of this live fire, the units moved into field training excises.

For tank units, the events that happened after gunnery are what separated them from the other combat units. SFC Williams had this to say regarding post-gunnery activities:

> After gunnery is over there is usually either a huge barbecue or a big meal for the tankers. We threw some burgers, hotdogs, and steaks on the grill and sat back and enjoyed for a minute. I've been in units where we do gunnery first and then do field training or vice versa. As tankers, we get ridiculed sometimes for the amount of fun that we have. But we work just as hard as the infantry guys, we just devote most of our time to tanks while they worry about squad-level tactics and physical training.[140]

Post-gunnery, field training for tankers consisted of them being put into different situations and forced to react based on their training. For example, they could find themselves conducting a mounted patrol when their vehicle was disabled by an IED (improvised explosive device). They then used their SOP[141] (standard operating procedure) regarding vehicle recovery.[142] They would do scenarios like this for every aspect of combat that they might encounter in Iraq. One thing that was different after 2003 was the fact that during these field operations, tankers also had to dismount and focus on dismounted patrols, room clearing, and returning fire from the vantage point of an infantryman.[143] They conducted day and night operations from both the turret of the tank and an infantry squad configuration. After the 60-day training event, the tankers returned to their duty station where the tanks and their weapons were thoroughly cleaned, and thorough maintenance checks of the tanks were conducted.

CHAPTER 2

Tank Preparation, and the Invasion of Iraq

It is also important to investigate the vehicle or machine that these tankers use, which during the time that we are discussing, is the M1A1 Abrams Main Battle or its sister variant, the M1A2/M1A2 Sep. These are the machines that had to be mastered and employed during this conflict to make sure that victory was achieved for the coalition forces.

All soldiers, no matter what their MOS, must qualify with their personal weapons. This is to ensure that all soldiers can defend themselves and destroy the enemy in combat if the situation arises. For tankers, gunnery is different. Gunnery tables were created to allow tankers to use every single weapons system on the MBT and be proficient at it, whether against enemy dismounts or enemy armor.[1] Tankers used what were called "tank tables." These were a series of training engagements meant to allow tankers to focus on skills needed for the combat theater at the time—Iraq. The qualifying table at the time was table eight, which used all the weapons systems. Each table before eight would focus on one or two weapons systems; some tables would be only for the commander and his .50-caliber machine gun, while others would use a combination of the main gun and the machine gun. Tank tables are scored between 0 and 1,000 points, with 700 being the bare minimum needed to pass.[2]

Field training is something that all units go through in hopes of preparing their soldiers for combat. Operation *Iraqi Freedom* was a bit different because many of the leaders did not know that they were going into a counter-insurgency battle. Many of the tankers that fought in this campaign also fought in the Gulf War during Operation *Desert Storm/ Shield*.[3] These tankers had the advantage of knowing what the enemy could throw at them, or at least they thought they did.

In September 2002, the 2nd BCT (brigade combat team) of the 3rd Infantry Division (Mechanized) found themselves on rotation in Kuwait. The goal of this rotation was to give the soldiers a sense of what life was like and the terrain that they could expect to fight in during the upcoming campaign in Iraq.[4] This was supposed to be a six-month tour. During this time the men of 2nd BCT—consisting of approximately 4,300 soldiers—shot gunnery, practiced scenarios, and continued to gel within their tank crews to become a more lethal force in combat.

The 2nd BCT was under the command of Col. David Perkins.[5] Perkins was an armor officer who had graduated from the prestigious West Point Military Academy. The training that tankers received in both garrison and, for some, in basic training, was needed as they were now being asked not to shoot gunnery for bragging rights, but to prepare them for combat. 2nd BCT was equipped with two armor units, 1-64 AR and 4-64 AR, which had 44 Abrams tanks each.[6] During this time, if a brigade was considered "heavy," it was not uncommon for the leadership even at the brigade level to be tankers. Perkins, the CSM, Otis Smith, and the XO, LTC Eric Wesley, were all tankers. This made things in the brigade run through the lens and actions of tankers. During this time, the full assembly of CABs had not been instituted yet. In its place, the army used a task force (TF) configuration.[7] The TF organization meant that in most cases, armor battalions would "trade" one of their tank companies with an infantry battalion. This would serve as the precursor to the combined arms battalion.[8]

Making this switch allowed the infantry to have a significantly greater amount of firepower during the campaign. To start at the brigade level, the CSM's role is the same as in garrison: the welfare and discipline of the enlisted soldiers. It is also vital that the CSM be the eyes and ears of the enlisted men for the commander.[9] This allows the commander to stay in touch with the senior NCOs at the company level and to have a better understanding of what they need or need to accomplish to achieve the mission. CSM Smith had this to say about his role during the initial training in Kuwait:

> We were doing a regular six-month rotation to Kuwait at the time. The big picture then was training up the brigade combat team, which consisted of armor, infantry, engineers, field artillery, and all your logistical support elements, including signal and military intelligence. We had to train up the unit as a brigade combat team and this was our first opportunity to go out and do training like we'd do at Fort Stewart or going out to the National Training Center, but on a much larger scale. This gave the commander the latitude and the time he needed to train these units to be a cohesive brigade combat team. A big advantage to that was that we were able to put an entire brigade combat team in a situation in the desert so all the elements could function at one time with movement techniques across the desert. We did that during the day. At night, we did a brigade combat team live fire exercise with all the elements involved.[10]

During his time in Kuwait, the CSM made sure that the entire brigade was properly preparing for combat with the Iraqi forces. The main force expected to pose resistance to the American forces was a group called the Fedayeen Saddam. The other was a group called the Republican Guard.[11] These militant groups were thought to have been the best-trained and best-equipped group that the coalition forces encountered. For tankers, this meant that they had to prepare for fighting infantrymen or dismounted troops. During this time, tankers trained in garrison for the possibility of being in direct combat with other Iraqi tanks. However, the Abrams tank was more than equipped to face dismounted troops. The gunner's coax and the loaders' 240 machine guns are both mounted weapons that are used to combat dismounted troops. The gunner also uses his "canister" round to destroy dismounted troops.[12]

Smith had the duty to make sure that not only were his tank battalions properly preparing for war but that they were properly integrating with the mechanized infantry companies to build cohesion for the fight to come. In the 2nd Brigade, there was one infantry battalion: 3rd Battalion, 15th Infantry Regiment (3-15 Inf). An infantry company was configured very similarly to a tank company. The difference of course was the number of men. The impact that infantry has, and had during that time, on the armor is profound. The mechanized infantry companies were fitted with a Bradley Fighting Vehicle and were known as "Bradley companies."[13]

This vehicle was a heavily armored squad personnel carrier equipped with two main weapons: the first is a wire-guided missile called a TOW missile. The other is an M242 Bushmaster chain gun, a single-barrel chain-driven autocannon.[14] The Bradley does not have the same firepower as the Abrams, but it provides mechanized infantry with significantly more firepower than its light infantry counterparts. The goal of organizing by TF was to allow the armor the ability to dismount in case they were in a combat situation where they had to face infantry troops. Tanks are not made to clear buildings; that is simply not their function. Their goal is to eliminate enemy armor and provide support for dismounted troops.[15]

The integration was perhaps difficult for all soldiers involved. The differences in culture made it difficult to coexist in garrison. On the battlefield, however, it is a different story. Tankers and infantry were a lethal combination in this fight. Armor units softened the battlefield and the infantry went in and engaged and destroyed the remnants of resistance from the Iraqi dismounts. Life became a bit more difficult as the enemy

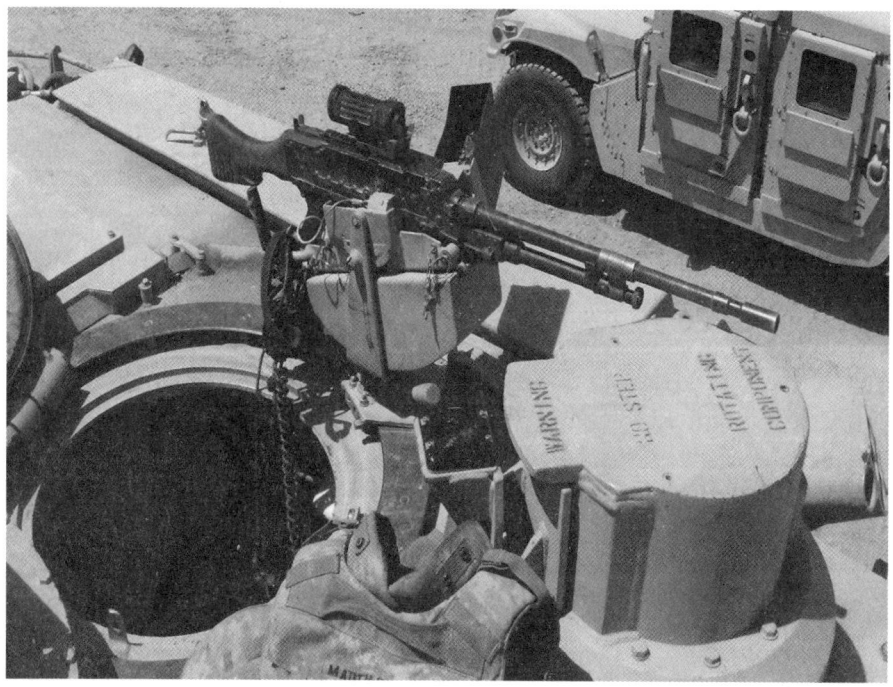

M1A1 Abrams tank-loader's machine gun. (Jeff DeRosa)

Bradley Fighting Vehicle (BFV). (U.S. Army)

started to learn the ways of the combined arms battalions. Smith had to take off his proverbial "tanker hat," and become a well-rounded senior NCO who could lead all combat and support soldiers in battle. The brigade commander found himself in a similar situation. David Perkins grew up in the military with the same culture and love of tanks as his command staff. He found himself in a position where he was asked to lead a group of men that trusted him and needed him to find a way to bring them home and achieve victory.[16] This meant finding a way to form a cohesive unit and present a formidable force to defeat the Iraqi army. The most important aspect for Perkins during his stay in Kuwait was training. He was fortunate to have CSM Smith to be his eyes, as Smith had over two decades of military experience.[17] The reality was, however, the goal for Perkins was to make sure that his brigade was trained. They spent the time in Kuwait making sure every possible outcome was covered and it still did not cover everything that could and did happen in combat.[18]

Perkins spoke in length about the training of his brigade during an oral interview with Dr. Tony Carlson in May of 2013. He had this to say about his goals while in Kuwait:

> We trained a lot. I will tell you probably one of the most important aspects of training. We trained combined arms maneuver and combined arms live fire. We had a huge training area, the Udari training area in northern Kuwait, so we fired multiple launch rocket systems (MLRS), artillery, and tanks: Bradleys. Probably the most important thing we did is, almost every night I had what I called sort of a science project.[19]

Perkins and his CSM ensured that not only were they in tune with each other, but their vehicles as well. Combat maintenance became something that many of the tankers had to focus on and learn on the fly. In garrison, if there are any problems with tanks, it is fairly easy to get parts and maintenance issues fixed. You simply fill out the paperwork and have a conversation with the company or battalion mechanics.[20] In the field, or in combat situations, this isn't necessarily the case—parts for a tank or Bradley were hard to come by during the initial months in Iraq.

During the early phases of the training in Kuwait, soldiers learned quickly how effective or ineffective their vehicles would be. They often found that their vehicles got bogged down due to the sand and the wet mud.[21] Tankers were used to training in the desert as all armored units during this time passed through the training halls of the National Training Center (NTC) located in Fort Irwin, CA. Even in this training environment, tankers often found that the weather there could be described as a "dry heat."[22] This weather was significantly different than what tankers faced in Iraq. During the six-month training, tankers found that many of the maneuvers that they attempted simply did not work in the sands of Iraq. This led to tankers, and their leaders, having to adapt and adjust to what the Iraqi sand did to tanks.

Tankers have a series of parts and equipment listed on a chart to describe what types of liquids, lubricants, and parts they use.[23] This chart was important as it gave the brigade and division commanders an idea of what their units were using and what they lacked. Later in the war, these items became much easier to come by. During the infancy of this training and the beginning of the war, however, the military, in general, was simply not prepared for the equipment usage that the tanks went through. Ammunition was also something that had to be taken into account. This was something that not only tankers had to go through, but the entire U.S. military. The questions about what lay before them became more important as they inched closer to combat. They needed to know what the enemy was using and for tankers, what types of tanks they could face.[24] The tankers of the 2nd BCT found those answers as they crossed over into the demilitarized zone of Iraq.

Iraqi Defenses

The initial, most dangerous enemy the tankers would face was enemy tanks.[25] The Iraqi defense was composed of three main armored adversaries: T-72 and T-62 tanks, along with the BMP (Boyevaya Mashina Pyekhoty 1), all Russian-made. The T-62 tank was built and used by the Soviet Union and later by the Iraqi army. This tank has a 115 mm main gun and is less armored than its sister tank the T-72.

The T-62 tank suffers from several issues that make it less than ideal for the tank crew. The space inside of this tank is extremely cramped and uncomfortable for the crew.[26] The main gun also suffers from directional firing issues: it cannot fire at one target and then quickly fire at another that is in a different direction. The main gun of this tank has a significantly slower turn rate than the Abrams tank. This makes it especially difficult if the tank fires and misses the target as it simply is not fast enough to reengage the target.[27] The main gun is slightly less powerful than the Abrams' as well. The Iraqi Army also did not commit to armored training as their American foes did. Many times, the Iraqi Army simply had hasty training for their armored core and this makes it almost impossible to have a mastery-level grasp of the tank. When the T-62 had mechanical issues or broke down, the Iraqi tankers did not have the wherewithal to fix the tank, and often it was abandoned on the battlefield.[28] The Iraqi armored corps was simply not used to fighting an enemy that was prepared and determined to achieve victory, and that was never more obvious than when they encountered tanks from the U.S. Army.

The T-72 tank is a more modern Soviet tank. This tank had the capability to be more of an adversary to the Abrams, but a lack of tankers and training also doomed it. The T-72 was perhaps the most observed enemy tank during this conflict.[29] A lightweight tank, it is more agile and mobile than the T-62. This tank has a 125 mm main gun and a three-man crew. It served as the main armored resistance during the initial invasion, able to fight toe to toe with the Abrams simply because of the main gun.[30] One of the biggest issues that this tank has is optics. The tanks that were used by the Iraqis during the invasion were built in the 1970s and 1980s. They never had the opportunity to use advanced technology.

These tanks were still being used during Operation *Desert Storm/ Shield*. They were never designed to fight M1A1/2 tanks that had the newest technology and state-of-the-art equipment.[31] These tanks were involved in several major attacks against the American forces during this invasion and were able to have success against units that were either lightly armored or simply did not have a major armored presence. The Iraqi Army used their intelligence to decipher which units were not armored and they would put their armored forces against those units.[32] TFs were only in their infancy, and they did not extend to light infantry brigades. This would often lead to many intense firefights when light infantry units would be forced to go up against armored units of the Iraqi Army.

T-72 Soviet tank. (U.S. Army / DVIDS)

One of the things that the army did during the initial invasion was to "cross-lend" units.[33] Lieutenant Colonel Ernest "Rock" Marcone commanded 3-69 AR during the initial invasion of Iraq. He talked about how the armor units would cross-lend units during his oral interview in 2022.

> I think that one of the biggest things that were interesting to me was how I was able to divvy up my armor units within the brigade and within the coalition forces in general. One of the airborne infantry units from the 101st was having some significant issues with the Iraqi forces and they made it clear that they could use some armor support. One of the things that I would point out is the fact that one tank platoon has more firepower than an entire light infantry company. I offered to give them one of my tank companies in exchange for a light infantry company. This gave my task force a bit more flexibility regarding combating dismounted infantry and it gave the infantry a squared-away tank company that could take the fight to the enemy.[34]

This cross-lending of armor units was something that became common during the entirety of the invasion of Iraq. This became a precursor to the CAB configuration and gave armor TFs the ability to clear rooms and fight the "infantry fight" during the invasion. The training and professionalism of tankers made cross-lending possible and successful. Tankers not only had to conform to fighting the enemy through the lens of an infantry battalion, but they had to conform to the different atmosphere of infantry leadership. Priding themselves on being masters of adaptability,[35] tankers knew that they were vital for this fight. At this stage of combat, they also knew that the old ways of the pure battalion were coming to an end. They understood the army was changing and they had to learn to function within that new way if they were going to continue to be viable. These changes within the armor also allowed tankers to see the battle from the eyes of their rivals and show that they were more than "gearheads" that sat on their tanks all day.[36]

One of the other obstacles that tankers and coalition forces had to face was the Iraqi infantry. As stated earlier, the two main forces that the coalition forces would face during the initial invasion were the Republican Guard and the Fedayeen Saddam.[37] The Republican Guard was the personal security of Saddam Hussein and the city of Baghdad.[38] These soldiers were heavily armed and very well trained. They were the elite infantry fighters of Iraq and the ones that gave coalition ground troops the most resistance. This unit was not a large force. There were an estimated 2,000–3,000 Republican Guard forces (RG) fighting throughout the invasion.[39] This number became a bit more problematic for the army and its tankers as they spread throughout the invasion route. Tankers found themselves in prolonged firefights with the RG simply because they chose not to fight a conventional war and used their small numbers to their advantage. The RG spread themselves thin, choosing to engage coalition forces in small groups of 20–75 soldiers at a time in some cases. This would force the larger forces to engage in firefights[40] to destroy the enemy. Tanks engaged the RG the same way that they did any of the dismounts during the initial portion of this conflict. If it was possible to use small arms munitions, that's what the tanks did. They routinely fired the loader's coax and gunner's 240 machine gun. They also used the TC's .50-cal, although there was always a caution with using this due to the exposure of the TC.

Both the RG and the Fedayeen Saddam (FS) were armed with essentially the same type of weaponry. The main rifle that was used by both groups was the AK-47 (Avtomat Kalashnikova-Russia).[41] This rifle uses 7.62 ammunition (the same munition as the gunner's coax and the loader's 240 machine gun) and was used by the Soviet Army during the reign of the USSR. The Iraqi resistance favored this weapon because of the accuracy of the automatic burst. They could merely point the weapon at their enemy and if the auto switch was selected, it would unleash a 3–4-round burst in the direction that the weapon was pointed in.[42] This was deadly for the coalition ground troops but also for the TC and loader

AK-47 rifle. (Courtesy Wikimedia Commons)

when they were exposed from their tanks. The Iraqi resistance also used a rocket-propelled grenade (RPG). Launched at the enemy, this would explode on contact—fatal for anyone in the vicinity of the explosion. This was also problematic for the tanks as well. Many times, during the invasion, the resistance would fire at the tanks and either hit the bustle racks that stored the crew's personal equipment or the rear of the tank that holds the engine (depending on which way the tank is facing).

These would be two forces and weapons that tankers would fight and face during the initial phase of this war. They would be forced to align the munitions that they brought and used with the enemy that they would be facing. Heading into the invasion, the amount of ammunition and type that each tank would use was dependent on the command staff of that unit. For many of the armor units during the invasion, the main round used would be a sabot or HEAT round. These rounds were preferred as the enemy would routinely hide in areas that small arms rounds could not penetrate and the HEAT round was perfect for destroying bunkers, buildings, or other hiding spots.[43] Another concern from tankers that arose during the initial invasion was enemy "technicals." Technicals (techs) were enemy soldiers that used either vans, small cars, or trucks, and attached machine guns to them or simply shot out of the windows of the vehicles to oppose the initial convoy of coalition forces.[44] These technicals were dealt with primarily by tankers or mechanized infantry and armored cavalry troops. Technicals made it difficult for coalition convoys to move quickly as they became more of a nuisance to the forward movements or armored convoys. Tankers had to use their training and instincts to quickly identify who was the enemy and who was simply a civilian trying to move through the highway. Identification was an issue as many of the resistance fighters would be in plain clothes and not in uniform. This made fighting the enemy difficult for the entirety of OIF[45] and it became more difficult as the coalition drove further into the heart of Iraq. Coalition forces were expecting the roads to be clear, but they were met with hundreds of civilians running through their ranks.[46]

All of these enemy elements led to the daunting task that faced the tankers in their drive to Baghdad. They knew that they had to fight a mixture of both armored and light infantry fighters. The commanders within the 3rd Infantry Division knew that as well. They made sure that during the six-month rotations in Kuwait, the BCTs were ready to fight whatever enemy they faced. Much like the garrison environment was different for tankers during the BDU era, the same can be said for the infantry units. They were pushed in a different way than the army infantry units that followed them. Toughness and discipline were paramount in those units with a premium on physical fitness.[47] Whether it was mechanized or light infantry units, during this era, it was demanded by the leadership at all combat levels, to be in the best shape humanly possible. This mentality and combat approach was vital to have as a companion to the armored corps. Tankers needed to know that when they softened the battlefield, without a doubt, a physically fit and determined infantry force could come in and destroy the enemy dismounted troops.[48]

CHAPTER 3

Thunder Runs

The invasion of Iraq and "Thunder Run" was a tanker's dream. They were able to unleash their full arsenal of weaponry against the soldiers and tanks of Iraq. The initial push was known as a "turkey shoot."[1] This was because many of the tanks that were spotted and fired upon did not have any Iraqis inside of them. They were abandoned once they spotted the army's tanks approaching. As they would inch closer to the city, they would encounter a much larger and more determined enemy.

Battle of Samawah, March 23, 2003

The 3rd Infantry Division, commanded by Major General Buford Blount, led the charge for the army as far as the invasion of Iraq and the eventual "Thunder Run." Blount was a career armor officer and veteran of *Desert Storm/Shield*.[2] The division comprised three heavy brigades (HBCT or heavy combat brigade teams). The corps level comprised several combat divisions or regiments, which answered to one corps commander and CSM.[3] The corps commander was a three-star general (lieutenant general). The role of the corps CSM is no different from other senior enlisted roles that have been discussed, except that it is on a much larger scale and the interaction with the enlisted soldier is minimal at best. The 3rd ID was under the control of the V Corps during this initial invasion and the corps command staff was given a large role. The entirety of the coalition forces fell under the command of the Coalition Forces Land Component Command (CFLCC). CFLCC decided that the best way to approach this invasion was to bypass smaller cities that could delay the progress of the main ground elements.

The first major engagement for tankers and the army, as they attempted to obey this plan, was the city of Samawah in March 2003.[4] The 2nd BCT, 3rd ID, had the impression that as they headed south towards Samawah, the city would embrace the U.S. forces and could possibly be a place to rest and refit. The intelligence, however, was incorrect. As the brigade's recon battalion, 3rd Battalion, 7th U.S. Cavalry Regiment, made its way towards the city, they were greeted with RPG and small arms fire.[5] Lieutenant Colonel Bryan Batson served as a battery commander with 1-39 Field Artillery Regiment during the initial invasion into Baghdad and had this to say during an interview with the Army University Press in 2019: "We were told that the people of Samawah and other areas around the region would be happy to see us and to expect a greeting. No, the greetings were bullets, and the welcome was RPGs."[6] The battalion comprised three line companies and a headquarters company (HHT).[7] This squadron was composed of two armored recon or scout companies and one armor company. The scout companies came under fire as they passed the city. Instead of bypassing the city, the battalion engaged the enemy for over two days. This would be one of the few times during the initial invasion that the coalition forces would face both FS and the RG in large numbers. The enemy was dug in and prepared for the coalition forces and waited for them to approach before they unleashed a barrage of fire on the tanks and Bradleys of 3-7.[8]

Tankers within a cavalry squadron or troop are often asked to act as the long arm of the recon unit. They are to provide armored support and protection to the recon units as they scout and observe the enemy deposition.[9] During the battle of Samawah, tankers were unleashed to go on the offensive. Due to the city's small and compact construction and architecture, tankers refrained from sending a barrage of main gun rounds into the city. Instead, they chose to use the loaders' coaxes and TCs' machine guns. This would be the first time that the tankers would see how determined the enemy was and what they needed to do to be successful in this type of urban environment. 3-7 Cav, along with U.S. Special Forces, continued to probe the enemy and destroy them when engaged. Special Forces and the cavalry used the armor and protection that the tanks provided to secure information about the enemy's disposition and what would be needed to destroy them in Samawah. This probe mission for the tankers of 3-7 Cav lasted for three days. "Apache" (Alpha) Company was the armored force of the battalion.

By the time the battle was over, the battalion was responsible for nearly five hundred enemy deaths.[10] Tanks had fired nearly one hundred main gun rounds, with the majority of those rounds being HEAT or canister. The goal of this mission was to simply distract the enemy with tanks and Bradley fire, while at the same time using reconnaissance units to pass the information along to the unit that would engage and clear the city for the coalition troops. The 3rd ID was instructed by V Corps to relinquish the task of taking the city to the 2nd Brigade of the 82nd Airborne Division. This unit was a light infantry brigade and had the numbers to go in and individually clear houses and destroy the enemy through the use of close-quarter combat to achieve the mission of clearing the town.[11] The 82nd went on for the next several days, combating the enemy in Samawah. They would eventually clear the city on March 30, 2003. The infantrymen of the 82nd were able to achieve their goal and destroy the enemy in large part due to the efforts of the tankers. The use of the main gun proved to be the difference in the battle as the

Rocket-propelled grenade (RPG). (Courtesy Wikimedia Commons / Michal Manas)

tank companies pounded the enemy fighters with main gun to which they had no answer. The armor companies of 3-7 were able to use the urban combat training that they developed before the war, to soften the battlefield for their infantry brothers.[12]

Seizing Saddam International Airport

One of the next major landmarks that the armored corps of the coalition forces faced was an operation to secure Saddam International Airport (SAI) located in Baghdad. SAI was not simply an airport, but a beacon. Coalition forces and in particular the army targeted the seizure of this airport not only to take it away from the enemy resistance but to show the Iraqi people that the FA and RG were no longer in charge.[13] This would be the stiffest test that the 3rd ID had faced up to this point. Military intelligence had reports stating that the airport was guarded by Saddam's best T-72 units. The task of securing the airport was given to the 1st Armored Brigade (Raider), comprising three battalions that had armor—3-69 AR, 1-64 AR, and 5-7 CAV. The brigade would rely on its armor to secure the airport. The attack began with artillery fire on April 3, 2003, at 11 p.m.[14]

The goal of this artillery fire was to ensure that as many T-72 tanks and antiair pieces as possible were destroyed before the Raider brigade began its assault. The fear was that the T-72s may attack the vulnerable dismounted infantry and heavy losses could be sustained. Even with the artillery that helped destroy much of the enemy armor capability, the 1st Brigade found itself amid some very intense close-quarter combat. The enemy was still able to muster up over three hundred enemy fighters during this collision with the Raider brigade.[15] The tanks that were used during this battle used mainly the coaxial machine guns and the TCs' .50-cal. This was due to the close proximity of the enemy during the fight. Tanks can use their main gun at any range but were given orders about when and where they could use their main gun during this battle. This was a battle where it was important to deploy the integration of the combined arms model on the enemy. The tanks were tasked with ensuring that the enemy was unable to use armored vehicles to flank or tank down the more vulnerable infantry. The tanks needed to be able to keep the enemy armored vehicles and/or technicals at bay to allow the infantry the opportunity to move close and destroy the Iraqi resistance using close-quarters combat.[16]

The fighting proved to be more intense than any up to this point. Because the 1st ABCT had the advantage of being mechanized and using their tanks, they were able to destroy the resistance and ultimately take the airport. The fighting lasted for over two days. This was another example and proof that the resistance that the coalition forces were facing was perhaps different than many of the veterans of *Desert Storm/Desert Shield* had faced.[17] After the airport was secured and in the hands of coalition forces, MG Brooks spoke for the coalition forces as the airport was renamed Baghdad International Airport. This was important not only for the coalition forces but for the people of Iraq. This airport was a beacon of power and prestige for the Saddam regime. The perception was being fought just as much as the enemy by the coalition forces. The coalition had to prove that although they came in with a lot of bravado and equipment, when it came down to the combat aspect of the war and putting rounds down range at the enemy, they would be victorious.[18] CFLCC commander LTG Wallace now had to decide what to do about Baghdad.

Wallace knew that he simply did not have enough information about Baghdad to plan the next military action against the city.[19] One of the options given to him by his subordinates was to conduct a series of small raids into the city. This would give the commander the ability to discern the city's defenses while at the same time probing the road leading up to Baghdad for any potential hazards that could delay or even destroy an armored column. Wallace's goal was to militarily own the city without taking it by force, or at least not by force at that very moment. Deciding to use a reconnaissance effort to determine the next course of action, Wallace opted for this action to be an armored reconnaissance effort instead of using light forces.[20] Wallace made this choice due to the unknown situation in Baghdad. If he had chosen to send in light cavalry with "soft" vehicles, they could find themselves fighting an entrenched enemy and perhaps roadside bombs or other ambushes that would put coalition lives in unnecessary danger. Knowing that an armored brigade would at least be able to withstand a significantly larger amount of enemy fire than a light infantry brigade, Wallace gave the task of conducting this initial recon of Baghdad to the 2nd ABCT of the 3rd Infantry Division.[21]

This armored brigade was commanded by Col. David Perkins. Perkins knew that this would be a daunting task for any unit, but as a career-long armor officer, he also knew what Abrams tanks were capable of. He entrusted the initial recon mission to the 1st Battalion 64th Armor Regiment commanded by LTC Rick Schwartz.[22] Schwartz was the commander of what would be called Task Force "Rogue." Schwartz explained the composition of this task force during an interview where he also explains the goal of the initial Thunder Run:

> Task Force Rogue consisted of 731 officers, non-commissioned officers, and soldiers. The actual makeup of the organization was tankers, infantrymen, engineers as well as the associated scouts, mortars, medics, mechanics, cooks, and truck drivers. We crossed the line of departure with 30 tanks, 14 Bradleys, 14 engineer vehicles, and about 220 pieces of rolling stock, and that included everything from shooters to trailers. Regarding your second question about what the intent of the operation was, the answer is threefold. Gain information about the enemy, destroy defending forces, and finally, send a clear message that coalition forces were in the capital city. First, the mission was intended to gain information that we badly needed. Up to this point, in five previous battles, we had little actionable intelligence that we could use to our benefit. For the longest time, that bothered me. I felt that going into this as the lead element, I would have access to information about the composition and disposition of the enemy. Instead, we were the reconnaissance-by-fire force, the probe-and-get-information force, but with the speed of our movement, that's the way it had to be. There were no human intelligence (HUMINT) sources that we could keep forward because we were moving so fast that we'd just overtake them. That's the first important note. We were going in to determine what was there, and the attack on the 5th of April—known as the thunder run—was essentially 17 kilometers and two hours and 20 minutes of moving to contact, identifying what was there, destroying it, and at the same time trying to gain an understanding of what the future environment would look like.[23]

During the initial push into the city, several things disturbed Schwartz and had to be overcome. One of the bigger issues that plagued him before this push into the city was the lack of information that he received from those in charge.[24] Schwartz was told by Perkins that he would be going into Baghdad and the goal, of course, would be to discern the enemy defenses throughout the city to ascertain if the entire brigade and other BCTs could enter the city. The issue that Schwartz had was for the safety and security of his tankers. Several of the Iraqi mechanized infantry and armored divisions had already been destroyed by coalition forces up to this point. The Marines and other army units had seen the enemy and made sure that any coordinated attacks by the resistance forces would be minimal because the enemy lacked numbers and leadership.[25] One of the things that had ceased was the enemy's ability to maintain artillery strikes on the coalition forces and in particular their armor. The Iraqi forces used artillery as a way to deter tank units from progressing on their position. The coalition forces had targeted their artillery pieces and this allowed the armored core to move forward at a steady pace.

One of the issues with this pace for Schwartz and 1-64, as they prepared to move out and complete the first Thunder Run, was the wear and tear that this war had already taken on the Abrams. Several of Schwartz's tank companies had been hit hard by the war at this point. Charlie Company was one of the hardest hit as they served as the vanguard for a good portion of this conflict up to this point.[26] They had two tanks down and two more that were heavily hit by enemy fire. Perkins discussed why he was so willing to send in his tanks and the confidence that he had in them during a video interview in which he stated, "The leverage that I'm using for my tanks is that they are extremely large, they go really fast, and they can take and put out a lot of firepower."[27] This meant that while other "soft skin" vehicles were sent through certain areas of Iraq with more caution, Abrams were sent through these areas first not only during the infancy of these battles but throughout the war.

Schwartz had seen 1-64 destroy countless enemies, but now he had to see what the cost of that success was on his tanks. One of the important things to note about Abrams tanks is that they take a significant amount of maintenance just to keep going. It takes a constant effort to make sure that Abrams tanks run at the optimal level. Oftentimes, this sort of dedication to the tanks is misconstrued by other soldiers. Captain Woodward of C-Co 1-16 had his to say about the topic:

> Infantry guys may see us as lazy because we sit and work on our tanks all day instead of rucking and running 100 miles. But it's important to know that it takes discipline to stay on that beat and fix problems day in and day out. Tanks break down a lot and the crews have to know what they can fix and what they can't. This is something that is only learned through the garrison training they receive from the section and platoon sergeants.[28]

One of the things that Schwartz made sure to instill in his tankers was how to react if a tank went down. He made sure that every tank company knew who would tow the tank and what to do with the remaining crew after the tank was eventually removed.

This was important for the company commanders and company first sergeants as they had to make sure their men were properly trained for whatever situation they found themselves in. Schwartz would not leave his men and as the battalion commander of an armor unit, he would lead by example as the TC of his tank. This meant that during the initial reconnaissance of Baghdad, he would be in the enemy's crosshairs as well. The CSM would be in an APC (M113) as well as the company's senior enlisted men, right alongside their units.[29] Although Schwartz had to go into this mission shorthanded on armor, the mission still had to be completed. This honor was given to the tankers not only because of the vehicle they rode but because of the training they had received and the trust of the commanders.

One of the biggest issues that plagued the armor units as they drove into Baghdad was the enemy placement up Highway 1. Going into the fight, tankers went up the highway blind about what the enemy would do to defend the city. One of the things that caused the most damage to the tank columns would be the enemy hidden on the side of the road and bushes as they traveled to Baghdad.

On April 5 at 0530, the TF moved out and began the mission to Baghdad. During the initial movement to Baghdad, tanks found themselves under constant fire by the enemy in an unconventional setting. The enemy was well aware of the fact that they could not merely go toe to toe with the greatest armored force in the world so they found ways to attack the armored column in a way that could annoy and disrupt the column as opposed to defeating it. It is important to note that this first Thunder Run was a battalion-size task force. 1-64 Armor was given a company of mechanized infantry and other combat enablers, but this was still a relatively small force for the mission that they were undertaking.[30] The initial barrage that the task force was met with was enemy RPGs. This rocked many of the soft-skinned vehicles in the column but caused little to no damage to the tanks. The fear was that the RPGs could hit the engine located in the back of the tank and force a tank to stop or slow down the column.

There was an instance where a tank was hit by a recoilless rifle (long-tubed portable artillery piece) that hit the back of the tank and permanently disabled it.[31] Lieutenant Colonel Ricky Nussio and other tankers tried for nearly an hour to put the fire out using water containers strapped outside of the Abrams. In the end, the order was given to abandon the tank and it would eventually be destroyed by the Air Force to prevent the Iraqi forces from being able to use its parts.[32] This was of course disheartening to the column and the tankers for several reasons. The Iraqi military under Saddam was trying to push the narrative to the people of Iraq that the coalition forces were being defeated and that the Iraqi military would prevail. They used the image of a destroyed tank to reinforce this story in the public view. This had the potential to be damaging to the armored corps of the U.S. Army. They needed to not only complete the current mission of reconnaissance but also to assure the people of Iraq that this war would be the end of Saddam and that the armored forces would not be stopped. This was an eye-opening moment for both Schwartz and the soldiers of TF 1-64. They were aware that their tanks were not indestructible, as some tankers might have felt.[33] This notion continued to be true as the armored column pushed forward toward its objective in Baghdad.

With all the training that tankers must go through, there are still combat scenarios that test that training. One such incident was when both the gunner's coaxial machine gun and the TC's .50-cal failed during an intense firefight involving the tank of SSG Stevon Booker. Although there are tables during gunnery where the tank crew must manually fire the main gun, this, of course, is not while they are under fire by a determined enemy. It was during this time that Booker showed the true heart of a tanker and the courage of an American soldier and exposed himself to enemy fire while lying in the prone flat position on his tank. He used both his sidearm pistol and his M-4 rifle to attempt to repel the Iraqi dismounted troops as they charged toward the column and his tank.[34] SSG Booker gave his life on April 5 defending his tank and his crew members. This sacrifice shook the TF to its core. But it also showed the type of leadership that existed within the armored corps and the army as a whole. The mission had to continue for the task force, even with the loss of Booker. The problems that presented themselves with his death continued to plague 3rd ID's column. They had to continue to fight a faceless enemy that did not conventionally present itself. This made it difficult for the tanks, but it also taught them the importance of properly identifying their targets before engaging them.[35]

Staff Sgt. Stevon Booker. (3rd Infantry Division)

The TF continued to slice through the enemy defenses en route to their objective. They continued to engage the dismounted troops using primarily the coax and the TC's .50-cal. This tactic preserved main gun ammunition but also put extra stress on the coax and the .50-cal, causing several of the tanks in the column to have issues with those systems, just as Booker's had. In some instances, tank crews were forced to manually turn the gun tube to use it or simply used their personal M-4 rifle and sidearm.[36] This advance was perilous for the 1-64, to say the least. They had to continually fight both the enemy forces as well as the malfunctions on the tanks. The first Thunder Run tried the continuity of the tank crews and the resolve of the armor commanders. It would have been easy to conclude that the tanks could not take the beating that they were receiving and simply attempt to pass this assignment to other units that had fewer vehicle demands to worry about. However, this is not the way of the armored corps. No matter the issue or task that lies in front of them, tankers simply find a way to complete the mission and that was the case for the thunder runs. By mid-morning, the task force had completed the task and arrived in Baghdad.[37]

Schwartz returned the TF to the airport to report back to Perkins about the conditions that he faced on the trip to Baghdad and if the trip would be possible again for a much larger force. Perkins was curious about the success of the TF as well as what changes would need to be made to allow a larger force to become a fixture in Baghdad, at least for the moment. Perkins would also be joining the second attempt to recon the city.

Before any planning took place, the TF held a memorial service for SSG Stevon Booker. For his valor and dedication to his crew his tank, and the army, Booker would posthumously be awarded the Army Distinguished Service Cross.[38] Later that day, Perkins would meet with his senior officers and enlisted advisors. This meeting would be to determine what the next stage of this fight would entail. Perkins was given the mission to return to Baghdad and set up a base of operations from corps commander LTG David McKiernan, and then from MG Blunt who commanded the 3rd ID (mechanized).[39] Perkins did not have a reputation as a "micro-manager." He knew the importance of using his subordinates to carry out missions and made sure that although this mission was large in scale, the company commanders, platoon leaders, first sergeants, and platoon sergeants would be involved in the planning and execution of this mission. Perkins discussed this philosophy:

> When you then sort of look at the mission and do an analysis of it, we were an Armor Brigade, so we didn't have a lot of dismounts. We had one Infantry battalion, but a mechanized Infantry battalion, so we didn't have a lot of dismounts. We were going to have to conduct very dense urban warfare with an Armor force, which pretty much in any school I'd gone to in the Army up to that point, was exactly the wrong kind of force that you wanted to put into it—one would think. Now, as I said, one of the main tenets of Mission Command is trust up and down and empowering subordinates. Subordinates, as I said, can empower superiors quite often. We don't think about that. A great resource that had on the brigade was CSM Gallagher, the command sergeant major of the 3-15th Infantry. He was also in Mogadishu as SGT Gallagher, who was the non-commissioned officer in charge (NCOIC) of the quick reaction force (QRF), who was going in to rescue the Rangers. Back when we were in Kuwait, he would come to me and we would do these training exercises and have these visualization discussions about how we would do Baghdad. He'd always constantly go, "Sir, make sure this does not turn into a Mogadishu. Make sure we can get in and out." In other words, he was empowering me. He was giving me a great understanding of the perils of urban warfare because he had been there, done that. Purple Heart and Silver Star from Mogadishu, so literally he had done that. He is now CSM of a light infantry battalion. We started to think about the problem set differently.[40]

Perkins and Blunt decided that the next step would be to send a brigade-level force into Baghdad. The TF 1-64's XO, Major Ricky

Nussio, was given the monumental task of ensuring that the tanks and Bradleys of the TF were conducting day-long maintenance and refit operations. Nussio stated that he had never seen men so focused on their vehicles and supervised as the TF got their vehicles ready to go.[41] The TF was still mourning the loss of Booker and this played heavily on the hearts of the men as they attempted to get ready to go back into the heart of Baghdad. 1-64 was still reeling from the constant barrage of fire that they took while entering the city the first time. Many of the soldiers faced enemy fire for the first time in their young military lives. This was something that they all had to come to grips with because the armored force was then, and always will be, the tip of the spear when it comes to the army. The soldiers fixed what could be fixed and made sure that all the crew-level PMCS was completed.[42] The soldiers were told that the second run into Baghdad would take place on April 7. The biggest difference that the TF would experience, at least at the beginning of this mission, was the fact that they would be going into Baghdad with the entire 2nd BCT. This meant that they would have more armored support as they tried to set a base of operations in Baghdad.[43]

Perkins revealed to his commanders that several objectives needed to be met for him to decide that the mission was a success and that the brigade could stay in Baghdad. Perkins felt that a base of operations needed to be set up in downtown Baghdad, to set up operations for the coalition forces at a later date.[44] He was unaware of how long his brigade, or the coalition forces, in general, would be in Iraq. But he did know that they were not leaving anytime soon and he wanted to make sure that a base to run tanks and mechanized infantry was possible for American forces. It was also important that the tanks within the brigade were able to set up a defensive position once they reached their objectives. As an armor officer, Perkins knew the capabilities of tanks and he felt the best way to use them would be to act as the big brother of the brigade.[45] Another reason that Perkins knew he had to send in the brigade was simply as a tool to defend against the misinformation of the Iraqi resistance. Mohammed Saeed al-Sahaf (also known as "Baghdad Bob"), was the minister of public information for Saddam during the initial phase of this conflict.[46] Sahaf tried to paint a picture to the Iraqi people that the forces of Saddam would not be defeated and that there were no American forces near the Baghdad area.

He wanted the people to feel that the FS and the RG were repulsing the coalition forces. Validity was added to these false accounts when the tank from TF 1-64 was disabled during the first Thunder Run. Sahaf used the tank as a talking point to let the people of Iraq know that the American tanks were no match for the forces of Saddam. Perkins knew that if he could park several tanks in downtown Baghdad, this would dispel that notion and bring credibility to the coalition forces, and show that they would indeed complete the mission that they were there for. Perkins laid out the four main objectives that he had to his commanders as preparations were being made by the tank crews. The first thing that would need to be set up was preparatory fire by 1-9 Field Artillery, the brigade's artillery unit. The goal was to destroy as much of the enemy's capabilities before sending in a brigade-sized element into the heart of Baghdad. The first run into Baghdad was simply a show of force. This assault would be a move to assert control and set up a permanent base in Baghdad.[47] The armored column would first take enemy fire around 0630 on April 7.[48]

The enemy had prepared for this second incursion into Baghdad and appeared to be more prepared for this fight as opposed to the first incursion which was a surprise to much of the Iraqi forces. The armored column would take heavy AK and RPG fire from the sides of the road as they moved up Highway 8. One of the biggest threats that 2nd BCT faced was crossing through an underpass. This was dangerous for both the loader and the TC as they were often outside of their respective hatches to use their assigned machine guns so that the TC could have a better view of the battlefield. Perkins gave instructions to the tank crews about not only the underpass but the move to Baghdad in general: "I told the tank crews that we were going to go screaming into Baghdad. I gave them specific instructions: do not stop! When you are going through an underpass you are going to take heavy fire so get down inside the tank and button up. If a tank is disabled immediately put that crew on something else and keep moving."[49] As a tanker, Perkins was well aware of how it got inside a tank during garrison operations. Now, his tankers were stuffed inside of a tank while the heat was well over 100 degrees and they were taking enemy fire.

These orders were given to get the tanks to their objective as quickly as possible without losing any of his soldiers.[50] One of the things that plagued the column as they moved from objective to objective was the type of enemy that was attacking them and the weapons they were using. During the second Thunder Run, the column was not only facing fire from dug-in Iraqi fighters but also from enemy technicals mixed in with the civilian population.[51] This would take the form of Iraqi fighters riding bicycles with AK-47s and minivans with machine guns sticking out of the back window.[52] This made engaging the enemy very difficult for the tank crews. Even with their targeting systems and sights, they still could not use their main gun while the enemy was mixed with the civilian population for fear of harming innocent bystanders. When there was an opportunity to engage these technicals or at least those using minivans or other vehicles for cover, tankers would often engage them with a sabot round. This had the desired effect of destroying the enemy and killing those inside the vehicles, neutralizing the threat.

Oftentimes, the Iraqi fighters simply wanted to deter the tank as it moved to its objective. In all reality, they knew that they would never be victorious against an Abrams. The goal was simply to go and distract them or perhaps wound or kill a crew member while they were in their hatch, as was the case with Booker.[53] This combined with the constant barrage of enemy fire led to another tank being disabled during the push into Baghdad. Perkins immediately ordered the tank towed to the rear of the column and proceeded with the mission. Along with the current mission of getting his tanks into Baghdad, Perkins also had to manage and focus the fight that was going on within the brigade. Before the second Thunder Run, TF 3-15 was involved in some heavy fighting along the three objectives dubbed Larry, Curly, and Moe.[54] These three locations were located on a cloverleaf interchange. These interchanges were the site of intense fighting that was led by TF 3-15 IN. This TF was a mechanized infantry unit that was supported by two tank companies. These tank companies came for both 1-64 and 4-64 AR.

The fighting at these interchanges was intense and lengthy. Perkins had to make sure that he kept in communication and that the situation would not be dire for the men there. 3-15 had to be reinforced by another mechanized infantry battalion to hold their grasp on the area. Perkins took an entire infantry company from the task force and used it for the second run into Baghdad. This put a strain on the task force and forced them to use other traditional assets to be able to maintain the interchanges.[55] The

Diagram of a cloverleaf interchange.

tank companies that supported 3-15 during this fight had the duty of being the support of the infantry units that were the main force. For the majority of this fighting, they used their coaxial machine guns and the TC's .50-cal to fight off the enemy.[56] The TF soon found themselves short on ammunition as the enemy continued to attack and counterattack. The Abrams also found themselves short on fuel during their battle for these interchanges.[57] During this battle, the tank companies could not continually use the main gun due to the proximity of the enemy forces. Several tanks used two times the combat load for small arms on their tank. This led to the deaths of nearly two hundred enemy soldiers during the battle for the interchanges.[58]

As the armored column continued its path from one objective to another, the fighting continued to be intense for the brigade. The two tank battalions (1st and 4th Battalion, 64 Armor Regiment) fired nearly 400 main gun rounds en route to objective Moe.[59] Once the brigade reached objective Moe, Perkins evaluated the movement of the column and decided that his objectives had been met to the level that met his, the division, and the corps commander's approval. He made the decision for the brigade to remain in Baghdad overnight. The tank battalion was used to set up a perimeter and provide overwatch for the rest of the brigade as they moved into a position of guarding the terrain that they had taken as opposed to being on the attack.

The tank units paved the way for both Thunder Runs. It was Perkins' experience as an armor officer that led to the planning and overall completion of this mission. This mission was needed for the coalition forces to set up Baghdad as a permanent station from which they could set up patrol and resupply for all coalition units. Ultimately, during these two recon efforts, tanks proved how valuable they were against both the infantry and the vehicles that they would encounter. The notion of using tanks to deter and destroy the enemy would be a common theme for the rest of this war.

CHAPTER 4

The Second Battle of Fallujah

The second battle of Fallujah officially began on November 9, 2004. AQI had grown and taken over Fallujah, declaring it an Islamic state. Under the direct guidance of Abu Mus'ab Zarqawi, enemy forces had gathered in the city—there were estimates of 2,000–5,000 enemy fighters.[1] The battle was meant to be a Marine-led operation to drive out the insurgent forces in Fallujah and deny them a safe haven within the city. There were several different ideas as to how and who should carry out the actions of this fight.[2] While it was Marine-led, it was not a Marine-only operation—it was amazing how often this battle has been characterized with many documentaries or books stating something along the lines of: "Marines went in house-to-house and captured Fallujah." The Marine Corps did lead the assault on Fallujah and were the main fighting force. But to say that entitles the Marines to take sole ownership of this battle is ridiculous and disrespectful to the United States Army.

Units from the army's 1st Cavalry, 2nd Infantry, and 1st Infantry Divisions all played a significant role in the second battle of Fallujah, known as Operation *Phantom Fury*.[3] During the early phases of this conflict, there was a shift in command in MNF-W and the I MEF. Major General Richard Natonski became the new commander of both forces and Fallujah fell within the realm of his command. Two regimental combat teams (RCT) were tasked with being lead elements for the 2nd battle of Fallujah. RCT 1 and 7 would lead the assault. Natonski, the Marines, and MNC-I (Multi-National Corps-Iraq) realized that more armored and mechanized infantry units would be needed to avoid some of the shortcomings of the first battle.

During the first battle of Fallujah (which was also Marine led), the Marines lacked a large armored/mechanized force to go in and inflict the necessary damage on the enemy, as would be proven effective in other battles such as Baqubah, Ramadi, and Sadr City. The Marines had been assigned several units to provide support for them as they conducted operations in the city.[4] The MNC-I reserve strike force, a Stryker battalion, was assigned to the Marines to give them a unit to implement an outer cordon and allow the Marines the ability to focus solely on the inner-city fight that would come. During the battle of Najaf, the Marines fought side by side with the 2-7 Cavalry Regiment from the 1st Cavalry Division.[5] During this time, the Marines that fought with them gained a profound respect for them and remembered the efficiency and discipline that was displayed during the fight.[6] The Marines would request that 2-7 Cav join them in the upcoming battle with the insurgents of Fallujah. The way that units are set up and identified in the 1st Cavalry division is slightly different from most divisions in the army. Armored cavalry regiments and cavalry units in general identify each unit as a "cavalry" unit. For example, the 3rd ABCT had 4 different units in their brigade but they are all classified as cavalry units. During this time, these units in all actuality were infantry, armor, and recon units that just fought under the cavalry banner.[7] The 1st Cavalry Division had already begun to experiment with the idea of combined arms. Several units that had traditionally been mechanized infantry had now integrated with armor units.

2-7 Cav was assigned to RCT 1 under the command of Col. Shupp. 2-7 was under the battalion command of LTC Rainey, an infantry officer who commanded the mechanized infantry battalion. During this conflict, a tank company from 3-68 Cav was task organized to 2-7 to give them armor capabilities.[8] Charlie Company 3-68 Cav was commanded by Capt. Peter Glass. Glass was an infantry officer who branch transferred early in his career to the armor. A highly respected officer, after the transfer he indoctrinated himself in tank culture and knowledge. Those who were around him could not identify the fact that he was anything else but a tanker.[9] Another move that was made within TF 2-7 was the reorganizing of several infantry platoons to give them armor or recon capabilities. Rainey wanted to attempt to give Glass an infantry platoon within his company and he also took one of the tank platoons and gave it to one of his mechanized infantry companies. The goal was to increase the firepower and maneuverability of the TF.

Within RCT 1, most of the fighting power of the Marines was infantry. The goal of this joint operation between the army and the Marines was to combine the strength of both services and to make this battle different from the previous attempt on Fallujah.[10] The army had a history and tradition during this war of bringing armor and mechanized infantry to areas that were considered "bad areas" or areas needing military cleansing. This led to success for the army but also a reputation for causing large amounts of destruction.[11] During the interview with 1SG Yuen, he had this to say about the destruction that armor units inflict:

> Sometimes you have to put a main gun round into a building. Sometimes you have to use the coax on dismounted troops. Sometimes you must use the TC's .50-cal on a vehicle. The enemy asked for the combat power of a tank when they refused to surrender and chose war with the U.S. Army. Once that line is crossed, there is no turning back.[12]

It is important to discuss the acceptance of destruction when deploying an armor unit in an urban city. Tanks bring with them a certain amount of devastation to the enemy. No one would argue that. But they also bring protection, increased firepower, and a psychological advantage over the enemy that light infantry simply do not.

The other major armored force in this battle would be from TF 2-2 Inf, known as the "Ramrods." They were commanded by infantry officer LTC Pete Newell, who was told that he would be taking a combined TF into Fallujah to assist the 1st MEF in October 2004. There was much debate going on between the Marines and TF 2-2 about what was the best way to organize a unit into the battle plans that the Marines had set in place. When it came to T-F 2-2, one tank company would join the TF and that would be Aco-2-63 AR. They were commanded by Capt. Paul Fowler who was an armor officer. His company would include a mech infantry platoon to give them the ability to deploy dismounted troops if need be.[13] Fowler and his company would be able to aid and assist the Marines due to their lethality and the firepower that they brought to the battlefield. It was important for Fowler and his tank crews to provide a strong level of tank fire throughout their mission as they would be the support and overwatch for dismounted infantry for both the army and Marines. Newell would be away on leave for the early stages of planning for this mission. Once he returned, he dove into the mission and rehearsals to get up to speed with what was being asked of him by the leaders of the Marine Corps.[14]

This battle would be different from others fought during this time due to the cohesion and interservice understanding that would be needed between the army and Marines. One of those issues was with the armor. The way the army views its armor is simply different from the way the Marines view theirs. During an interview with CSM Jackson on Ft. Riley, he had this to say about the army's view on tanks: "The armor is the backbone of the army. If you look at the majority of the major battles in Iraq, they were armor-led or led by a heavy

Operation *Phantom Fury* briefing between the army and Marine Corps officers. (U.S. Army)

brigade. That's not a coincidence."[15] Tanks were seen as a pivotal piece to heavy combat during this war and thus, the Marines wanted to make sure that they had a good source of armor while fighting this battle. For Marines, the rifleman is the spearhead of battle. They simply are not as mechanized as the army and they often prefer to attack head-on with their dismounted troops while the army use their vehicles to soften the battlefield if those vehicles are available.

The goals of the two units would differ based on the Marine regiments that they were attached to. For 2-2, the goal would truly be to assist and help the Marine infantry clear rooms while providing tank support for the rest of the regiment. The tank units in 2-2 would be equipped with over 11,000 rounds of coax ammunition, 2,000 rounds of the TC's .50-cal ammo, and another 4,000 rounds for the loader's 240 machine gun.[16] Along with the normal full load for the main gun, the tanks were expecting an all-out war during the second battle of Fallujah. 2-2 would be in a situation where they would scatter their task force to provide the Marines with help where they needed it and infantry bodies that could support Marines during close-quarter combat.[17] The "Ramrods" would uniquely use tanks as they would be asked to provide a cordon for the infantry and to fire on buildings that had become a safe haven for enemy infantry.[18] During several firefights in Fallujah, tanks were asked to fire on enemy positions to free up the infantry to fight and clear rooms. One of the issues that the tanks faced in Fallujah was the layout of the city. As much as the Marines needed the armor and mechanized infantry of the army, finding a way to deploy them within the city was difficult, to say the least.

Tanks were vital during the firefights as they helped 2-2 when they got bogged down and attempted to help them avoid being bogged down at all. SSG David Bellavia was a squad leader with Alpha Company 2-2 Infantry (A-Co 2-2 Inf). In his book he had this to say about the tankers of 2-63:

> The tankers that fought beside us were studs. I saw tankers fire and destroyed Iraqis on the street who were firing at us. It was amazing. I also saw them fire at buildings that had snipers in them and completely rock the structure of the buildings. They may not be grunts, but I was sure glad to have them on our side during this fight.[19]

In his book, he depicts how helpful and valuable the tanks of A 2-63 AR were to the TF. Alpha Company would also be divided within the TF to provide certain sectors with overwatch and to increase the firepower in areas that were being cleared by dismounted troops. The goal was to completely lock Fallujah down and disorientate the enemy-dismounted troops with the use of both mounted and mounted troops. This was made more possible by the ammunition that the tanks chose to use. The main source of ammunition that tanks would use for this fight would be HEAT and IMPAT rounds.[20] The IMPAT round provided tanks with the ability to fire at buildings in Fallujah, giving the dismounted troops cover fire and becoming unpredictable to the enemy forces.[21]

Canister and HEAT rounds were also used in abundance by Alpha Company. Over two hundred main gun rounds were used by Alpha during this conflict.[22] It is important to know how large a number that is for one single company during mere days of combat. During several of the conflicts in Iraq where tanks were used, main gun rounds were used at a minimum in order to reduce damage. For this battle, the goal was to destroy the enemy and the army put that at the forefront as opposed to damage control. Canister rounds were vital to the tank crews during the street fighting that took place. Alpha was involved in the fighting that took place for both the Army and the Marines. Street fighting would bog down coalition troops on one side of the street and often, the fighting was so heavy that troops could not advance. Instead of firing countless rounds at the enemy, tanks could use this shotgun–like round to clear out several enemies at once.[23] In 2-2, the TCs and loaders' personal machine guns were used as much during this battle as they were during the initial invasion due to the presence of snipers and the enemy's overreliance on IEDs. Still, during this fight, Alpha fired over ten thousand rounds of the loaders' and TCs' weapons. This showed that even during the most intense fighting, the tank crews still had to rely on their gunnery training and weapons proficiency.

TF 2-7's mission was less of a supporting role and more of a lead role for RCT 1. Under the command of Col. Shupp of the Marine Corps, TF 2-7 Cav had the honor of being the main force for the main force. They were asked to assist and accompany RCT 1 as they would lead the assault on Fallujah. Captain Glass was tasked with having the main armor force for this assault and would be relied upon to lead the tanks. The main ammunition that the tankers used was HEAT rounds,[24] similar to how they were used with 2-2. Cougar 6 (company commander of C 3-68 AR) was asked to provide cover and support for the breaching elements of the Marines and to assist the army mechanized forces as they set up blocking positions and conducted room-clearing operations.[25] One of the important aspects of this fight was the use of phase lines (PLs). This is an assignment along the path to an objective that had been laid out by Shupp and his staff and coordinated with Rainey. The use of PLs helped coordinate the many units that were used during this conflict. These PLs would allow the units to report back to the higher command and give a status that paralleled the mission goals, allowing the commander to make decisions based on the location of the unit.

During the initial fighting, the TF were under the impression that they needed to bypass smaller enemy forces to maintain a speed of maneuver that was acceptable for the RCT. But the army units were told not to bypass enemy units even if they were smaller than platoon-sized elements.[26] As was the case with 2-2, 2-7 was given initial instructions on how to proceed and how they could be best used to assist the Marines in their assault. Glass gave up one of his platoons to receive one mech infantry platoon within the TF and to allow the tanks to be used in other areas of the fight to aid the lightly armored Marines and dismounted army infantry. This platoon was led by Lieutenant Matthew Wojcik, 3rd Platoon, Charlie Company, 3-8 they were assigned to Alpha 2-7. This gave Glass the ability to fight the enemy on a different level than most armor units. The goal of the operations was to surgically attack and destroy the insurgents that were dug in.[27] It may have been difficult for the armor forces to do that without the aid of the infantry units and without utterly destroying the city of Fallujah (which eventually suffered great damage regardless). Cougar 6 used the infantry to infiltrate and destroy the enemy on a micro level, while he used the two tank platoons left in his company to take out larger enemy targets and enemy vehicles or technicals.[28]

The mission for the tanks started with a breaching operation done by the engineers of the Marine Corps. This mission was necessary because train tracks would be difficult for tanks to cross over and could potentially be an issue that would slow down the TF.[29] During an interview with Combat Studies Institute (Ft. Leavenworth, KS), Glass had this to say about the initial breach operations and what happened after:

> Before we entered the breach, there was a large air campaign that took out strategic targets, obviously oblivious to the company. We didn't receive any fire going through the breach. We actually thought we would. We turned up Phase Line April and headed due east up April. Came into Phase Line Henry, which runs north/south, and that was the boundary between RCT-1 and RCT-7. We were the furthest flanking. Alpha Company, 2-7 CAV was to secure the Jolan Park area and then the Marines were going to come through and clear that out. They cleared that sector in the first 24 to 48 hours. We were taking sporadic small arms and RPGs [Rocket-Propelled Grenades]. We didn't receive any mortars. We did see a lot of IEDs [Improvised Explosive Devices] and stuff like that, but they were not detonated against us. We just saw them on the road. We engaged those IEDs with our .50 Cal and coax just to neutralize them because in that operation we couldn't afford the time to wait for EOD [Explosive Ordnance Disposal] to come out there. So once Alpha Company got in and secured Jolan, we kind of moved in unison with Alpha Company, securing their flank, and we moved all the way up to Phase Line Fran. We were held there while the Marines were dealing with securing the Jolan area and rooting out all the insurgents. That's when they started doing that deliberate clearance, going house to house and room to room, and making sure they cleared. I would say within 36 hours, I had to go to the Martyrs Cemetery and secure that as my objective. That was supposed to be the endpoint and that was supposed to be the end of Operation Phantom Fury. We were going to secure that and they were going to continue to clear out the Jolan District.[30]

Glass and his men were met with a more defined defense from the enemy as they continued their way south on Highway 10. The tanks were slowed down during this portion of the mission by sniper fire. Sniper fire prohibits or deters tankers from having both the loader and TC out of their hatches during any type of movement. While they both have the ability to use either their manual or electronic sights, having them outside of the tank allows them a better view of the enemy, especially one that attempts to close in on the tank and take away the advantage of the main gun.[31] TCs instructed the gunners to attempt to use their sights to locate where the muzzle flash was coming from. If the muzzle flash was located, this gave the gunner the ability to identify which building the sniper was located at and fire into the building.[32] The sights located in the gunner's and TC's station gave the tankers a distinct advantage during OIF. The enemy tried to hide and conceal where they were firing from, but the armor units had the ability to magnify any position with their sights and attack the enemy forces.[33]

The tanks also faced RPGs, as they had during the Thunder Runs. The enemy attempted to time the deployment of an RPG to hit the engine or the crew members themselves.[34] For most of the battles that armor units participated in during OIF, the enemy's attempt to slow down armor units consisted of firing the often-used AK-47 at the tanks which had little to no effect. RPGs were a deadly use of firepower by the enemy for both infantrymen and tankers during this battle. If the driver had his hatch open, or the loader or TC was out of their hatch, often the enemy would fire directly at them, wounding and in most cases killing the crew members.[35] Tankers would use their machine guns to destroy these RPG teams. The gunner would either use his coax or leave it to the commander and his .50-cal. This was the most effective way to kill the RPG teams which would gather in three- to six-man squads with one or two people using an RPG and the rest with small arms to protect them.[36]

Between November 8 and 9, Glass used his forces to cordon off certain areas around PL Fran. He used his tanks to surround the area and provide cover fire and allow his mech infantry platoon to go in and clear schools, stores, and other abandoned buildings.[37] This was effective against the enemy that were hiding as they could not escape and they were forced to stand and either absorb the firepower of the Abrams or go toe to toe with the army's infantry. Glass used this tactic to ensure his company's ability to destroy the enemy while taking the least amount of casualties. One of the advantages that often gets lost when discussing armored warfare is the ability to keep the enemy in hiding and make it easier for dismounted troops to come and kill the enemy who refuses to stand against the barrage of coalition firepower.[38] Glass and his armored TF would continue this form of combat through November 10. He would continue to give his tankers the ability to destroy the enemy in a "weapons-free" status in the hopes of overwhelming the enemy forces with the main gun and preventing coalition losses. This was also a quick and effective way to meet the objective of RCT 1.[39]

One of the important lessons that Glass and the army learned during the battle of Najaf in 2004 was that the insurgents favored daylight when fighting the coalition forces. This battle pitted the 11th Marine Expeditionary Unit (MEU) and the Army's 1–5 Cavalry Squadron against the Mahdi Army led by Muqtada Al Sadr in the summer of 2004. During *Phantom Fury*, the heat would soar well over 100 degrees in many instances and the insurgents were trained and raised in such heat and were used to it. The coalition forces were bogged down with 40–50 pounds of body armor, water, and ammunition; they had to endure and fight the heat as well as the enemy.[40]

By November 10, Charlie 3-8 had made it up Highway 10 and were headed west towards the bridges. They would use the cover of night to continue the order of march towards their objective in Fallujah. Glass used his Abrams to lead the way and mix in the mech infantry platoons within the column.[41] Glass did this because he was well aware of the IED threat that loomed in Fallujah and knew that his tanks were best suited to take the brunt of the explosion that an IED would cause. This comes from not only knowing the ability of the Abrams tank but knowing the ability and training of your soldiers and how they will react under combat stress.[42]

Glass knew that the role of his tankers was to be the shock force and provide armor support for RCT 1. As stated earlier, tanks are a constant maintenance project. The leadership must be vigilant and make sure that the proper maintenance of the tank is being conducted even during battle. CSM Joshua Bittel had this to say about keeping the tanks in the fight:

> Tanks are no good sitting in the motor pool or sitting in the back disabled. They need to be in the fight to be effective. That's the job of every tank crew to make sure that their tank is operational. If there is an issue that they can't fix, they need to let higher know so the 1st Sgt. and XO can get the parts or the maintenance personnel to fix the issue. That's the thing that separates us from the infantry in the man-hours that we put into our tanks. It's an art. It's a craft and not everyone can do what we do in terms of keeping our vehicles running. When you see combat documentaries or read books about OIF, all you see is the main gun being fired or the gunner lighting up the enemy. But how do you think the tank was able to get to that point in the first place? Even

during heavy fighting, you have to find a way to make sure that your tank and weapons systems stay functional. When there is a lull in fighting, it's up to the section Sgts. to have crews check the weapons systems and do a hasty PMCS of the tank to keep it going.[43]

Glass, and the rest of Charlie 3-8, had the burden/honor of being the only armor force for the army in the 2-7 TF. They had to carry this burden with pride and continue to move towards their objectives despite the issues with the tanks or the enemy. As Charlie Company moved towards the bridges, they were given the mission to continue to clear the Jolan district. At that point, it was Glass's understanding that the task force's mission was to secure the main highway between RCT 7 and RCT 1, which was Phase Line Henry.[44] During his interview, Glass goes into detail about this change of mission and what it entailed:

> Iraqi towns are square boxes and they're made up of north, south, east, and west-running streets. When we received the follow-on mission, if you follow on the map—Phase Line Fran and Phase Line Grace. We split up and I had a tank platoon cover four lanes in the west, a tank platoon cover four north/south roads in the east, and my infantry platoon in the center. So, we were platoons online heading from Phase Line Fran to Phase Line Grace, and we went in and tried to identify insurgent positions. We didn't do any room-to-room clearing but we could identify them through our optics and stuff like that. Any vehicles we saw—intelligence suggested that those vehicles were suspected VBIEDs [Vehicle Born Improvised Explosive Device] because that's where the majority of the VBIEDs in the Baghdad area of operations were coming from—from Fallujah. So, any fixed fighting positions we could identify—places with sandbags around windows and on buildings, fortifications, and any cache we could identify we engaged. We continued to push down to Phase Line Grace and all the way down south to Phase Line Isabella and Phase Line Jenna in that same fashion.[45]

One of the issues that Glass and his company encountered as they continued to Phase Line Fran and Phase Line Grace was the positioning of the tanks. Glass found that often his tanks did not fit in the narrow alleyways on the PL. This forced the tanks to back out of the alley and relocate just outside the entry point, which often led to the TC being exposed as snipers were still a threat to the tankers during this movement. One of the reasons that this movement was vital was the Marines of RCT 1 and their involvement with the armor units of the army. During this conflict, the Marine Corps bore the brunt of casualties; they had the most of any of the units during this fight.[46] The role of the armor units during this fight mirrored its role during the entirety of the OIF. Glass observed that the Marines suffered fewer casualties when the army's armor was positioned in front of them, pinning the enemy down. As they reached these phase lines, they took the lead role and once they were in position to observe buildings and possible enemy positions they went to more of an overwatch role as the Marine infantry would go in and clear the buildings that were in the area.[47]

The role of the armor during OIF was a role that did not simply benefit the army and their dismounted troops—it benefited the entirety of the coalition forces during the war in Iraq. It is important not to look through too small of a lens when trying to decipher the role of the armor as they were able to help multiple units and military branches achieve victory and limit casualties during this conflict. As Glass and his company continued on Highway 10 near the vicinity of Phase Line Jenna, right along Phase Line Henry, the task force began taking heavy RPG and AK-47 fire from a mosque. This was problematic for the tankers as the ROE (Rules of Engagement) had specific rules about firing into mosques. Captain Glass was given strict orders by the battalion and regiment leaders that mosques could only be fired at after the enemy was positively identified and it was confirmed that the enemy initiated the engagement from the mosque.[48] During this moment in the battle, it became difficult for tanks to make the distinction between an RPG that struck their tank, and the fact that the tank had run over an IED. This would often make the crews question what happened, and they would not immediately look to the mosque for the enemy. This area would take Glass and his company 48 hours to occupy and clear.[49]

For the duration of this particular fight, Glass and his company remained in this position and were ordered to continue to post tanks in an overwatch position to deny the enemy a path to set up sniper or RPG teams in the mosque. Glass would align the tanks along the intersections of the phase lines as they were the best suited to provide a lookout for the company given the sights located within the Abrams tank.[50] During this time at the intersection, Glass and his men were routinely confronted with enemy troops that were either merely trying to test the defense of the tanks or trying to sneak around the positioning of the tanks to find positions in and around the mosques. The tanks under Glass would engage these enemy forces with their bevy of machine guns and coax weapons. This showed the training and synchronization of the tank crew to be able to identify and engage the enemy at a very high kill rate.[51] This was due to the tank tables in gunnery that focused on the loaders' and TCs' machine guns. Having the confidence to engage the enemy no matter the situation was a learned behavior by tankers through garrison training. Tankers constantly trained on how to engage the enemy and what rounds were best in each situation. For the tank crews that had been together prior to OIF, the transition to actual combat was a bit easier.

The next phase of this battle for Glass and Charlie 3-8 Cavalry consisted of waiting and watching. During this time, Glass wanted to be proactive and use his tanks and go on the offensive. He requested permission from LTC Rainey to go on what he called "mini Thunder Runs."[52] These would be nightly runs in and around their area of operation (AO). Glass was permitted to conduct night-time reconnaissance operations, but during the first outings, he discovered that the enemy was nowhere to be found. This seemed like a strain on the fuel resources of the tanks to have them continue to go on these recon missions knowing that the enemy was not going to fight at night. Glass then requested that he be allowed to go on recon missions during the day instead to gather information on the fighting positions of the enemy.[53] Rainey granted permission to Charlie 3-8 to conduct these daytime operations and the result was much different in terms of enemy contact. Glass used his Abrams to conduct the recon missions as the goal and guidance were not to get into a full street fight with the enemy forces during the missions.

Glass moved the mech infantry Bradleys into the positions of the tanks. While he conducted the recon missions during daylight hours, Glass noticed the enemy was more active and willing to engage with his tanks. During the missions, Charlie Company continued to be relentlessly hit by RPG fire.[54] Glass and his tankers relied on the main gun to engage the enemy during these recon missions as opposed to their machine guns. Given this tactic and the Abrams crew's freedom to fire the main gun, the tank crews often found themselves going through an entire rack of main gun ammunition.[55] This forced Glass to have to rotate his tank crews to the resupply point to keep their tanks full of main gun ammunition. The need or reasoning to use the main gun for these engagements was based on speed and shock value. Tanks bring with them a great amount of vehicle speed and their firepower is second to none. Within a matter of seconds, the loader and the gunner on a proficient tank crew are in sync to the point where they can engage multiple targets and be prepared for a new

Col. Peter Glass. (U.S. Army)

engagement.[56] This is an important aspect of tank combat as the crews hope to overwhelm the enemy with their firepower. This meant that during these runs, the enemy was more likely to continue to hide in their defensive positions than fight an armored vehicle with a 120mm main gun.

HEAT and IMPAT rounds were the main rounds used during these runs.[57] These rounds caused significant damage to the enemy ground forces while also destroying their positions. These runs were important to the overall mission of the armored forces and the army in general, giving the army a solid picture of what the enemy's strengths and weaknesses were during this battle. Tanks were used during this portion because of the firepower that they possess and the ability to engage and disengage with the enemy without casualties.[58] That is not to say Glass and his men did not suffer casualties during this conflict. Tanks themselves may be powerful and hard to bring down, but the men that use and operate these tanks are no different or less vulnerable than any other soldier. The goal for the tankers is to train to become one with the tank and to ensure its success is the success of the tank crew.[59] Captain Glass and his unit were able to go and destroy several small-scale forces during these runs and prevent them from engaging with the dismounted troops of the TF.

Glass spoke about the losses that occurred during his company's time in Fallujah:

> Yes. I'd like to talk about the casualties we suffered. Remember I was talking about Staff Sergeant Reyes, the tank commander that got hit by an RPG, the gunner that got a flash burn, and the loader who took some shrapnel as well. Because of our battalion aid station and because we were on the move, I put our company command post/aid station with Alpha Company's CP, because they were in a holding pattern waiting for us to continue moving south. That tank crew made the smart choice to try and go to the battalion aid station. As they were going through the breach, the tank flipped and rolled. By this time, my company's first sergeant had actually linked up with Staff Sergeant Reyes at the site of the breach point. That was our alternate plan. They transferred the casualties. Staff Sergeant Reyes had gotten off and Specialist Edwin Modeste had gotten off and they were cross-loaded. Sergeant Jonathan Shields had actually taken over as tank commander. He was the gunner, and even though he was wounded, he realized that the tank had to get back because it wasn't functioning properly. It took shrapnel to the main gun and they were worried about penetration on the sleeve of the main gun. As they were taking it back, they fell into a deep hole on the side of the road that no one knew about. The tank actually rolled and flipped and instantly killed Sergeant Shields. It rolled on top of him and crushed him. Specialist Troy Caicedo was the driver of the tank at the time. He survived, but Sergeant Shields didn't make it. We didn't take any other casualties from my company other than him. We continued the mission. We stayed in that area and operated out of our CP. Using those grid squares, we'd go in and clear the streets and avenues of approach, engaging fixed and fortified positions with our main guns, as well as houses that were obviously fortified. And we had great effects. The Marines were going into buildings and finding lots of stuff. I got one report that they found six enemy KIA [Killed in Action]. They had weapons and a cache in there, but they were all embedded with concrete in their bodies from the 120s. So, we called these "mini" gun runs. Similar to what the helicopters would do—kind of circling a target, engaging fixed positions. Then the Marines would come through. My tank got taken out by an anti-tank mine, probably around November 17th or 18th.[60]

Glass and his men were able to achieve success for RCT 7 due to their training and their ability to fight alongside the infantry during this conflict. As much as the armor and infantry are service rivals, they need each other on the battlefield. The army is a better force and more lethal when they are combined with a viable dismounted force to destroy the enemy. One of the biggest obstacles to that victory during this battle was the differences between the army and the Marines.[61] The Marine Corps had a different setup and organization to their regiment that often made it difficult for the two services to collaborate and often led to infighting about what was best for the battle. There was even an incident with 2-2 where the Marines threatened to return fire on them if they felt the army was firing too close to their position.[62] The other armored element of the task force was the brigade reconnaissance troop (BRT). This unit would be the true recon element of the TF. There were several first-hand accounts of this unit and what their mission was during this battle; Captain Neil Prakash described it as "go in and soften several targets for the main force."[63]

This unit was attached to 2-2's task force during their battle in Fallujah. Most BCTs during that period had at least one cavalry squadron in their brigade that was tasked with the recon duties for the brigade. Having a single troop attached to a battalion allows the BC the flexibility to be able to send that troop to conduct recon missions without the permission of the brigade commander or the DCO.[64] Prakash was a platoon leader with Alpha 2-63 AR during the beginning of his combat tour in 2003. He was a part of the reorganization of the battalion to prepare for the battle in Fallujah; he and his platoon were split up to integrate with the BRT for the upcoming fight.[65] This would be the first time that Prakash would work with any type of infantry unit as the army still used "pure" battalions at this time. He would join the BRT and his platoon consisted of two tanks, two Bradleys, and two infantry squads. This unit mirrored what the other army units of the TF were doing to get the most out of the Abrams and Bradleys. One of the benefits for Prakash of being in a recon troop and platoon was the opportunity to use different systems that he had not had experience with outside of training. One of those items was the long-range advanced surveillance system (LRAS).[66] This system is used by light, armored, and Stryker cavalry units, and gives the recon element advanced vision and line of sight of the enemy. The BRT knew that at least initially there were two ways that they were probably going to be used in this fight. They either needed to be used as a true recon element and go out and observe and record the enemy's movement and report back to the commander to give him a better picture of the battlefield, or used as an extension of Alpha 2-63.[67]

Long-range advanced surveillance system (LRAS). (U.S. Army)

Either way, having this system benefited the troop as they engaged the enemy no matter the capacity. Prakash found that he and the tanks in his platoon were asked to support the infantry in his unit. The idea that cavalry immediately means recon is simply not true, at least not in the context of OIF. His unit often conducted overwatch missions as the main dismounted forces for the RCT. Earlier in this work, it was discussed that often the leadership in charge of armor was infantry. As the war progressed, infantry commanders became more familiar with how to utilize tanks to achieve success. During the infancy of this war that was not always the case. The BRT was commanded by Captain Kirk Mayfield, a career-long light infantry officer.[68] For many of the light infantry divisions up to this point in the war, Abrams tanks were simply a vehicle that they would see in passing and not something that they used in combat. Prakash knew that because of Mayfield's lack of experience, he and his tanks would be allowed a little leeway in how they operated. This flexibility came to fruition during a firefight that took place on November 9, 2004.[69]

During this firefight, Mayfield and the rest of the BRT came under small arms fire by the dug-in insurgents of Fallujah. Mayfield attempted to react as an infantryman and tried to send his dismounted troops in the direction of the fire while also attempting to pin them down with the machine guns mounted on the Humvees. The number of insurgents that attacked the recon troop became overwhelming and the infantry could not defeat the attack alone.[70]

Abrams were often used for "counter-sniper operations" during OIF. The sights on the Abrams made them ideal to spot and destroy snipers during combat operations. The issue for tankers during these operations is often not spotting the enemy but the unit's approach to suppressing fire. For many commanders, the idea of simply destroying buildings once the enemy is spotted was not sustainable or desired.[71] Deploying infantry to counter snipers is often the tactic of infantry officers that do not have tanks or armor experience at their disposal. Prakash went into detail about what his commander's reaction was to this situation and how he employed tanks during this firefight.

It was good and I was glad it was like that. It would have been a bad idea to bring logistics in there. So anyway, we get down to the cloverleaf and got our first taste of going into the city. When you're going into an area you're unfamiliar with, you should always let the tanks go first, then the Brads, and then the Humvees. In this case, though, the Humvees went first and they started getting shot up by sniper fire. There were a couple of scattered buildings as well as these barriers. There was concertina wire, HESCOs, bunkers and all the stuff the Marines and the entire coalition had previously put in there for themselves and the Iraqi Army, yet the city had not been patrolled for six months. No one had been there since 9 April when the Marines got hit really hard trying that ground assault they did to go after the Blackwater guys who got killed. So, from April until November, the intel we had said there was no patrolling going on in the city, no maintaining of a presence at all. All these bunkers were either ready to explode, they were full of IEDs, and or they were enemy strongholds, so we were just lighting them all up. With the main guns. After that, though, as the dismounts were trying to go forward, the Humvees were getting shot at.

Captain Kirk Mayfield, the BRT commander, seemed really pissed off because he was getting sniped. Captain Boggiano had told me previously that Captain Mayfield had spent 16 years in light infantry. He hadn't messed with tanks too much so I would probably get free rein. It's great when you're a tank attached to the light because they really want to use you, but oftentimes they don't know how. However, when the bullets start flying, it's just no holds barred and the gloves come off and all that good stuff. So he starts getting sniped and I call him on the net as we're moving down towards Fran. He's telling me about taking sniper fire and he's just pointing at houses and saying, "Shoot that shit!" so we just unloaded main gun rounds on all these houses he thinks he's taking sniper fire from. This was day two, 9 November.[72]

After this encounter, Prakash and the rest of the BRT went into a series of what he called "probing missions."[73] These missions would consist of the troop going and either clearing the building, conducting recon by fire, or doing overwatch on a series of buildings or an area.[74] This would allow the unit to be useful to the rest of the RCT but also allowed the armor of the BRT to able to influence the battlefield by way of their main gun. This idea was important as Prakash stated that the Marines had a lack of an armor presence during this fight.[75] The lack of Marine tank units was for several reasons but all had an impact on the army, not only in Fallujah but in OIF. The Marine Corps at one point only had four tank battalions in the entire service; the army had 19. This is due to the distinct fighting style of each service and how they employ their mechanized and light forces. Fallujah was a fight that was dominated by infantry forces, but the army was brought into this fight specifically for their mechanized infantry and armor.[76] The lack of an armored presence for the Marines was exactly the reason that the army was able to come in and have an impact in this battle both in terms of taking and securing areas and in killing the enemy.

The BRT would go from having company-orientated missions to platoon-level missions. This handed the authority of when to kill the enemy into the hands of the young lieutenants. The training for the young armor officers was something that they received while in garrison.[77] Gunnery was always important for the tank crews, but it also played a significant role for the armor officers during the infancy of the battles of OIF as they simply did not have the combat experience to rely on.

It was the responsibility of the brigade staff and master gunner to set up combat scenarios to help the officers learn to command their tank units in the face of combat pressure. This training was important to prepare the tanks for the types of maneuvers they would use in Iraq. Prakash and his tank unit continued these missions until they were given new orders by the troop commander.

Phase Line Fran would be the next area that the BRT would be asked to recon.[78] Capt. Mayfield was given orders by the battalion commander that the southern portion of Fran needed to be reconned. Prakash and his tankers were told that they needed to conduct a series of mounted patrols around the city as well as route security.[79] During this static defense and overwatch, Prakash and his men were alerted by another unit in the TF with the call sign "Outlaw 1," that their men were taking fire from a series of houses near the overwatch position. Prakash and his tanks were ordered to go and reinforce the Outlaw element. Arriving at the firefight, they were directed to the location of the houses and ordered to suppress and destroy the enemy forces that were firing from there.[80] Prakash and his tankers decided that the best way to defeat the enemy was through the use of the main gun of the tank. HEAT rounds were used as the main weapon during this skirmish. For the next 45 minutes, Prakash and his tankers lobbed round after round into six designated houses. This not only destroyed the enemy that had attacked the TF, but it deterred other enemies in the area. Before it was over the tankers fired 20 main gun rounds into the houses. During this skirmish, tanks were viewed as the best course of action to defend the dismounted forces.

In this instance, tanks were used for their shock factor. This is the ability to scare and deter the enemy from returning fire due to the overwhelming firepower of the Abrams. This tactic became a staple in the army's way of using tanks in future battles of this war. Prakash stated that during this portion of the fight, the BRT was used in the best way possible. According to Prakash, it was a win for both the army and the Marines. The army was able to field a recon element that had both light infantry and tanks working together while also giving the TF another company of armor to fight the enemy.[81] Prakash had this to say about the goals and conditions of the BRT:

> There were two things that went on. First of all, he pretty much gave me free rein. I think that was more the nature of combat, though than the choice he had. Second of all, ask anyone from 1st ID or any of the tankers from Fallujah: this shit is easy when your orders are to kill everything in front of you and when you're limitless on fuel and ammo. Food and sleep? Don't worry about it. That's what we live for.[82]

During the battle, CSM Timothy Mace was the senior enlisted NCO of TF 2-7 and played a critical role in the preparation for Fallujah. Mace served under Rainey and advised him on the best course of action for him and his men. Admittedly, Mace was a career-long light infantry fighter.[83] He had gone from being a paratrooper to being a drill and senior drill sergeant. He had virtually no interaction at the command level with armor before OIF. As discussed above, all senior enlisted jobs are not the same. Even as a CSM, there are unique differences between the 101st or 82nd Airborne Division and the 1st Cavalry Division. The biggest difference between the two is the deployment of the vehicles and the cultural differences between the armor and the infantry. When armor units were commanded by an all-armor staff, this bred a certain mentality when everyone felt the same way and was trained the same way.[84]

Mace was tasked with mentoring the senior enlisted NCOs, while also giving sound advice to Rainey and making sure the task force was on the same page in terms of what needed to be done to assist the Marines in achieving victory in Fallujah. Mace had the advantage of having a battalion that was battle-hardened due to the fight they encountered in Najaf in 2004.[85] Mace was one of the first battalion leaders during this conflict to have the unique responsibility of being in command of a unit that had been integrated. One of the things that the cavalry had been famous for in the past is their unique configuration when it came to troops. Captain Woodward had this to say about the armored cavalry formations:

> It is always funny to me when you hear soldiers talk about the old, armored cavalry units and how disciplined they were and how much the army has changed over the years. But I think that the thing that made the ACRs great was their diversity. They incorporated mech infantry, tanks, and armored cavalry units. Bringing all that fighting power on the enemy was a lot for them to handle. For tankers, the good part of those units was that they were all run by armor personnel.[86]

Mace credited the readiness of 2-7 to Rainey and the staff that had been put together at the battalion level. Although the unit had been successful against the enemies in Najaf, they still had to shift their focus and firepower to Fallujah. This included some of the smaller tasks that only the senior NCOs were responsible for. Gunnery on a large scale was new to Mace as he came from units where going to the range was a single day and night event, and the light infantry soldiers only had to worry about their personal weapons that needed to be qualified.[87] This was an adjustment for Mace and he relied on the battalion staff to help him with this portion of leadership. During the initial breach, 2-7 (C 3-8 CAV) used plows on the Abrams to successfully breach the enemy's defenses. Mace gave credit to Glass and his tankers for their ability to be the leading force for the TF and how they were able to fight and destroy the enemy while using their mounted capabilities.[88] While the primary role of the senior enlisted advisor is the same in every army unit, their ability to provide the commander with expertise in the field that they are commanding is exactly why the army puts (or used to put) infantrymen in an infantry battalion and tankers or cavalry scouts in command or in an advising role of an armor unit.[89]

Initially, Mace had the responsibility of riding with the BC in the command Bradley. He was tasked with coordinating with the XO and making sure that the TF was supplied with food, water, and ammunition during the fight. When units came to resupply, Mace would supervise the company's first sergeant and make sure that all the men and vehicles were supplied and combat ready. He also had the duty of overseeing the medical evacuation of the wounded soldiers (medevac).[90] He would ride with the commander to constantly give Rainey a status on the enlisted soldiers from a supply and logistical aspect, allowing the commander to focus on the planning and actual fighting that was taking place in Fallujah. Mace was a man who tried to put interservice and service rivalries aside for the sake of his men and the mission. It is impossible for any command sergeant major or company first sergeant to not feel a certain way about his own MOS simply because the pride and love for the army and that specific MOS has been embedded in the NCOs from the moment they arrived at their basic training.[91] Mace had this to say about the rivalries and how he feels they impact the battlefield:

> The rivalry crap between the Marines, the Air Force, Navy—that stuff doesn't survive the first bullet. Everybody we worked with—the SEALs, the Air Force, tac air guys, the Marines, my counterparts, sergeants major in the Marines—it was almost like an automatic friendship. Great admiration for all the services, and that's doctrine; that's how we fight. It's easy on a battlefield when everyone is working towards the same thing. The soldiers were very impressive and I think a lot of that had to do with An Najaf. You're probably going to survive, but it's luck of the draw,

so you might as well just put it out of your mind because you don't know. I did see one kid, one of the new guys that came in. A few days into the fight, we were downtown at one of the mosques, and the colonel and the PSD and I ran into a little bit of fire getting to the mosque. The Marines and our guys were out there. Well, I saw this kid barf; he was looking like, "Oh my God." But the PFCs, the specialists, the E–5s, and the lieutenants, that's the strength of the Army. All of our training and just leading people right paid off in that battle. I have great admiration for the Marines. They took the brunt of casualties because they were dismounted and cleared the stuff. We were under armor, we blew through and overwhelmed the enemy, so we were more well-protected. Those guys had the hard job of going door to door, floor to floor. When I was talking to one of my counterparts at the train station, their aid station took fire a few times. There were several times daily right there, getting pounded, but you know, Marines are Marines: they're going to do the damn job. Very impressive. So, all in all, how we train, our good leaders, good soldiers, and a good mission we believe in—and that's the thing. Everybody knew these guys we were fighting are not good people. They're just bad people, and every time you pulled the trigger, the world got a little bit better.[92]

Mace also spoke about the support that was needed for the mission and how the Marines and the army had to constantly work together to strive to achieve logistical success. Mace was aware that tanks would require much more logistics than he was used to as a light infantryman and relied heavily on the help of the Marines and the army to make this happen.[93] He gave praise for this work to Col. Shupp and RCT 1. Shupp and the Marines knew that the army was going to need supplies that the Marines simply were not used to carrying, at least in such a large quantity. It was important for Shupp and his staff to work hard to help the armored and mechanized infantry element logistically to win this fight.

One of the biggest concerns that Mace had going into this battle was civilians on the battlefield.[94] For the infantry, the weapons they carry often do not have the same impact as vehicle-based weapons. During the anonymous interview with the army master sergeant, he had this to say about the differences in firepower between the infantry versus the armor:

> If you look at the weapons systems of the armor and the infantry or the light infantry, it's no comparison. One tank platoon has the firepower of an entire light infantry battalion. There is a need for the dismounted troops for the sake of the boots on the ground and the numbers. A tank cannot clear rooms or man checkpoints in terms of actually patting people down. But on the reverse side of that, no infantry unit remotely has the firepower of an Abrams so I guess they needed each other.[95]

In the case of civilians, Mace had to constantly monitor the situation to make sure that the firepower was used in a responsible combat manner.[96] Mace made sure to have constant interactions with the first sergeants to convey the commander's intent while also making sure they were instructing their men on the importance of target acquisition. For the days and weeks leading up to the battle of Fallujah, the Iraqi government used pamphlets, gatherings, and television broadcasting to instruct the civilian population to leave the city.[97] This allowed a large number of civilians to leave but also a large number of enemy insurgents. Those that stayed and fought often blended in with the population. One of the tactics that the insurgents used would be to fire at or kill coalition forces then hide the weapons and blend in with a local family.[98]

For Mace, the issue was always: were the tanks going to be used in a manner that would kill these civilians en route to killing the hiding enemy? The thoughts and concerns that an 11B (enlisted infantrymen, 11A infantry officer) have are different from those of a tanker. Mace knew that he had to blend his experience of being a senior enlisted NCO with

M1A2 SEP Abrams tank during Operation *Phantom Fury*, November 2004. (U.S. Army / Captain Scott Kuhn)

being a veteran infantryman.[99] This mixture of the two allowed Mace to identify the needs of every element of the TF to serve the battalion more effectively. Mace admittedly had trouble at first connecting with the tankers due to the lack of familiarity. However, he believed that a CSM was universal and that his job was to supervise the enlisted NCOs no matter what their job was. One of the highlights of this mission was the enlisted support that the TF received. Mace stated that the division, corps, and regiment (Marine) sergeant majors all made their way down to the soldiers and showed their support for them at some point before and during the intense fighting in Fallujah.[100] This gave all the soldiers the feeling that they were being supported by the chain of command. This action was common among tankers as they are accustomed to the senior enlisted advisors coming to inspect their vehicles before combat.

During this portion of fighting in Iraq, the corps and division CSM were both armor NCOs. Another dimension of this fight is the vantage point of the men that fought the battle.

The soldiers of 2-2 had a different experience than those of 2-7. This was due both to the mission that was asked of them and to the overall structure of the 1st Infantry Division (Big Red One). One of the men closest to the battle and the tanks was SSG David Bellavia, a squad leader within Alpha Company. Although he was an infantryman, his experience with the tanks on the battlefield is vital to show their importance and how they were used for this fight. Bellavia detailed his unit's fight in his works *House to House*, and *Remember the Ramrods*. These books give great detail about how 2-2 was used in this fight, and how the infantry and the armor were able to coexist during Operation *Phantom Fury*. As stated before, TF 2-2 was a combined arms unit that was pieced together while in Iraq to confront the enemies of the coalition forces.[101]

When it came to the infantry interaction with the armor, Bellavia states that the armored forces were there to back up him and his squad. The tanks that supported Alpha were not there as offensive weapons of war. The BC, LTC Newell, used the tanks to shadow the infantry companies as they cleared the rooms and houses. This allowed the dismounted infantry to clear the rooms with fear of being ambushed by the enemy. One of the things Bellavia also pointed out was the work of the tanks regarding snipers. During this operation, many of the infantry companies started operating in squads. The platoon leader would be the center of command and keep in constant contact with his infantry squads.[102] He would also direct the tanks where to go and what the proper positioning of each Abrams should be. Many of the tanks were separated from their company. A platoon-sized tank element (four tanks) would accompany the infantry companies as they conducted operations. Bellavia stated how effective the tanks were in this role and marveled at the power of the main gun on the Abrams.[103] Bellavia was aided during his time by elements of 2-63 Armor.

These men were commanded by Captain Paul Fowler, a young armor officer who had gained experience as a combat tanker as his company took part in the 1st battle of Baqubah in July of 2004. During that time, A 2-63 was called upon to support the 3rd brigade of the 1st Infantry Division led by Col. Dana Pittard.[104] During this battle, Fowler was forced to use his tank company to engage with forces loyal to Abu Musab al-Zarqawi. It was there that Fowler learned how to maneuver his forces and support infantry troops during combat. He would divide his company up and give two tank platoons to 2-2 in exchange for two "rifle platoons."[105]

Bellavia and his squad were the beneficiaries of this new merging of forces that the army was testing in this combat environment. Bellavia got to see firsthand what Abrams were capable of as several times during this fight he requested and directed the tanks assigned to his company where to fire to suppress the enemy and destroy sniper positions.[106] Bellavia and the other infantry dismounts of 2-2 were able to use the tanks freely; they were not required to get permission to fire the main gun from the BC as other armor units would later on during OIF. Bellavia was able to have success with his squads in part due to the firepower that was at his disposal and the effectiveness of that fire from well-trained M1 tankers.[107]

During Bellavia's interaction with 2-63, their most effective moments came when they fired on RPG teams and snipers. These RPG teams proved to be deadly for dismounted forces during this battle and throughout the war. They often fired on unsuspecting units conducting patrols or deliberate assaults on designated areas. The optics of the Abrams allowed them to see enemies that the normal dismounted troop could not and enabled the tankers to identify and destroy the enemy quickly and save the lives of infantry troops on several occasions.[108] Bellavia and the Ramrods were able to aid the Marines in destroying the enemy strongholds in Fallujah while also showing the importance of working with other services and cooperation within the branches. Bellavia and his unit had to rely on tanks as well as field artillery to be successful and to survive the attacks of the enemy.

One of the important aspects of this battle for the 1st ID was the loss of the battalion CSM, Steven Wayne Faulkenburg. Although he was an infantryman, Faulkenburg put aside his own personal pride and love for his branch and made sure that every enlisted soldier within the TF felt important and knew that they were supported by the battalion leadership.[109]

On November 9, 2004, CSM Faulkenburg was serving with the 2nd Battalion, 2nd Infantry Regiment, and 1st Infantry Division while deployed in support of Operation *Iraqi Freedom*. In the early morning hours that day, CSM Faulkenburg's unit was engaged in combat action against enemy forces during the initial assault into Fallujah, Iraq. CSM Faulkenburg was dismounted and organizing the soldiers around him after they had just finished leading a battalion of Iraqi soldiers through the breach lane. As enemy small arms fire burst out from two sides, CSM Faulkenburg issued fire commands to his gunner and, as they raced forward into the contact, he was mortally wounded. CSM Faulkenburg was posthumously awarded the Bronze Star Medal and Purple Heart for his actions during Operation *Phantom Fury*.[110]

The second battle of Fallujah was important for both the armored corps and the U.S. Army. It saw the first major integration of tanks and infantry on a large scale up to this point of the war in Iraq, and for this particular battle to go well would give validity to the idea of combined arms within the army. The army was convinced that the future of modern warfare would be to go away from the old "pure" battalions and to move into the combined arms model. This model, however, was still in its philosophical phase before this battle.[111] It had been used situationally to allow the infantry to have the backing of the armor and the armor to have the backing of a dismounted force. This battle was the precursor to the combined arms battalions that are still being used today by the U.S. Army. The tank units that fought in this battle did not have the benefit of fighting within their units as 3-8 Cavalry and 2-63 Armor were broken up to meet the needs of the RCT 1 and 7 for this fight.

This meant that the tankers were fighting with men that they never met and leaders that they never served under for the duration of this fight. This fact cannot be understated as one of the main goals of garrison training is to allow the soldiers to learn how to fight as a unit and learn the expectations of the leadership in any given circumstance.[112] Credit must be given to the commanders of these tank companies that fought alongside both RCTs during this battle. Peter Glass (C 3-8 Cav) and Paul Fowler (A 2-63 Armor) led their units into battle and relied on the training and brotherhood that was fostered during garrison and NTC training.[113] These units would not have been successful if it was not for the NCO leadership of their companies. The involvement of the first sergeant in an armor unit may have been heavy during garrison, but it also allowed the men to come together and know what the standard was and how to achieve it. The overall effort of the army and its units were felt, and it is safe to say that they played a major role in the success of Operation *Phantom Fury*. This operation needed the help of the army's armor and mechanized infantry to defeat the dug-in insurgents and because of the firepower and mentality that they brought to the battlefield, it was a success, and the army was able to kill a large number of enemy forces while keeping their own losses to a minimum.

CHAPTER 5

Ramadi

The battle of Ramadi took place between March and November 2006.[1] Ramadi was a battle in which the old guard of the army was facing the new enemy of the Iraq War. Al-Qaeda in Iraq (AQI) had declared Ramadi to be the new capital of its insurgency. They were determined to make the area a safe haven for enemies of the coalition forces. They knew that if they could muster enough forces, and cause enough damage and coalition losses, they could force the coalition, and mainly the U.S., to stay away from Ramadi. For the most part, this was working early on for AQI. They had become so powerful of a force that there were places designated as "no man's land" meaning these places were laced with IEDs or being overwatched by enemies who had snipers embedded in the area.[2] It could be argued that this operation was not initially given the attention that it deserved. Before the 1st Armored Division and in particular, the 1st BCT took over and secured Ramadi, it was under the stewardship of the 2nd Brigade of the 28th Infantry.[3]

This unit was formed under the banner of the Pennsylvania National Guard. In truth, it was made up of a 20-state conglomerate of "part-time soldiers." This meant that, unlike the regular or active forces, these men came together monthly and had minimal training compared to the active-duty army BCTs. This was the unit that the army's leadership chose to send into the most dangerous place in Iraq at the time. For many commanders close to the situation, this felt like a mistake and mismanagement on the part of the U.S. Army. Marine Major Teddy Gates observed the National Guard unit come under fire from the enemy, and he had these observations:

> The national guard guys simply could not hit the enemy that was firing at us. They were hitting sandbags and objects in front of the insurgents that we were engaged with but did not inflict damage on the enemy. To have the national guard in Ramadi during this time was simply asinine.[4]

This notion was shared with both Marine and active-duty units during this fight. The arrival of Col. Sean MacFarland and the 1st BCT of the 1st Armored Division was needed, but the unit itself was unexpected.[5]

The coalition units that had occupied Ramadi thus far had been infantry units. These units bring the numbers with them that ABCTs simply do not. As the war progressed after Fallujah, the army shifted their battalions into a permanent combined arms module for many of their heavy or armored brigades.[6] More units that were coming to Iraq had fully transitioned from the "old guard" to having two tank and two mechanized infantry battalions (at a minimum). This beefed up the units and allowed them to have more firepower. This was not the case for MacFarland's brigade. They had not yet transitioned to the new way of fighting and still had the older model of two tank battalions, one mechanized infantry battalion, and one armored cavalry squadron.[7] MacFarland also had to fight the perception of the armor officer during this conflict. Although several of the major operations had been conducted up to this point with armor officers, including Thunder Run (David Perkins, Buford Blount), the battle of Ramadi was seen as an infantry fight and many commanders on the ground thought that there should be an infantry officer running the show. Another reason for this bias was the fact that many people believed that armor officers simply wanted to come in and destroy everything in their sight.[8]

MacFarland had to show that although there was a reason for the armored brigade coming to Ramadi, he was fully aware that he could not simply go in and destroy every building in Ramadi as that would not achieve the success that the coalition commanders desired. That was one of the fears that the commanders above MacFarland had. It is important to know that this operation was coming off the heels of Operation *New Dawn* (*Phantom Fury*). The operation itself could be viewed as a success.

However, the damage that the city was dealt was not lost on the commanders of the operation. In fact, MacFarland was given specific instructions from his superior to "fix Ramadi, but do not turn it into Fallujah."[9] Much like the *Phantom Fury*, this operation was under the command of the Marines but relied heavily on the army and its armored forces to achieve victory. It was the commander of Multi-National Corps Iraq, Gen. George Casey, that assigned command of the Ramadi battle to MacFarland.[10] Before MacFarland took command of Ramadi, the 3-8 Marines (3rd Battalion 8th Marine Regiment) were heavily involved in the battle for Ramadi.

The Marines faced several issues in Ramadi before the arrival of the 1st Brigade. Firstly, the enemy (AQI) had a large inventory of weaponry that they were using against the light rifle battalion of Marines. This made it difficult for the Marines to combat the insurgents in Ramadi without the aid of another mechanized or armored force.[11] Much like the situation in Fallujah, it became necessary to have the army come in and support this operation as they had the necessary military equipment to combat the enemy. The other issue was the fact that the Marines lacked the numbers to take and hold the area of Ramadi alone. During OIF, they had been asked to hold certain areas, but the reality is that to truly take and hold an area, you need tanks, Bradleys, and an abundance of supplies and manpower.[12] The Marine Corps is substantially smaller than the army and thus often used as a "strike force" as opposed to an occupational force.

MacFarland was relatively new to his command when he accepted the task of taking over the 1st BCT of the 1st Armored Division. He worked for the operations and planning section of the 1st AD (Armored Division) before being assigned to the 1st BCT. Initially, MacFarland came into a situation where the brigade was conducting gunnery before their deployment. There were several issues with the deployment before it even started. The army and the division had decided that 1st Brigade needed to be chopped up.[13] MacFarland had this to say about the composition of his unit as they prepared to deploy:

> The train-up program was based on the ability to conduct full spectrum operations in Germany and we were initially told that we were going to be configured in a nonstandard way. We had one additional infantry company attached to us

from my sister brigade in Baumholder, Alpha Company, 1-6 [Infantry], and we were told that a certain percentage of our brigade was going to be motorized. All the infantry guys would be mounted on Bradleys, but we were only going to have two tank companies mounted on tanks. My other four tank companies would be mounted on HMMWVs and then my artillery was only going to have one firing battery and two of the batteries would be converted into motorized infantry. So, that was a bit of a problem for me because the intent was to train all tankers and infantrymen, and artillerymen in how to shoot tanks, Bradleys, and Paladins, as well as train them on their up-armored HMMWV motorized tasks. We were able to accomplish both, but it created one of the more intensive gunnery experiences that I have ever gone through. I also became concerned that we weren't bringing enough of our tanks with us and, over time, was able to persuade the folks in Germany to let me bring two additional companies worth of tanks. But I still ended up leaving two companies worth of tanks in our motor pool, which, as soon as we got to Iraq, I began scrounging around and was able to eventually outfit all my tank companies with tanks, which they desperately needed. So, there was some friction in terms of our train-up because the task organization that we were told to deploy under didn't resemble the mission set that we were going to execute. On the patch chart that gets distributed, we were lined up against the 3d CAV (Cavalry). So, while the 3d CAV originally started south of Baghdad, they had moved up to the Tall Afar area in West Ninewa and this was long before we deployed. So, I made it known to the powers that be that I didn't think that we were going south of Baghdad and that we were going to go up to West Ninewa. However, our train up was still based on the south of Baghdad scenario with this motorized set. Then, the other thing was that the 3d ACR [Armored Cavalry Regiment] was not operating as a primarily motorized organization and I thought we should look more like the unit we were replacing. Well, that, more or less, fell on deaf ears; although, like I said, I was able to win a partial victory there on tanks. Then, the other thing that began to percolate, as we got closer to deployment, was the possibility that we wouldn't stay in West Ninewa and that we might end up going to Ramadi.[14]

Eventually, MacFarland and his unit received the tanks they needed to be successful in Ramadi. The notion that the fight in Ramadi would be an infantry fight was valid, but the idea that a large number of tanks were not needed was illogical and went against the reason that the brigade was sent to Ramadi in the first place.[15] MacFarland and his brigade were seen as overconfident in their tanks and Bradleys by the National Guard unit they were relieving. The outgoing commander did not like the tactics that MacFarland had planned on using as he and his men took over Ramadi.

During a transition of authority during combat, the army do something called a "left-seat, right-seat ride."[16] For the left-seat ride, some of the leaders from the unit that is taking over ride in the same vehicle as the unit that is leaving. For a tank unit, this often means that the leaders will either swap spots with a loader or ride in another vehicle alongside the tank unit while they conduct a patrol. MacFarland and his men did this with the National Guard units before they left. This left-seat ride will happen for a week or two while the incoming unit becomes comfortable with the terrain and the people. During the left-seat ride, the incoming unit does not interfere with the actions of the current unit. They are simply "interested observers."[17] After the "initiation" of the new unit, they transition to the right-seat ride. This occurs when the incoming unit takes the lead and the outgoing unit assumes the observer role. It was during this time that MacFarland and his staff let it be known what their intentions were for the upcoming battles.

One of the things that he wanted to do was to take an offensive and aggressive approach to the fight. Although the 2-28 had done an admirable job, they had left too many areas unpatrolled, and they did not take the fight to the enemy; they were in static defense for the majority of the time.[18] MacFarland had already had it in his mind that many of these areas needed to be patrolled. The only question was whether or not these areas required a mounted or dismounted presence. MacFarland understood that he was going to lose men in this fight. No amount of tanks or Bradleys would ensure the survival of his men. He knew that although his men were in for a harsh and costly fight, it was vital to pick the correct strategy that would end in victory in the long run for the brigade and the coalition forces.[19] The combat outpost (COP) was the secret to victory for MacFarland.[20] He wanted to move into neighborhoods that were controlled by the enemy and take away the notion that the enemy had free rein throughout Ramadi. These COPs were built hastily but were fully functional in about 30 days.[21] Several items needed to be addressed in every COP that was built. The first thing was to secure the COP itself, either by building a secure area or by reinforcing the area that already surrounded the building that was selected for a guard tower and or sniper position. This would be important as it would allow the soldiers to identify and engage enemy forces that were still within shooting range of the COP after it had been secured. Each COP was meant to house a company-sized element. This meant that companies that were "pure" needed to have some dismounted elements within them as they could not go on patrols without that element and be completely effective.[22]

The enemy did not allow the 1st BCT to simply come in and take these areas without a fight. During the creation of the COPs, the 1st BCT saw fierce fighting simply to go in and have a place to lay their heads.[23] This was the initial portion of the fight where the Abrams would be used to combat the enemy. Abrams were positioned to guard the units that were building the COPs and tankers used their machine guns on the tanks due to the proximity of the enemy to the soldiers that were building the COPs. These tanks were supported by Navy SEAL snipers during this battle and in particular during the building of the COPs. While the optics on Abrams were state-of-the-art, the snipers put fear in the enemy by not allowing them to get close enough to be hit by the tankers.[24] With the support of the tankers and the SEAL teams, the COPs became an integral part of the success that the "Ready First" brigade and the coalition forces had in Ramadi.

One of the things that this brigade had going for it was experience. The idea of building COPs and moving into the enemy's neighborhood was not used originally by MacFarland but by Col. H. R. McMaster during his battle for Tal Far (2004). During this fight, McMaster led the 3rd Armored Cavalry Regiment (which later would be reorganized into a Stryker regiment) against insurgents and achieved great success. McMaster was given a regiment that had several squadrons that were militarily diverse and had the pleasure of having a good mix of mechanized infantry, armored cavalry, and armor units. He was able to move into the cities and gain a foothold over the insurgent forces while using a heavy regiment.[25] He got the support of the people in Tal Far and used that support to drive out the enemy forces from the region. Initially, McMaster had to go in "guns blazing" to drive out the enemy forces in the area and remove them from the COPs that they wanted to secure. McMaster was not able to complete the mission in Tal Far hastily. He had to move in and secure it piece by piece. This meant that the process had to be meticulous and even though McMaster was an armor officer, he had to rely on the infantry to go in and do the day-to-day grind of room clearing and dismounted patrols.[26]

MacFarland was the man who replaced McMaster in Tal Far. He was able to gain knowledge from him about this strategy and the best way to implement it. This was the vision that MacFarland had for Ramadi. The question was simply whether those in charge would allow him to implement his plan, and if his subordinates could stand behind his decisions.[27] Major General Richard Zilmer was the commander of the 1st MEU. He had operational command of the battle of Ramadi during the time that MacFarland was there.[28] Zilmer was known for giving his commanders leeway when it came to command and what they wanted to do within the brigade AO. MacFarland used this leeway to set up his plans for the upcoming operations. He knew he wanted to separate himself from the way that the 2-28 handled business before his arrival. That was not because they performed poorly, but rather because he wanted to attempt to implement a plan that could drive out the enemy for good.[29]

One of the things that MacFarland wanted to do was to be more aggressive when it came to room clearing. He wanted his dismounted elements to go in and clear rooms aggressively and that would serve the purpose of showing the enemy what they could expect if they were caught, and showing the local populace that they were serious about clearing rooms. MacFarland used 1-36 Infantry, (Mechanized), 1-6 Infantry (Mechanized), 1-6 and 3-8 Marines, along with 1-506 Infantry (Airborne)[30] to confront the insurgent forces during his time in Ramadi. The two leading tank elements for this battle would be 1-37 Armor and 1-35 Armor. MacFarland deployed these tank units in a variety of ways to get the most out of them in combat and to allow their power to be felt by the enemy. One of the ways that would happen at first would be to use them in support of his aggressive dismounted campaign. During his interview, MacFarland stated that there were an estimated 3,000–5,000 enemy soldiers in Ramadi during his time in command.[31] He was a staunch supporter of "presence" or "visibility patrols"—patrols that served no purpose other than ensuring the Iraqi people saw soldiers on the ground.[32] MacFarland wanted to move with a purpose and a sense of urgency throughout Ramadi. In his mind, wasted movements could be detrimental to his men and the overall mission.

This aggressiveness made him unpopular with those that he was replacing and many of his Marine counterparts. During the right-seat ride, he showed his it by hastily moving people from their homes while setting up COPs. This was seen by several Marine officers as too extreme and an easy way to get the populace to turn against the coalition forces.[33] LTC V. J. Tedesco was seen as the most aggressive of the battalion commanders serving under MacFarland. Tedesco commanded 1-37 AR and had proven himself as a competent battlefield commander according to MacFarland. Tedesco felt that tanks were a valuable asset during OIF. He made this statement regarding tanks: "During Thunder Run, tanks proved how valuable and lethal they could be in an urban environment. They simply need to be commanded and situated properly. Thunder Run removed the shroud that tanks could not be combat effective in Iraq's terrain."[34] Tedesco and his men were in charge of setting up a COP codenamed "Falcon." He took seven houses that were occupied by civilians and turned them into a base of operation for the battalion. Each family was given 2,500 U.S. dollars (3,272,500 Iraqi dinars).[35] IEDs would be the biggest obstacle for MacFarland during this fight. They evolved from a mere nuisance during the infancy of this war into a full-fledged battle component that had the ability to rip an Abrams tank in half if properly placed and fueled. The Marines thought that dismounted troops patrolling the city were less likely to encounter these IEDs, or were more likely to see them and call in EOD (explosive ordinance disposal, Army units whose sole purpose was to dismantle bombs or explosive devices). MacFarland's plan was to send a combined force of mounted and dismounted units into the city to cleanse it of the insurgents that had overrun it.[36] The Marines simply did not have the luxury of having armored and mechanized units before the arrival of the 1st BCT. Although the Marines and the army had a different way of conducting combat operations, MacFarland and the Marines agreed overall about the direction that Ramadi needed to go. Lt. Journey BC of 1-6 Marines had this to say about MacFarland and how he conducted business in Ramadi:

> I was surprised by how much Col. MacFarland and his men saw eye to eye with us as far as the best way to pacify the city. He did not try to force a new way of thinking down our throats or try to make us find a new way to skin a cat. He gave us guidance about how he wanted to do business and left the way we did that business up to us.[37]

MacFarland knew that he had the daunting task of trying to fix Ramadi. But he also knew that although many of those who were in command were comparing this fight to Fallujah, he simply did not have the combat power that was allotted to the commanders during Operation *Phantom Fury*. This became clear during an operation that took place on August 2, 2006. MacFarland decided that he wanted to test the strength of the enemy fighters while at the same time going on the offensive and using his tanks and Bradleys to drive out the enemy as he had intended. Tedesco used Charlie Company under the command of Capt. Mike Bajema to lead the assault. The tankers were assisted by infantry from 1-36 and Navy Seals from the TF "Bone Crusher" under the command of Lt. Com. John Gretton "Jocko" Willink. Bajema was also an aggressive commander within the armor ranks; a smart and well-rounded commander according to Tedesco.[38] The goal of the operation was to allow the tanks to set up an outer cordon (outer security) and then allow the dismounted troops to go in and confront the enemy.[39]

This was the first major operation for MacFarland during this fight. He was confronted by a determined enemy. MacFarland expected this mission to take 6–10 hours. He wanted the company to clear from east to west.[40] The role of the tankers during this mission was to provide the infantry troops with armored support and to set a cordon around the area that was being cleared. This was a very similar role that the armor forces had played in the war up to this point. During the march into position, Tedesco and his men led the way and were poised to set the cordon. The order of movement was the tankers first with mechanized infantry mixed in between.[41]

Bajema and his company task force would lean heavily on the snipers from the SEAL Team TF. The TF attempted to set up positions on buildings and inside cleared rooms to spot enemy forces that were coming to attack the armored column. Bajema rode inside the commander's tank and made sure to keep constant radio contact with the forces under his command. The commander's tank in an armor unit is not simply another tank in battle. To clarify, the commander has the same combat obligation as any other tanker: once the enemy has been identified, destroy the enemy with extreme prejudice.[42] But the commander also has to be the eyes and ears of the battlefield for the BC. That is another reason why every single tank crew member needs to qualify and be proficient on their tanks during gunnery to give them the confidence they will need to fight the enemy during combat situations. Lieutenant Colonel Nathan Davis had this to say about officers being on tanks during combat: "You see armor officers are different from other officers when it comes to combat and combat expectations. Yes, the commander has to make sure to orchestrate what's going on during a firefight or an operation, but they also must be able to maneuver their tanks in a way that makes them effective against the enemy."[43]

Bajema observed the situation before the TF and decided that the best course of action was to regroup and come back at night when the sights on the tank gave the tankers an advantage and the optics of the dismounted troops allowed them to conduct a nighttime raid without alerting the enemy.[44] After getting permission for Tedesco to withdraw, he attempted to turn the column around, still using the tanks as the lead element. Bajema's tank was the last to exit. Just as he passed through an alley, he and the TF were attacked by one hundred enemy fighters. The insurgents calculated the movement of the column and waited until the tanks passed to attack the Bradley and the soft-skinned Humvee vehicles. Bajema soon found himself surrounded on all four sides by insurgent forces armed with AK-47s and RPGs. The enemy started to fire on the column, and they were so close that the vehicles had issues returning fire. Tedesco's XO got on the radio and demanded a situation report (sit-rep) from Tedesco.[45] He then asked what he (Bajema) needed to fight back the enemy forces. It was during that portion of the fight that Bajema requested danger close artillery fire.[46] This was the first time during MacFarland's reign that artillery was used in combat during his time in Ramadi.[47]

Shortly after the request, artillery fire landed and was able to create space between Bajema's TF and the enemy insurgents. This allowed for better target acquisition for the tankers, and Bajema and the tankers used the main gun and coax to fight off the enemy fighters. The Abrams used mainly HEAT and IMPAT rounds from the main gun.[48] The sound and use of the main gun was effective in driving the enemy fighters away from the tanks and Bradleys but the dismounted troops still had to endure a tough and determined enemy raining small arms and RPG rounds at them.

One of the units that bore the brunt of this attack was the Navy SEAL team. A brotherhood had grown between the soldiers of the 1st Armored Division and the SEAL team. There are several reasons for that, one of them being the fact that the SEALs believed in the direction that Ramadi was headed after MacFarland had come in command.[49] The SEALs believed that the new aggressive approach could enable the city of Ramadi to be taken the correct way and not allow it to fall back into the hands of the insurgents once the coalition had completed its mission.[50]

This brotherhood allowed the SEAL leadership to come to the aid of the soldiers without question when they were engaged in a firefight. This was the case during the operation on August 2nd, 2006. Before the involvement of the SEAL team, the tankers were busy laying waste to much of the dismounted enemy forces. Bajema's tankers were responsible for 37 enemy kills during this fight.[51] By this time in Iraq, the enemy was well aware of the capabilities of the Abrams tank. They hid and only peeked the weapon out to shoot. They also fired their AK-47s at the tanks to no avail, with the hopes of catching either the loader or the TC out of their hatch. The small arms fire did little to no damage to the tanks as it bounced off its armor.

Tankers also evolved during this conflict and moved away from loading their tanks with a heavy dose of sabot rounds in favor of more HEAT and IMPAT rounds.[52] During the interview with an Army master sergeant, he had this to say about the shift in rounds and why it was important to the tank crews:

> Early during the invasion and Thunder Run, we made sure that the bustle rack had a good number of SABOT rounds. Matter of fact, there were certain moments when SABOT almost exclusively occupied the racks. Over time though, we had to change and shift away from the use of SABOT rounds simply because the enemy was changing its tactics. They did not hit us head-on with Russian tanks anymore. They were attacking us using IEDs, and snipers, and by ducking and taking pop shots with their infantry. So, we had to start using HEAT, IMPAT, and canister rounds to destroy their hiding places and flush them out.[53]

The tankers were able to flush out the enemy fighters and destroy the places they were hiding which allowed the infantry to have a better chance of finding and destroying them. While this made the enemy more easily detected, it also brought more firepower down on the coalition infantry.

During this time, the tankers were able to reorganize their firepower and surround the enemy's dismounted troops. While this was taking place, the SEALs found themselves in a brutal firefight with the insurgents.[54]

It was during this time that SEALs lost their first operator during OIF, as Marc Lee was fatally wounded while clearing a room during the fight.[55] The SEALs continued to fight after Lee was taken back to base for medical treatment. Once they returned, they found themselves back in an intense fight. The tankers were able to help end this battle and save lives as they continued to engage the enemy with machine- and main-gun fire. This operation lasted from 4 a.m. until 5 p.m., and Bajema estimated that over 60 enemy fighters had been killed.[56] The majority of the operation had taken place during the hottest portion of the day. MacFarland stated that at its height, the temperature was just over 120 degrees.[57] Several things became clear to MacFarland after this operation. Firstly, the armor officer realized that he simply could not cleanse the city with armor or mechanized forces. Secondly, he knew that the Iraqi Security Forces (ISF) would be key to truly winning Ramadi.[58] MacFarland would commit to training the ISF, which would mean going out and recruiting Iraqi citizens. He would need to assure these recruits that the cause was worthy and that they would be supported by U.S. forces during this fight.[59]

MacFarland had this to say about his goals in Ramadi and the Iraqi Army (IA) and the ISF:

> So, to get to know the people in the areas we were occupying, we would put patrols out at night and go to every single house and, just like you would any normal census, we would find out everything we could about everybody in each one of those homes at an hour of the night where we expected to find, basically, everybody at home, to include vehicles, weapons, and you name it. Anything we could find out about the people that lived around us. Then, the other thing that became apparent as we were going along was that the soldiers on the combat outposts were getting pretty worn out from making sandbags and doing all those kinds of things when they weren't out on patrols and they were building up their force protection. So, rather than just dumping dirt out there and sandbags, what we started to do was we started Operation Jamestown, no work, no food, on Camp Ramadi proper, which meant that everybody, before every meal on Camp Ramadi at the main chow hall, had to fill two sandbags and put them on a PLS [Palletized Loading System] flat rack. So, with about

4,000 to 5,000 people living on Camp Ramadi proper, including contractors and engineers and Seabees and all kinds of people that didn't work directly for me, and with that being my base, I could make them fill sandbags if I wanted to and we could generate 10,000 to 12,000 sandbags a day on Camp Ramadi and push them out to the combat outposts and, that way, everybody kind of felt like they were contributing to the fight outside the wire, even if you were a person who never left the wire. So, that was one thing we were able to do. But clearly, we didn't have enough Iraqi Security Forces to establish the presence everywhere we went. And the Iraqi Army was okay; but they were not all that well trained and they weren't very popular with the locals either because they had a high percentage of Shia and, of course, the people there were all Sunnis. Then, the other thing about them was they were very under-strength. In fact, right before we kicked off our operation, there was an Iraqi Army outpost next to this railroad bridge, which I had visited, and that night or the next day, I think, a massive dump truck bomb drove into it and exploded and this was manned by an under-strength Iraqi Army company. And this was before I, officially, took over the battle space. This was on like 3 or 4 June [2006]. But it obliterated that company. I mean, they went from about 40 guys to about 20 guys. So, they went from basically an under-strength company to an under-strength platoon. Well, let me take that back. I guess they might have had about 60 guys, they lost about 20 in the attack, which put them down to about 40, and then they put the company on R&R [rest and recuperation] leave and only about half of them came back off leave and the first sergeant was assassinated on leave. So, that company was essentially combat ineffective. So, I realized that the ISF, especially the Iraqi Army, was very vulnerable to murder and intimidation and could be removed from the board like a chess piece just like that, in the blink of an eye. So, I knew that I had to generate more combat power and, when that company was wiped out, I pushed one of my own companies up there. But the lesson learned there was, "Don't put an Iraqi Army company out by its lonesome," and I made sure that wherever they were I was also to kind of bolster them.[60]

Tanks, and tank units, still played a major role in the coming mission. MacFarland used his armor battalion to support the ISF and IA as they manned police points and checkpoints. This was a needed action as the insurgent forces were constantly attacking these areas and having an Abrams nearby would often serve as a deterrent to enemy forces.[61] The training of the ISF and the IA was vital to the plan that MacFarland wanted to implement to take back Ramadi. While MacFarland needed his armored TFs to continue to fight back the enemy insurgents, it was necessary to ensure that the Iraqi people and their government could continue the fight once the brigade had moved on. MacFarland was not simply there to win a few firefights; he was there to fix the city and make sure that it could stand on its two feet without the aid of the American forces.[62] One of the issues that plagued the recruitment of these forces was the fear that the insurgent forces instilled into the local populace.[63] The goal for MacFarland and his men was to continue fighting and winning these "smaller" battles or combat operations to show the city that the enemy was not indestructible and that together, they could defeat the insurgents and be free from their tyranny.

This fight had to be spearheaded by the armored forces of MacFarland. The Abrams battalions (1-35, 1-37) needed to clear the way for the other dismounted forces to achieve victory and usher in a new wave of Iraqi forces who would align with the coalition forces. Before that could happen, there were several instances where the armor battalions needed to show their mettle and killing power. During this conflict, one of the battalion commanders, LTC Anthony Deane, commanded 1-35 Armor. Deane's battalion was divided once it arrived in Iraq, to become a true task force rather than the pure armor battalion that they had trained with before their deployment. Deane's battalion consisted of two tank and two mechanized infantry companies which were the standard for the combined arms or TF model. Deane had a much different view of Ramadi than MacFarland given he was often on the ground directing the companies during combat while MacFarland had to look at the bigger picture of the battalions and how they were functioning.[64] Deane was also a career armor officer who was put in charge of an AO to pacify the area of insurgents while also building a relationship with the leaders of the Iraqi government.

An anonymous U.S. Army master sergeant had this to say about the transition from the BC to the brigade commander as well as the CSMs and how the enlisted soldiers see the differences between the two commands:

> I think the biggest difference is the interaction with the soldiers. For example, the brigade CSM is never involved with soldiers at the company level in garrison. In fact, if you as an enlisted soldier ever have to see or talk to the brigade CSM it is because you did something great or you are in serious trouble. It's the same with the brigade commander. You never hear from him unless there is a brigade formation or something went wrong. Now in combat, you will see those two (brigade commander and CSM) a lot. Their role shifts a bit in combat as they are

in more of a micromanaging role in terms of logistics and orders. The CSM is always around to make sure that the brigade commander's orders are being followed and that the enlisted soldiers are meeting the standard. There's a lot that goes on if the CSM is a tanker versus if he is an infantryman. A 19K CSM will pay a lot of attention to the vehicles and make sure that they are up to standard and that the crews are also wearing the right gear and have everything they need. This is not just for the tankers but for the Bradley crews as well. That's the thing about having an armor command staff, they have probably been through the wringer and have seen every single armored formation that there is in the army. You could have an infantry guy (CSM or brigade commander) that has spent their entire twenty- or thirty-year career being light and they may not have the same sense for vehicle maintenance and standards. I used to hate it when I found out that we went from having a tank command staff to an infantry one. They just have different values and see garrison and combat differently. Back in the day like the 90s and early 2000s, if it was a heavy brigade (HBCT) or an armored brigade (ABCT), 9 times out of 10, the command staff would be tankers.[65]

This glimpse into the differences between the two command positions is important as it shows why there are many different aspects and viewpoints for the same tour of duty in Iraq. Deane found out very quickly how important his tanks were and the composition of the enemy as he conducted his first combat patrol without the outgoing unit which was 1-172 AR from the Vermont National Guard.[66] June 6, 2006, was the first major contact that Deane would be a part of during his command in Ramadi. Deane chose to use a Humvee vehicle instead of his Abrams tank, which was customary at that time for BCs who were armor officers commanding armor units.[67] During his exit to attend a change of command ceremony for another company under his command, the entry control point (ECP) was hit with mortar fire. Shortly after, one of the vehicles within his personal security detail (PSD) was hit by an IED. Deane chose to ride in the softer-skinned vehicles to divert attention from himself as opposed to bringing the added eyes of the enemy who would have found joy in attacking a convey of Abrams tanks.[68]

During this attack, several of the PSD soldiers were injured and Deane found himself using his rifle to fight back the enemy insurgents. Every patrol base in Iraq during this time had a platoon-sized element called the quick reaction force (QRF). This platoon is always on standby if the platoon that is on patrol encounters enemy contact.[69] The QRF for armored TFs usually consists of either a tank or mech infantry platoon.

This is because in many cases when the QRF is called, there is a dire need for firepower. During the attack on the ECP, the QRF was called to assist Deane and his men. Although Deane and the rest of his PSD were able to hold their own against the enemy insurgents, it was the tanks that came in and provided an outer cordon, shielding the soldiers from continued fire from the enemy insurgents. This led to Deane and his men being able to medevac his men and put an end to the firefight. This action proved how valuable tanks could be as a quick reaction force, but it also showed Deane how determined was the enemy that he was facing at the time. It was after this incident that Deane realized the severity of the situation in Ramadi. He needed to find a solution that could destroy the enemy but not turn the local populace against the coalition forces.

Colonel MacFarland's plan was simple on paper—seize, hold, and build. This concept was easy to spell out, but it was up to the battalion commanders to make this concept a reality. Every battalion commander was given their own little space that they were in charge of, and they needed to find a way to make that little space a safer place for the Iraqi people.[70] As stated earlier, this brigade in general was a legacy brigade and they had to mix several of the company elements to have a more complete battalion. Assigning a company here and there was not a problem for most battalion commanders but the camaraderie and making sure that everyone was on the same page was one of the bigger issues.[71] Deane and his men had to adapt to having infantry units within their battalion. The notion of this mix is well documented in this work, but every experience was different. Although Deane was an "armor officer," he was also a career tanker. He had not been exposed to the light cavalry world except for training in the basic course that all armor officers must go through. Before this war, the training that took place under his command revolved around tanks: being proficient at killing the enemy, and maintenance.

This mixing of companies also changed the first phase or "seize" portion of the operations in Ramadi. The armor battalions needed the aid of the infantry companies much as they did in the battle for Fallujah. Due to the lack of manpower for this operation, every single available unit within each battalion was vital. The seize portion involved action and firepower for the Abrams of 1-35, 1-37, and 2-37. This phase allowed MacFarland to go and clear sections of Ramadi piece by piece. This was perhaps the most action-packed portion but also the time when the tanks were used the most. During this first phase, nearly three hundred main gun rounds were fired by all the armor battalions within the 1st Brigade.[72] Even the 5-7 Cavalry squadron was involved in this initial barrage of fire. 5-7 was commanded by LTC Cliff Wheeler. Wheeler was also a career-long armor officer who had joined the army in 1988.[73] He and his squadron had the task of observing suspected insurgent forces and reporting back to the BC who would then report to the brigade commander.

Because the squadron is the only one within the brigade, it has the responsibility of ensuring that all of the battalions have the recon element readily available. Wheeler's unit was also divided, not due to the mission but out of necessity. Like most armored cavalry units, Wheeler's squadron was divided into three companies with one infantry, armor, and cavalry company.[74] This meant that the infantry company, although mechanized, was a "scout" company. Their job, at least on the surface or doctrinally, was not the same as other infantry companies, but to assume the role of their squadron which was to identify targets for the large force.[75] Their battalion was augmented by the tank company, and their job of course was not to identify the targets by dismounted means but to provide overwatch and use their optics to observe and report. Having Abrams came in handy for the squadron when the enemy fired upon the recon forces. The firepower that the tanks provided for the recon element also served as a way to keep enemies at bay as often the enemy fighters would stay back, knowing the capabilities of the tank. 5-7 did not participate in as many firefights or enemy engagements as the other battalions but they were responsible for much of the information that the brigade used during the seize portion of this fight.

Deane and the rest of 1-35 Armor used this information to pinpoint either the house or location of the enemy fighters. In many instances, the goal was not to find a house to kick in or search but to find weapon caches or IED manufacturing sites.[76] These sites often proved to be more valuable than attacking a building or putting a main gun round downrange.

The seize portion for 1-35 took a combination of patience and action. Allowing intelligence to dictate what houses needed to be hit and battles needed to be fought became vital for Deane and his men. Unlike other operations of this magnitude, the opening salvo consisted of a series of smaller battles for 1-35 Armor.[77] The day-to-day grind consisted of men carrying body armor, water, and ammunition when the heat index was well over one hundred degrees. During this phase, the work of the 1-35 was grueling hard labor. For many of the soldiers, it appeared that they were constantly in a firefight. This notion was different for the men on the ground as opposed to the commanders. It is important to note that the experience for the squad leader or section reagent was different from that of the CSM or the BC. There are risks that the leadership takes on when they decide to have an aggressive approach to combat as opposed to one that puts the men in static defense.[78]

First Sergeant Marshall Yuen spoke about the fight on the ground and how it was viewed by the soldiers.

> I think a lot of times we live in our world. The battalion commander gives the orders to the company commander and it is my job as the senior NCO of the company to make sure that the commander's intent is followed. But they do not see the hours and hours of maintenance. They don't see the stress of the individual solder. Now to be fair, it is the CSM's job to relay that information to the BC and let him know about the status of the soldiers and how they are doing. But they are focused on the overall mission and sometimes they get out of touch with what the soldiers are going through.[79]

The soldiers in Ramadi did not worry about the overarching goal of the mission. Their job was to simply get through the day and carry out the mission at hand. This part of the phase for soldiers meant routinely getting into smaller skirmishes with the enemy forces as they would invade their homes in search of enemy occupants. These searches became almost routine for 1-35 and they would often find the dismounted troops having to return fire on the enemy.[80]

Deane and the brigade as a whole found success during this phase: they were able to kill nearly 300 enemy fighters during the first month of this fight.[81] For the tankers, this was also a time that they yet again proved their worth on the battlefield. During this phase in general, tankers knew that they would be called upon to bring the fight to the enemy as MacFarland wanted this phase to set the tone and send a message to the enemies of the coalition and the Iraqi government. Thousands of rounds of machine-gun ammunition were used during this first portion of the battle from the tanks. Deane was an aggressive but smart commander much like MacFarland and he knew that the tankers needed to be implemented in the battle plan but he also valued the role of the infantry and knew that they were necessary to achieve success during this first phase.[82] 1-35 found themselves on the front lines at this time and it was imperative that they were disciplined and decisive as they engaged the enemy and prepared for other operations later on that would eventually allow the Iraqi people to be to focus on ruling themselves without the aid of U.S. forces.

As MacFarland and his battalions fought to destroy the enemies of Ramadi, other factors slowed their progress apart from the enemy's rifle. One of the things that affected tankers and all U.S. forces in Ramadi was the perception of the job that was being done by the ground forces and their commanders. It is important to emphasize the fact that the army and Marines saw the fight in Ramadi very differently. For many Marines, the fight probably felt like a losing proposition as they did not have the manpower or equipment themselves to win in Ramadi. The Marines that fought alongside the "Ready First" brigade benefited from having an armor and mechanized presence.[83] This is where perception meets reality. Although Marine officers were in charge of both the corps and force levels in Iraq at the time of the Ramadi fight in 2006, the army and more specifically the 1st BCT of the 1st AD was selected to go in and replace the National Guard unit that was fighting, as well as to be the lead element under Col. MacFarland. This move had the potential to drive a wedge between the two services as very seldom during this fight did the Marines have to directly answer to an army commander.[84]

This difference of opinion about the fight in Ramadi between the Marines and Army led to certain leaders within the Marine Corps feeling that from the vantage point of the Marines, Ramadi and the Al Anbar province were lost beyond redemption.[85] In August 2006, a report by Marine Col. Peter H. Devlin—who served as the senior military intelligence officer in the province—would become famous for the negative remarks and overview that it gave to the military and civilian followers alike. Initially, this report was to be kept between military personnel as this was an official report of Devlin's findings and his views would serve other commanders who oversaw the province.[86] But the report was quickly leaked to the public and not only did the people of the U.S. find more reason to doubt the idea of victory in Iraq, they also now had reason to doubt the leaders and the plan that was in place to conquer the enemies of the coalition forces. The news that this information was leaked made its way to Gen. Casey. He was disappointed in Devlin for several reasons according to sources.[87]

Casey visited Ramadi and, more importantly, Devlin. During their talks, he made Devlin aware of how this report reflected on the coalition forces in Ramadi. It did not simply state that the situation was hopeless, but that the coalition forces were nearly powerless to stop the onslaught of attacks by the enemy insurgents.[88] Perhaps the biggest issue that Casey had with this was the fact that the new commander and his brigade had been making headway in Ramadi. The enemy attacks had gone down and the forces under MacFarland had killed a significant number of combatants. Now, to be fair, the number of enemy KIA does not mean that an area is safer or that a plan is working, especially given the fact that the enemy was facing U.S. forces. But the fact that an aggressive, offensive plan was in place and appeared to be working made this report premature and damaging. Casey called the plan and the outlook by Devlin "defeatist."[89] Casey stated that Devlin needed to focus his attention on giving the MEF and MNC military intel that could help defeat the enemy and not on negative reports that downplayed the success that MacFarland and his men were having.

As this report was being prepared, the brigade TF continued to push forward with the mission. They now had a foothold in Ramadi and the areas that needed to be cleared were either done or being worked on. This included COPs as well as stores, schools, police stations, and government buildings.[90] MacFarland continued to use the tanks as the outer cordon while the infantry would go in and clear the buildings. Tanks often had to use their main gun round during this phase but the goal—to fix the city without destroying it—was achieved during phase one.

MacFarland learned a lesson that many of the commanders learned during the battle of Fallujah when it came to tank warfare: to use the tanks to encircle the enemy and then use the infantry to attack those that were inside. Abrams were vital during this phase of the fight as they helped usher in the infantry and allowed for the COPs to be taken by the brigade.[91] The next task would be the clearing; this phase went hand in hand with the seize phase and was swift as the forces of the 1st Brigade would go in and make sure that the buildings that were seized could be used and were clear of enemy forces. This was both a combat and a civil mission.[92] The army would go in and investigate the buildings to see what needed to happen to fix them or restore power.

The next phase was the "hold" phase. This involved holding areas that they had taken and cleared during the first part of the MacFarland/ McMaster plan. The important portion of this phase was the training of the IP, ISF, and IA. 1-37 Armor took on the task of training these units and in particular the IP and IA. One of the companies in charge of the training was Alpha Company which was commanded by Captain Joseph Albrecht. Albrecht was an armor officer who had helped clear several of the areas during the initial seize and clearing phase. The mission for Albrecht and his company was not simply to give the Iraqi soldiers ammunition but to train them to defend the city and the province on their own. There were several steps to achieving this goal. The first step was the recruiting aspect. Albrecht and his men would set up meetings with local Sheiks and tribal leaders to find the best places to go in and recruit IA and IP candidates.[93]

This experience was much different from any that Albrecht had before this transition. It is important to discuss the role of 1-37 Armor in its entirety before the transition to becoming the main force for training. Albrecht had this to say about the role of his unit before his reassignment:

I was assigned to secure the northern side of Hit. I was assigned to Task Force 1-36 and we had two infantry companies and one armor company; interestingly we were all Alpha Companies. It was Alpha 1-6, Alpha 1-36, and Alpha 1-37. We were originally supposed to have Alpha Company from the engineer battalion but we ended up with Delta Company so that kind of messed up our name. We were going to call it Task Force Alpha—all of us little guys. Anyway, my responsibility was to basically secure the northern side of the river. The city of Hit straddles the Euphrates river. You have one neighborhood north of the river and the preponderance of the city is south of the river. I was assigned the neighborhood north of the river and I was responsible for maintaining security within the neighborhood and the areas outlying from there. I think it was 600 or 700 square kilometers of battlespace running along the Euphrates river from the town of Zuwayah, which means "corner" in Arabic, which is kind of funny. I had the responsibility of 15 or 20 kilometers east of that city and north of Lake Habbaniyah and west just shy of a town called Baghdadi. You could draw a little triangular shape that covers that shape of the desert. It was predominantly security within that city. I was responsible for the bridge that connected those two sides of the city was secured. Somebody had tried to vehicle-borne improvised explosive device (VBIED) it before so my job was to make sure the bridge was not destroyed. We also trained Iraqi Army forces. I had less than a company-sized element assigned to me and the size fluctuated anywhere from a platoon to three platoons' worth of soldiers. We worked with them to secure the city, do engagements with the local officials, and recruit people for the police and Iraqi Army. That kind of encompasses what we did.[94]

The biggest issue for Albrecht when he took over as the training officer for the ISF was numbers. Initially, the recruiting efforts took a hit due to some of the cultural differences between the Sunni and Shi'a Iraqis.[95] Albrecht stated many of the recruits of the IA were Shi'a in a predominately Sunni neighborhood. Often these Shi'a attempted to keep their religious affiliation a secret to blend in with the population and not face backlash.[96] The initial weeks of training for Alpha Company were trying to the least. The men had to be taught the basic soldiering skills and a translator was needed for every word that came from the mouth of Albrecht or his subordinates. Often, there were no translators available and Alpha Company simply had to physically show the IA what they needed to do. This made training unnecessarily arduous. Another issue that slowed down the efforts to train the men was the equipment. The United States was pumping hundreds of millions of dollars into this war at the time but that was simply for its own forces and the cost of fighting a war.[97] Now, a company of tankers was being asked to make sure that IA had the manpower and equipment needed to combat insurgent forces. The IA lacked the weapons and vehicles needed to patrol the area and engage the enemy if need be. The weapon of choice for the IA was the AK-47.

This weapon was cheaper and easy to find during this portion of the war.[98] Coalition forces were also able to gift the IA with old, abandoned

Humvees and makeshift vehicles to at least get them started. Coalition forces used personnel from within IA ranks to fill the leadership holes. Having men that were trusted helped the IA and the IP units find a cohesive balance and someone that they were familiar with to lead them.[99] Due to the limited number of men, Alpha Company and the rest of the battalion made sure to constantly be in an overwatch position with the ISF. After weeks of training, the commander signed off on the available forces. The battalion started to take these new forces out on patrol missions. These missions were often the same types of missions that the American forces had been used to conducting. MacFarland wanted to show the people of Ramadi that their own units were leading the charge against the insurgents of Ramadi.[100] Their assent was also a major part of this phase to retake Ramadi. During the initial patrols, American forces attempted to allow the ISF to take the lead. For example, during room clearing operations, the ISF were allowed to be the first in the building and to set up their own outer and inner cordon. American troops would follow behind and use their tanks to assist in the outer cordon.[101]

This assignment was different for the tankers of the 37th Armor Regiment. They were not being asked to blow holes into buildings or dismantle an enemy RPG team. They were being asked to create a military force from the ground up.[102] The ISF were started with one patrol a day. Albrecht would go on these patrols to ensure that the ISF was doing their job but also to make sure that they were being properly supported by their American counterparts. One of the benefits Albrecht had was that he and his men were in an area that was not heavy on enemy contact, at least for the majority of their deployment. This allowed the ISF to hone their skills without having to pay for their shortcomings in blood. Albrecht had this to say about how his men performed in their duties as a training force:

> I think they did pretty well. The NCOs did a really good job of training the Iraqi Army soldiers. They were patient and they took their time. They also understood that they weren't going to ever be U.S. Army soldiers and operate at that level of proficiency but they had something they could teach and give to the Iraqi soldiers to help them perform better. I think there are times when you get frustrated working with them. They would get tired. If it was too hot outside, they wouldn't want to do training. In terms of religious and cultural sensitivities,

they'd want to take breaks. Most American soldiers were gung-ho and just do it until you're done and get it right. I think sometimes that can be frustrating because you have to operate at a slower pace and have more patience and you also have the language barrier. We would regularly have two interpreters. One guy's name was Ronny and he was a Sudanese gentleman. We called him our Sudanese warlord. He spoke Arabic well but it was a Sudanese or North African dialect and he didn't whisper well. When you were asking for a translation, he would give you a translation but it would usually interrupt the discourse that was going on in general because he spoke so loudly. We had another gentleman who was from Diwaniyah who was an exceptional interpreter. We had two guys. If we had one or two other interpreters, they were almost worthless. We had one kid who was probably 18 or 19 years old. He wanted to be called Scooby; I don't know why. We tried to get him to be a little more professional and adult and take the job seriously but he insisted on being called Scooby. I think my guys spent more time teaching him English and its translations into Arabic than he could translate the other way.[103]

It was the training of the 37th Armor Regiment that allowed the eventual recruitment of the ISF to blossom. Over the course of several months, the ISF went from a platoon-size to a battalion-sized element. These new recruits were able to fill the roles of police and army soldiers for the people of Ramadi. This also allowed for the areas that were going to be built in the city to be safe and secure for the people living within the city.

The first two phases cost the lives of many members of the American forces. American troops, including tankers, were asked to go in guns blazing and take areas just for them to live and conduct patrols from. The insurgent forces made sure that every asset would be needed to achieve victory for the city and the province. An army tanker was put in command of one of the worst cities in all of Iraq. He proved the doubters wrong as he was able to implement a plan that was used by another armor force to achieve success in Ramadi. The tankers' role in this city was profound. They were vital in the initial surge and capturing of the sites used for COPs. Without their sights and effectiveness, more American forces could have been lost.[104] It was vital that during the initial phase, tankers used their training and firepower to destroy the enemy forces. Later, their tactical patience and intelligence were called upon to train the Iraqi people to defend themselves.

CHAPTER 6

Baqubah II

During the summer of 2007, the U.S. Army continued to attempt to drive out enemy forces throughout Iraq. Al Qaeda in Iraq (AQI) had built up its forces in the Anbar and Diyala provinces and the city of Baqubah had been designated as the new "Islamic State" by AQI forces. AQI was made up of both Sunni and Shi'a militants who were determined to have their safe haven and to defend it against coalition forces.[1] In 2007, MND-B (multi-national division Baghdad) was under the command of LTG Raymond Odierno. Odierno was the commander of the army's 4th Infantry Division during the invasion in 2003. He was a career-long field artillery officer—the only division or corps commander during the invasion of Iraq who was not either an infantry or armor officer.[2] He had a more aggressive approach to the war than some of the other division- or corps-level generals. He wanted to make sure that his soldiers were doing the right thing and obeying the ROE, but he also wanted them to be aggressive with their operations and destroy the enemy as opposed to simply being a presence in Iraq.[3]

There was a notion during OIF that when areas were viewed as troubled or "red," the best idea was to send in a heavy brigade to sort the issue out. This became a common theme throughout the war. One of the issues that plagued the Diyala province was the use of IEDs and deep-form penetrators (DFP).[4] The goal for AQI appeared to be to prevent the coalition forces bringing heavy armor to the fight. If they could stop them from bringing tanks and Bradleys, they could limit the amount of firepower that they needed to face.[5] Several areas in and around the city of Baqubah had not been patrolled regularly because coalition forces knew they were laden with IEDs. Although Odierno knew that was the case, he had to find a solution to the problem in the Diyala province. He also had to manage the other "surge brigades." Beginning in 2007, the U.S. decided to commit more combat troops to Iraq to combat the rise of the insurgency.[6] These brigades were from all walks of military life including airborne, light infantry, Stryker, and armored units. Odierno wanted to divide the brigades in and around the cities surrounding Baghdad to secure the capital first and then branch out to attack the red or troubled cities that had become safe havens for insurgents.[7]

The MNC was commanded by Gen. David Petraeus. His goal was to push out large-scale operations in several areas at once. He would leave the particulars of those operations to the MNC division leaders. Odierno would have direct interaction with the troops on the ground during the

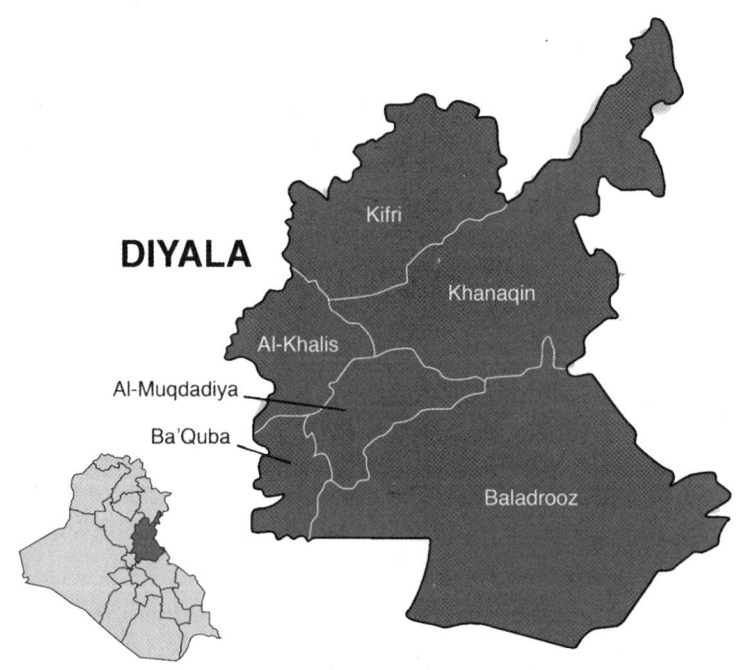

Map of Diyala province.

operations in the Diyala province.[8] The responsibility of the province was given to the 3rd HBCT (Greywolf Brigade) of the 1st Calvary Division. This brigade was commanded by Col. David Sutherland who was a career infantry officer. This brigade had already made the transition to a combined arms unit. It consisted of three combined arms battalions, one armored cavalry squadron, and one field artillery battalion. These battalions were all counted on to combat the enemy insurgents in the Diyala province. The battalion that was directly responsible for securing Baqubah was 1-12 Cavalry.[9]

In particular, at least during the infancy of this battle, the city was under the command of both Alpha and Bravo companies. Both of these companies would have tank platoons added to their ranks to supply them with more firepower. Charlie and Delta companies were both armor units going into the battle.[10] The issue for these units was the perception that the army had at this time about what was going on in Iraq. Many of the units and their commanders felt that the major armor fighting was done. This led to several armor units in Iraq making their tankers perform dismounted tasks to add more "boots on the ground,"[11] as described by Army 1SG Robert Colella, senior NCO during the battle, in his book *Battle for Baqubah: Killing Our Way Out*. His only experience with tanks was in Baqubah; he had been used to seeing tanks from afar but had never before seen them in combat up close. He admits that oftentimes, there is a schism or rivalry between the armor and infantry when it comes to garrison (time spent on the main base or location in the U.S.). Colella describes that the nature of the different jobs creates a rivalry and often gives the impression that tankers are lazy and infantrymen are too stupid to obtain a better job in the military, so they get stuck doing "grunt" or infantry work.

In Baqubah his mechanized infantry company was given a platoon of tanks from Delta Company to combat extremely heavy enemy resistance during their conflict. They were led by an infantry officer due to the lack of armor officers available within the brigade as the unit deployed.[12] Colella was pleased that the platoon he received had an infantry officer because in his mind this would help the tankers in their transition to infantry tasks. The issue was the fact that even with two companies on the eastern side of the city, the unit was woefully undermanned, and lacked the firepower to combat the enemy.

With the enemy firmly entrenched in their plan to prevent tanks and other armor from bringing the fight to them, the issue was that the army in general was allowing this plan to work. In areas where the infantry units had superior numbers, this was not a problem but in places like Baqubah, where patrols were constantly getting attacked, the situation was more dire. Bravo Company (Colella's unit) was regularly forced to send units out that were undermanned, and his men would come into some form of enemy contact one out of every three times they left the wire.[13] Although IEDs became the main issue for the units in Baqubah, Bravo Company still managed to find uses for tankers. During their stint with Bravo Company, tanks would routinely be asked to conduct overwatch missions. These missions were done to make sure that the undermanned infantry units still had the firepower to go in and destroy the enemy. Although the Greywolf Brigade was armored, they would rely on Humvees or dismounted patrols during the majority of this fight to limit the effect of IEDs.[14]

In an area laced with IEDs, Colella was forced to use tanks differently than many other leaders had the luxury of doing. He often had tankers dismount and fill in the ranks of his infantrymen to ensure they had enough troops to conduct dismounted patrols. Although this was done out of desperation, which complicated his decision-making about how to use tanks, it was a gross misuse of armor. During the battle and capturing of Baqubah, infantry patrols were met with enemy fire almost every other day. This meant that the infantry could have used the fire superiority that Abrams tanks provide. It is important to keep the infantry outlook in mind: not all of the sources in this work are from the perspective of armor personnel, and that can and will be beneficial as hearing from just a singular person or culture of people makes a work less objective.

Tankers still were needed and made an impact on this fight for Bravo. Nearly 20 main-gun rounds were fired during the early portion of the fight. This number may seem small compared to the early conflicts, but it reflects the small portion of Baqubah that was being fought for by Bravo Company.[15] The tanks during this fight were not on "weapons-free" status regarding their main gun. That is to say, they needed to get the company commander's permission to fire the main gun.[16] Later during OIF, tankers needed to get permission from the brigade/regiment commander or higher. These limitations on the main gun made it very difficult for the units that had armor to exploit the firepower they possessed. During this early portion in Baqubah, tanks were asked to be the big brother of the patrolling units. They were also asked to leave their tanks and perform room clearing and combat patrols with both Alpha and Bravo from 1-12 Cav. The impact that tankers had during the early portion could be felt not as much in the tank but in what they were able to do in terms of meshing with the mechanized infantry units they were attached to.

This was the beginning of a pause in "pure" tank combat for the armored forces of Iraq. The notion that tanks and armored vehicles were not combat-effective in urban cities was being floated around by the generals and even the civilians who were in command of the armed forces.[17] This notion was later proved to be false as the army would take the lead in Sadr City and tankers were again the lead element. But for this battle, there was an infantry numbers problem and the tankers were suffering because of it. The army was aware of this problem and the issue was what the right move was to fix Baqubah. The tankers in Baqubah were often asked to cross-train the infantry on the Abrams to allow the infantrymen to have sufficient knowledge to perform ECP guard duty.[18] This meant that the infantrymen could use the weapons systems on the tank should an enemy try and overrun the COP or joint security station (JSS). This was not ideal for the tankers or the infantry of 1-12. The fact was that the tankers were being underutilized and the enemy was exploiting that. Vehicles were constantly being hit by IEDs and destroyed, and men were lost throughout the brigade. These tankers were being limited in how they could affect this fight and the brigade was suffering because of it. This was not like Fallujah or Thunder Run. Tankers were essentially being told that they had to sit and watch the fight without bringing the main gun to it.

Luckily for the tankers of 1-12 Cav, and for the battalion itself, changes were coming that helped them succeed in taking this safe haven away from the AQI. Col. Steve Townsend commanded the 3rd SBCT (Stryker brigade combat team) of the 2nd Infantry Division.[19] Townsend and his brigade were the designated strike force for the MND-Baghdad. This meant essentially that they were the QRF for the division—if somewhere was becoming a bad or red area, Townsend and his men were sent there to handle the problem. Townsend discussed the state of affairs and the losses suffered by both the 2nd ID and the Greywolf Brigade with Sutherland:

> I was attending the hero flight memorial. That is the flights that they take the deceased soldiers away in. It was there that I met up with Dave Sutherland. We talked about the losses for both our boys from 5-20 INF and his boys in the Greywolf brigade. I was aware of the issues that they were having in Baqubah. The reality for commanders is that if the unit is not doing great or if they are taking a lot of losses, that's on the commander in the eyes of the army. The reality for Dave was that they were not having the success that they wanted because of the lack of numbers that were in the Diyala province. I don't know who said it first or whether I said, "Dave do you need some help?" Or if he asked me to come, but the gist of the conversation was that we agreed that Baqubah was not going to be fixed with his unit alone. Dave told me that if I came then he and his brigade would work for me and we'd try to get Baqubah cleared out. A few days later, General Odierno came into my brigade headquarters for a briefing and some of my staff members were a bit hesitant to tell him some of our ideas about Baqubah because a few days before we were told by MND-Baghdad that they weren't going to talk any more ideas about Baqubah at this point. General Odierno said "Hey, we're in a war. I wanna win, you wanna win, tell me what's on your mind." After that, we laid out a plan for us to go in and team up with the Greywolf brigade to help them sort out Baqubah. Twenty-four hours later, we had a warning order to go to Baqubah.[20]

This changed the fortunes of both the tankers and infantrymen. The notion that Baqubah did not have enough soldiers soon became a thing of the past as Col. Townsend would now bring nearly five thousand soldiers to the Diyala province.[21] The increase in men brought a change in the direction of leadership. Sutherland shifted into a deputy commander role and served as the second in command of the province, and the operation moved forward. Townsend led the two brigades in a new direction, and this allowed the tankers to go back into their more natural role of search and destroy. B-troop from 1-14 Cav and a Stryker battalion from 5-20 Inf (2nd ID) would immediately be thrown into the battle to add men and equipment to the fight for Baqubah.[22] At first, this only affected the tankers within the COPs. These COPs went from having one platoon and some ISF to having two or even three in some cases. Bravo 1-12 had been responsible for three separate COPs that had one platoon each. They used the COPs to patrol out of, but since the company only had three platoons, only one platoon could be on patrol at a time with one serving as QRF and one that was having a rest or "refit."[23]

The new units came in under the command of LTC Antonia and CSM Huggins (both career infantrymen). Just as the brigade had been laterally transferred to Townsend, the 1-12 Cav was now under the command of the 5-20 Inf. The mix of Strykers, Abrams, and Bradleys had not been seen on this scale before during the battle. The initial task of the tankers was to patrol the outskirts of the city and to keep enemy forces from coming in or out of Baqubah.[24] This task could seem menial for those on the outside looking in as tanks patrolled for hours in a city overwatch position. But this was exactly what the battalion needed. The enemy was in a position where they now saw the new soldiers come in due to the surge, and they were preparing for a fight. The enemy forces in Baqubah had been prepared for the fight that the 3rd Brigade had given them. This new fight that teamed all of these new combat elements together was different and it allowed the army to catch the enemy insurgents by surprise.[25]

Townsend and his staff decided that there needed to be a shift in the way that the operations were handled at the company level. The American forces in Baqubah had the manpower and resources to go on the offensive now and not simply sit back and try to stay alive or maintain a static defense.[26] The battalion combined and started to clear out the city blocks. Alpha 1-12 combined with 1-23 Inf (Stryker battalion from 2nd ID) to add numbers and equipment to their fight. All of the newly formed TFs were ordered to start systematically clearing areas in preparation for a larger operation that was coming shortly.[27] These combined operations consisted of room clearing and route clearance. The goal of these smaller missions was to allow the forces to start clearing the town in large numbers from all different directions. The biggest hurdle to this was route clearance. The 5-20 brought in their own engineers and EOD but this "bomb squad" would take time to clear some of the streets and alleyways that the TF needed. Tanks from Charlie and Delta were used to provide overwatch for these route-clearing missions.

During this portion of the battle and in the battle itself, tanks were still not at a weapons-free status but the authority to fire the main gun was given to the XOs and company first sergeants as well.[28]

This new line of communication made it easier for tankers as there was less chatter and less chain of command needed to use the main gun. On several occasions during the route clearance portion of this mission, Colella stated he directly permitted tankers to fire the main gun at enemy fighters that were attempting to destroy the EOD robots and the soldiers themselves who were trying to disarm a bomb. This process was very slow and deliberate, and the EOD relied on the tankers to be vigilant and maintain their scanning while it took place. It was also important for the tankers and the company and battalion leaders to be on the same page to ensure the enemy was being destroyed without civilian losses if possible.[29] The officers and senior NCOs had to trust that when tankers asked to use their main gun the threat was imminent and dangerous to the mission. This trust was built through the tankers not only proving that they were up to the task when asked to do infantry work but also being proficient at simple tasks such as patrolling the outskirts of the city.[30]

Odierno and his staff came up with an operation that was known as Operation *Phantom Thunder*.[31] This was put together with the sole purpose of moving the enemies of the coalition forces out of their safe haven and pushing them in a direction that was dictated by American forces. The operation had to be conducted simultaneously by several different combat brigades. It was perhaps the biggest operation up to this point as it covered a wide amount of terrain in Iraq and required the coordination of several combat brigades and their subordinate units.[32] One of the areas involved was Baqubah, where the mission was known as Operation *Arrowhead Ripper*. This operation was commanded by Townsend who brought the entire force of the combined brigades (3rd HBCT 1st Cavalry, and 3rd SBCT 2nd Infantry) down on Baqubah. This mission began on June 19, 2007, and the initial phase entailed the American forces going into blocking positions and cutting off the lines of supplies and communication for AQI. The first sequence relied heavily on the tankers from Charlie and Delta 1-12. As the companies had been divided before this operation to support the infantry companies at their COPs, they needed to be gathered and reorganized for this mission.[33]

Two platoons from Charlie Company were ordered into blocking positions and were the first to receive enemy contact during the fight. These blocking positions were vital to the fight as they stopped enemy forces from bringing vehicles or other enemy fighters to the city during the operations. Their positions, manned for several hours at a time before being rotated to another unit,[34] were set up strategically along roads and other places where the enemy may have had terrain advantages. Putting tanks there forced the enemy to resort to its dismounted or infantry fighters and this gave the brigade TF the advantage despite the enemy's knowledge of the terrain. The tankers initially arrived at these positions at 0550 and immediately started taking small arms fire from enemy forces. The enemy attacked the tankers with a barrage of machine guns and RPG fire.[35] The tanks returned fire with a combination of both main guns and small arms fire. During the initial blocking positions, the tankers of Charlie killed roughly 14 enemy soldiers.[36] The tankers were aided by a platoon of Strykers from Bravo 1-23. These Strykers were fitted with a remote-controlled .50-caliber machine gun. They were able to aid in the target and acquisition of the dismounted forces during the early phase of this sub-operation.

The communication and supply piece was commanded by the brigade staff. For this portion of the operation, aerial unmanned drones with missile launch capabilities were used to identify and destroy any communication towers that were still in the area. The lack of communication would be a key advantage for the coalition forces as the enemy could not send in new signals or strategies using radios.[37] These missions took several days during the opening portion of the campaign. While they were taking place, the rest of the brigade TF used this opportunity to resupply and refit for the coming fight. Tankers conducted a hasty PMCS of their vehicles and resupplied the bustle rack with main gun ammunition. Before this or any large battle after Thunder Run, tankers often only carried a small number of main gun rounds while on patrol. This was due to the shift in philosophy and also because if the tanks were hit with IEDs, the hope was to cause minimal damage to those around them by not having the ammo rack full of main gun rounds.[38]

Tankers during this fight were loaded with their normal full rack of main gun ammunition before taking up the blocking positions.

The main type of main gun rounds used for this fight was HEAT and IMPAT rounds. These proved to be the most useful as the tanks were called upon to provide support by fire into buildings and structures for the remainder of the operation. Before it began, the enemy fighting force was estimated to be between 2,000 and 2,500 soldiers.[39] Having tanks during this fight proved to be a force multiplier and deterrent for enemy-dismounted troops. Although the tanks and Strykers had been put in positions to stop vehicles from maneuvering, the threat of enemy technicals was still a valid fear. This operation would be fought on the ground by the infantrymen. Although the infantry still had the Strykers and Bradleys there to aid them during this mission, they were called upon to clear rooms and engage in street combat with AQI in places vehicles simply could not fit.[40]

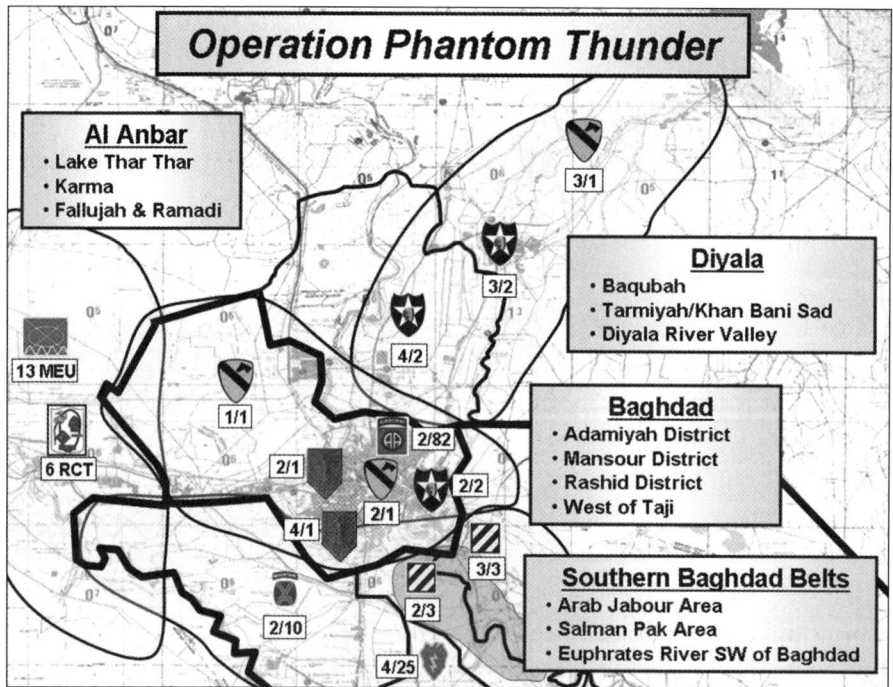

Operation *Phantom Thunder*. The numbers indicate what unit of that division is located where. For example, in the Diyala province "4/2" refers to the 4th Brigade 2nd Infantry Division.

This was precisely why having tanks in this battle was so important and the notion that armor was combat ineffective was proven wrong. The tank companies were able to continuously pin down the AQI forces by the use of their main gun and machine guns. This allowed the dismounted infantry troops to move faster throughout the city and not to give the enemy forces sitting targets that were bogged down due to small arms fire.[41] During the early days of this fight, one of the issues that continued to plague the Stryker unit was the use of deep-buried IEDs. These bombs could destroy Abrams tanks so, too often, Strykers stood no chance of leaving a blast unscathed. During the first week of fighting alone, Townsend's TF lost three Stryker vehicles to IEDs. This showed the TF that although the Strykers were fast and perhaps stealthier than their Bradley brother, they simply did not have the armor and resistance to enemy fire that the mechanized and armored vehicles did.[42] One of the ways that Townsend used the Strykers to avoid more vehicle destruction was to park them, dismount, and walk to the objective. This made the infantry more open to sniper and enemy infantry fire, but it allowed the vehicles to act in a cordon role that helped bring the vehicles to the fight and provide more cover fire for the infantrymen.

Another aspect of this fight was Townsend's use of air assault missions. These missions allowed the infantry to be dropped off using army helicopters and the soldiers then used a rope to rappel down to the objective.[43] This shielded the infantry from having to walk long distances to reach their goal. During this portion of the fight, the enemy tried to take advantage of the infantry leaders staging their troops by engaging the TF with sniper and AK-47 fire. Townsend and his staff had a plan for this and used the tanks and the Apache helicopters to counter this attack by the insurgent forces.[44] The tankers from C and D companies of the Greywolf Brigade were already in an overwatch position as the infantry were getting into place. This synergy by armor and infantry gave the TF a leg-up in defeating the enemy during this Operation. The tankers identified the houses and areas where the enemy chose to set up sniper and small arms fire from. They then used their main gun to suppress the enemy.[45]

The tankers of the Greywolf Brigade were able to pound the enemy positions while the infantry prepared to go in and clear Baqubah.

The tankers kept the enemy preoccupied with the power of the 120 mm main gun so they simply were unable to focus on the infantry and what they were doing. Townsend also used airstrikes to suppress the enemy fighters as his men got into position. During this portion of the fight, 10 airstrikes were called in. While this called considerable damage to the buildings of Baqubah, it also caused severe damage to the enemy fighters even before the clearing operations started.[46] The airstrikes were followed by more main gun rounds pounding the buildings of Baqubah. This forced the enemy infantry to run and hide inside the buildings and structures of the city. 1–23 Inf took the lead as the clearing operations began.

An issue raised by roping the enemy into houses was the fact that the tanks could not be used in room clearing. They positioned themselves outside of the houses and continued to provide overwatch and suppress the enemy with the use of their machine guns.[47] Gunners continued to use their sights to watch the buildings and areas where snipers could hide. Once snipers were identified they were engaged by the tank crews. Tankers had to be careful as their infantry brothers were now in the homes they were overwatching, so firing a main gun into the house was no longer an option. TCs took the lead and used their .50-caliber machine gun while also commanding the tank and ensuring proper scanning was still taking place. SFC Timothy Williams had this to say about scanning and its importance for tankers during combat while being interviewed in 2022: "It's up to the section or platoon Sgt. to set the tanks up with their fields of fire. The crew has to stay focused and watch every nook and cranny of those fields. When you are in a firefight, it's easy to stay focused and for the gunner to keep his fingers on the Cadillacs ready to fire. It can be hard when it is 120 degrees and you have been inside a hot tank and doing overwatch for three-plus hours. But the second you stop paying attention, that's when the snipers get in position and that's on you if you had a chance to identify the sniper and put a main gun round in the building to stop him."[48]

For the next several weeks while the tankers continued to lock down the buildings and rooftops, the infantry spent hours clearing thousands of houses and structures in Baqubah.[49] This went on for day and night operations. The TF used both Stryker and mech infantry dismounts, to kick doors in and engage the enemy fighters. This was the most intense fighting of the campaign according to General Petraeus.[50] The enemy was cornered and instead of lying down and surrendering, they continued to fight and gave the American forces every piece of the battle they were prepared for. For the month of May, the fighting was particularly fierce for Bravo 1-12. The company was assisted by the 5-20 Inf as they cleared houses on the eastern border of the city.[51] The Stryker element added speed to Baqubah but as stated, they were not immune to the dangers of IEDs. Bravo and Charlie (5-20) constantly ran into IEDs. They were frequently slowed down and forced to call in for QRF, and for the battalion's towing assets. This was not just for the Strykers but the Abrams as well. During the end of May and the beginning of June, the attached tank platoon lost another two tanks while four soldiers were WIA (wounded in action).[52] This not only slowed the order of movement for the TF but also limited the amount of firepower that Bravo had. Although the TF was continuing to pound the enemy in general, they were still sustaining losses on the way.

Townsend's plan did not change regardless of the enemy's tactics. He continued to have the infantry clear rooms and the armor would post up on the streets and attempt to suppress the enemy snipers and give support to the dismounted troops.[53] Maj. Anthony Gore was a company commander at the time with the 5-20 Inf that was originally a part of the division strike force. He was given a company before deploying to Baqubah and he had this to say about joining the 1-12 Cav:

> Baqubah was a little different than most of the missions that the battalion as a whole had experienced before. We were sent to Baqubah to assist the 1-12 CAV unit that was there which was part of the 3rd Brigade, 1st CAV. 1-12 had taken about 20 plus killed in action (KIAs) within the battalion and about 60 wounded in action, non-return to duty over about a four to six-month period. One of the unfortunate things was that there wasn't much information on why things were so bad. When we got to Baqubah we did a leader's recon where we got a PowerPoint presentation on what the brigade commander wanted us to do. We went back, packed up all our stuff in Baghdad, and moved to Baqubah and then were told to do 24-hour presence within the streets as soon as possible. As far as a flavor for everyday operations, on my first day during patrols, we suffered one KIA, seven wounded in action non-return to duties, one Stryker destroyed, and

two Strykers attacked by improvised explosive devices (IEDs) and rocket-propelled grenades (RPGs). From there as a company commander and as a company we adjusted to focus on, "This is not Mosul or Baghdad. The intent is to kill bad guys as quickly as possible." We focused more of our patrols on light infantry-type patrols where we'd use the Strykers to get to a certain point, dismount, move on to a strong point or a local defense within the town, and then try to kill insurgents. That was the flavor for our operations for the first few months in Baqubah and afterward, it started changing to battalion-led clearing operations. The battalion-led clearing operations were a lot better than what we were doing separately as company because it was a consolidation of combat power to clear out enemy areas one at a time. Initially going into Baqubah we were going at it piecemeal. There was a brigade plan, established by the CAV commander, to do clearing operations but it had to be coordinated overtime with resources and all of that. Until that could happen the company-led operations were very piecemeal and it seemed like we'd go out daily and kill a few dudes but it really didn't matter because they'd just sprout up like weeds. It didn't seem like we were actually affecting anything. The people in the town would not talk to us. They knew that after we got done with our several hours of clearing as a company, we'd leave, and the insurgents would come back and control the area. When we changed to battalion-led clearing operations I think it started showing the people in those areas that, "Wow. They're really there to change the dynamic between the people and the enemy. They want to maintain a presence. They're not going to let the insurgents intimidate us over a long period of time and maybe we can have some normalcy in our lives." That was the big difference with battalion-led operations and it started one by one. If anyone in the future looks at Baqubah you'll see six different neighborhoods so starting from neighborhood to neighborhood they started showing signs of success in operations which incredibly increased our morale and also changed the perception of the people in that area. They believed we were actually there to help them out.[54]

These clearing missions continued for the next several weeks. The American forces continued to stick to the plan that was laid out by Townsend and the 3rd Brigade leadership. The role of the tankers did not end or subside as the mission continued on through June and July of 2007. Nearly fifty main gun rounds were used during those months.[55] While that number is still relatively small compared to Ramadi or Fallujah, it is important to note that the task force only had two tank companies. In this fight, American forces suffered nearly seventy casualties (combined KIA and WIA). They were able to kill 482 enemy insurgents and detain over 150 more.[56] Tanks were vital to this fight which was dominated more by mech and Stryker infantry units than any other battles that have been discussed to this point. The fact that they were still able to make themselves useful and viable this late in the war for Iraq is a credit to the tankers of 1-12 Cavalry. They were able to fight in ways that they did not sign up for and then revert back to their traditional way of fighting when called upon. This was due to the training and tough mentality that had been instilled within the tankers of the armored corps of the U.S. Army.[57]

Tanks proved even in the fiercest fighting conditions that their abilities were vital to a victory for coalition forces. The sub-operation of *Arrowhead Ripper* ended on August 15, and the senior operation of *Phantom Thunder* ended on August 19, 2007. The operation was deemed a success by both Odierno and Casey. The enemy continued to have a small presence in Baqubah but would never raise the numbers that it did before the arrival of the 1-12 Cavalry. This operation showed the army and the coalition forces that problem areas in Iraq needed a combined effort to be successful. The old *Desert Storm* adage of "shoot everything you see" (relating to tank warfare) would no longer work to truly clear out the enemy insurgents and destroy AQI.

There were clear parallels between Ramadi and Baqubah. Baqubah was a battle that the American forces did not numerically access adequately. They sent a single brigade[58] in an area that should have had two brigades at minimum. This led to numerous engagements with insurgents and the army found that they were outmanned. Many times, the company-level leadership would have to take tankers off their vehicles and put them into the infantry ranks to have the numbers to go on dismounted patrols.[59] These actions made them less effective. One of the bigger issues that plagued units in Baqubah was the placement of IEDs. These bomb placements decimated the armored vehicles in this area. Tanks can only fight and destroy the enemy if they can get to the fight.

The second battle of Ramadi had a lot of political and military implications. It was a situation where a Marine Corps general had an army commander in charge of one of the provinces he commanded. This would often lead to issues between the two because the Marines and the army have different mindsets and ways of doing things.

Col. Sean MacFarland (CO, 1st Brigade, 1st Armored Division) was asked to come in and re-take control of Ramadi without destroying it.[60] The perception of MacFarland was also something that he had to combat. Not because he had done anything personally to destroy his reputation, but because often, armor officers face the stereotype of simply wanting to blast their way to victory and that is just not the case.

His time in Ramadi made MacFarland's career.[61] He was able to bring his armored forces in and re-take control of a city where Marines and army national guard units had failed.

CHAPTER 7

The Siege of Sadr City

The battle of Sadr City (March 2008) happened after American forces had already been embedded in Iraq and had a system for fighting the enemy. This battle also came after the coalition leaders had decided that tanks were not important or that they should be shelved in favor of Humvees. This battle was a startling reminder of why tanks were important, and they again showed their worth against the Mahdi army.

Sadr City was the last time that the armored core of the army would lead an assault in Iraq. This battle was also a time of transition for tankers. Many of the armor units had begun to take tankers off their tanks and require them to do infantry tasks, as was the case in Baqubah with 1-12 Cavalry. The difference at this point in the fight was the fact that tankers were not simply being taken off their tanks at the platoon level, but in many cases, entire battalions were leaving their tanks in the rear or trading them in for soft-skinned vehicles such as Humvees.[1] This played into the notion that tankers were not needed in the fight. Part of that notion was due to the army being under the impression that the fight was moving forward and did not require the large amount of firepower that tanks can provide. The hope for the army was to move into a role where they were truly occupying these large cities in Iraq and not clearing or laying siege to them to pacify them of enemy insurgents.[2]

The siege of Sadr City was proof that the war was far from settled and that tanks were always necessary for any major combat operation. During this time, Sadr City was under the thumb of the cleric Moqtada al Sadr.[3] Sadr was a Shi'a Muslim and commanded what was called the Mahdi Army or Jaysh al-Mahdi (JAM). At its height, this militia reached ten thousand men who would be responsible for major attacks against coalition forces, including car bombs, ambushes, IEDs, and sniper attacks.[4] In August 2007, Sadr and Prime Minister Nouri al-Maliki signed a six-month peace treaty to prevent major attacks by the JAM forces against the Green Zone in Baghdad.[5] During this cease-fire, the coalition forces were banned from entering Sadr City due to an event that happened with the U.S. Special Forces. In October of 2007, a Special Forces group conducted a nighttime raid to capture a JAM lieutenant named Abu Dura.[6] During this raid, the group were attacked by over eighty enemy fighters. During the firefight that ensued, the Special Forces requested and were granted an airstrike to help subdue the enemy fighters. The airstrike killed over forty JAM fighters, but it also killed eight Iraqi civilians.[7]

Although the mission itself allowed the U.S. forces to go in and kill the enemy fighters, the story that was shown on Iraqi and U.S. channels was that the U.S. was indiscriminately killing civilians in the war in Iraq. This gave Maliki enough evidence to sign a contract with MND-Baghdad to stop U.S. forces from entering the city or conducting major operations without his permission.[8] While the cease-fire and ban were in place, JAM forces were beginning to consolidate and continued making attacks against the Iraqi government that was joining coalition forces to attempt to change Iraqi policies. The Green Zone was within rocket-firing distance from Sadr City. Many JAM members disregarded the peace treaty and continued to ramp up attacks on coalition forces. These attacks forced Maliki to change course and request the aid of MNF-Iraq.[9] This aid would come in the form of an operation that would pacify the city and clear it of JAM forces. As the plan started to come together, it became apparent that no major operation could be successful in Sadr City without the use of tanks and the assistance and leadership of an HBCT or ABCT.

Several different events ultimately led to the siege and ultimately the pacification of Sadr City. The first was a change of command for MND-Baghdad. The new commander would be MG Jeffrey Hammond who was the commanding general of the 4th Infantry Division, a mix between light and heavy brigades. Hammond found a difference of opinion between himself and his subordinates.[10] He was under the impression that AQI was the main enemy in his AO. Other leaders, such as Col. John Hoyt of the 4th Brigade, felt that Sadrist and special enemy groups such as the JAM should be targeted. This clash of thoughts and ideas did not deter Hammond or his men from confronting the enemy that lay ahead within Sadr City.

This assault was different because there were more nuances to the city than just coming in and blasting the enemy.[11] One of the issues with Sadr City was the simple fact that it had been uninhabited by U.S. forces for months before the assault. This gave JAM forces the chance to beef up their numbers, but also, it gave them the chance to set up IED sites and sniper positions. Snipers and IEDs would be the biggest problems for coalition forces as they attempted to cleanse the city of enemy forces.

1-68 CAB was the lead armored element during this fight. This battalion had the usual configuration for this time which was two tank companies and two mechanized infantry companies.[12] It was commanded by LTC Michael Pappal. Pappal was a career armor officer but knew the importance of full-spectrum training for the men in his battalion. Much like Col. MacFarland in Ramadi, Pappal knew that to achieve success he needed to make sure that all the men in the battalion were able to fight in the battle ahead. Before coming to Iraq, 1-68 completed gunnery and MOUT training.[13] Pappal also made sure that his company commanders were able to communicate with Iraqi civilians. During their NTC rotation, Pappal ordered his officers and senior enlisted NCOs to have a lengthy dialogue with the Iraqi citizens to better prepare them for missions that were non-combative in nature.[14] For a large portion of their deployment, 1-68 did not even touch their tanks or Bradleys.[15]

The battalion were under the impression that for this deployment, they were going to be dismounted and used as infantrymen. For the actual infantrymen of 1-68, this was not uncommon or out of the ordinary and they felt that this was a sign that things in Iraq had calmed down to the point where tanks were no longer needed, which was a good sign for coalition forces.[16] For nearly six months of their deployment, they were conducting dismounted operations in Sadr City and were even given "infantry squad" weapons such as the 249 SAW (squad automatic weapon) to give them more firepower than the conventional M-4 rifle. Tankers from both Charlie and Delta companies (1-68) cleared rooms, set up dismounted checkpoints and engaged in dismounted firefights with enemy forces during the early stages of their development while only using soft-skinned vehicles. It was prior to their change of mission in the spring of 2008 that the battalion was told that they were going to Sadr City and that they would be retrieving their tanks for the mission ahead.[17]

This was an issue for the men and their tanks, which need constant maintenance to perform at their highest combat effectiveness. The tanks of both companies had been sitting at Camp Taji for months without such maintenance or care.[18] These tanks were the cornerstone of the mission ahead: to go in and destroy an enemy that had had months to prepare for them. It was important for the division to have firepower at its disposal. The brigade had more infantry units than in other battles that have been discussed thus far. Because the conglomerate of units within MND-Baghdad was not armor-heavy as they had been during the early portion of OIF, the division used several Stryker and light units for this fight.[19] The combat units that aided the tankers in this fight were 1-6 Inf (mechanized) and the 1-2 Stryker Cavalry Regiment. 1-2 SCR would consist of two infantry companies and one cavalry troop. These units would provide a much-needed boost of dismounted troops on the ground. The Strykers were able to bring speed to the fight. However, these vehicles lacked the armor of their mechanized counterparts and, like in Baqubah, IEDs proved to be an issue for the brigade TF and it leaned heavily on the mechanized and armor units.

The man that was put in charge of this TF was Col. John Hort. Hort was the commander of the 3rd BCT of the 4th Infantry Division, a career-long infantry officer who had experience with both mechanized and light units. Hort wanted to be aggressive while also making sure to implement plans that had a long-term effect on the city.[20] On March 23, 2008, JAM forces began a coordinated attack on the Green Zone. The goal of these attacks was to discredit the government led by Maliki as he and the Iraqi government had spearheaded an operation in Basra. The JAM offensive was designed to make Maliki seem incapable of conducting offensive operations against Sadrist forces and thus making him seem like perhaps he was not the leader that the people needed.[21] After these attacks, the goal of the enemy was clear and Maliki began to cooperate with MND-Baghdad in order to develop an operation to destroy JAM forces in Sadr City. Much like in Fallujah, Sadrists had the sympathy of thousands of people and followers within the city. This allowed the enemy to retreat to safe havens after attacking U.S. forces.

Hammond knew that the upcoming assault depended on several different aspects coming together for U.S. forces. Firstly, soldiers needed to attempt to remove civilians who did not want to be a part of this military operation. Doing this was vital as the perception of indiscriminate killing needed to be dealt with in a manner that illuminated the fact that collateral damage was at the forefront of the coalition forces' concerns.[22] Secondly, Hammond wanted to use his ground forces to attack and destroy several of the safe havens that the JAM forces had in Sadr City. Destroying these areas could help limit the rocket attacks on the Green Zone and help show the public that no area was safe from coalition forces during this fight. Concurrent with the rocket attacks, JAM forces started attacking ISF forces and in particular checkpoints along several coalition-controlled routes near JSSs and COPs.[23] Hammond, and later Hort, wanted to use tanks and mechanized vehicles to go in and support those checkpoints while also sending dismounted platoons to help man the areas until a presentable Iraqi force could be placed there. Many of the checkpoints were abandoned by the ISF, because a lot of ISF were aligned with the Sadrist regime and simply did not want to fight their brothers in arms. It is important to note that for many of the ISF, their family members were a part of JAM.[24]

On March 25, 2008, Maliki signed an order that allowed coalition forces to conduct both ground and air operations south of PL Gold (Al-Quds Street). Everything north of the PL was still considered off-limits without the approval of Maliki.[25] This operation was called *Striker Denial*. The fact that the coalition forces were limited to certain parts of the city was good for Hort and his men as they simply did not have the numbers or firepower to take all of Sadr City even with the aid of the ISF. Mortar fire became the deadliest threat to the Green Zone and stationary U.S. forces during the infancy of this operation. The order of movement for the early phases would put 1-2 SCR in charge of clearing and recon operations.[26] The goal was to have 1-2 clear the main roads and large areas on PL Gold and have the Iraqi forces hold them. For the areas that were not a high-level threat or that lacked enemy activity, this proved to be manageable. Later during this operation, the ISF had trouble maintaining areas where the enemy had larger numbers and more combat capabilities. 1-2 used its cavalry troop to recon the area for enemy forces and allowed its two infantry companies to go in and attack locations where the enemy was found and secure the area until they could hand it off to the ISF.

This strategy allowed the 3rd BCT to take the fight to the enemy and not get bogged down or have to give up valuable troops simply to hold areas. It also gave the public the sense that their own soldiers were helping to defeat the enemy.

The role of TF 1-68 CAB was to attack the outer edges of the city. This role was important because of the armor capabilities of the task force. Hort wanted to have the tankers and mechanized infantry attack the outskirts of Sadr City to keep the enemy trapped inside for the lighter forces to go in and clear. The two areas that were viewed as having the

Soldiers from 4th Platoon, A-Troop, 1-2 SCR load back onto their Stryker after a dismounted patrol in Sadr City on April 1, 2008. (U.S Army photo / Master Sgt. Christina Bhatti)

most launch capabilities were Ishbiliyah and Habbibiyah. These areas were targeted by 1-6 Inf. During the operations on the outskirts, 1-68 was divided up much like other units had been during OIF. Charlie and Delta companies were armor units, and they gave up two platoons each to Alpha and Bravo.[27] While conducting this mission for the TF, C and D companies faced mostly dismounted enemy forces trying to flee the city but also planting IEDs to prevent the use of armored vehicles.[28]

The two tank companies continued to combat the enemy using machine guns and HEAT rounds—the preferred main gun round used for this operation. Tankers often caught JAM soldiers setting up their mortars to fire them against American forces. If they could not contact the company commander or leadership in a timely fashion, then the TC .50-cal or the gunner's coax was used in order to kill the enemy.[29] The TF had a line of communication set up so the commander was not the only one that had the authority to order a main gun strike. It was important to have one officer that could authorize this as the company commander was often attempting to coordinate the entirety of the company's mission.[30] The tankers proved to be vital in this mission as they were trained to identify and destroy the enemy troops that were trying to undermine the vehicle movement of the American forces.

Some reintegration was vital for the tankers, and this had to be completed on the fly. The tankers of 1-68 had been away from their tanks for months and were asked to stop in their proverbial tracks, hop on their tanks and kill the enemy.[31] For the tankers of 1-68, the killer instinct was still intact, and they were able to make the transition from dismounted soldiers back to tankers without many issues. In a perfect world the tankers needed to at least shoot Table 8 (qualifying table at gunnery) before being put back into combat. But they simply did not have the time to do so before starting the operation. Instead of going through a long gunnery, the tankers were able to use ranges that were already set up at Camp Taji.[32] After some intense PMCS, they shot and zeroed every weapon system on the tank. Target acquisition was at the forefront of this hasty range day as the tankers needed to prove that they could hit both mounted and dismounted enemies. Once they met the commander's intent of target acquisition and PMCS, the tankers reported any issues within the tanks to the XO and the mechanics. Several of the tanks were unable to make the trip to Sadr City because they were not functional after the long layoff.

Capt. Looney commanded Charlie Company and saw the most vicious fighting of the tank companies during this conflict.[33] From March through April of 2008 was the fiercest fighting for the 3rd Brigade. The JAM forces fought viciously to protect their portion of the city and they wanted to ensure that they caused as much damage to the coalition forces as possible.

Looney and the rest of his company (dubbed Team Steel) were constantly tested by the enemy during the early portion of this battle, slowed down by the threat of IEDs. The difficult part for 1-68 was to provide sufficient overwatch for the area that they were in charge of. The main portion of this AO was two areas known as Jamila and Thawra I.[34] These areas were constantly overloaded with IEDs and often an EOD team was called to investigate an IED site. These investigations could take several hours and Team Steel and the TF as a whole were sitting targets for the enemy. The main focus of the tankers during these site investigations was to identify the triggerman. IEDs were generally triggered in two ways: they were either pressure triggered (they would explode once a certain amount of weight passed over the bomb) or they had an actual human press a button and detonate the bomb once they saw the enemy approaching.[35] Another aspect that 1-68 had to face was the notion of something called a complex ambush. This occurred when a vehicle hit an IED and then the enemy attacked the rest of the vehicles on patrol with sniper, small arms, and RPG fire.[36]

These ambushes proved to be the deadliest for the TF following an explosion. While the leaders on the ground tried to call in either a medevac or QRF, they also had to deal with the ensuing firefight. Through the first few months of the siege, 1-68 took heavy losses as they lost three tanks and eight soldiers KIA.[37] The armor units were often able to get new or used tanks from the main FOB (forward operating base) that had new tanks and Bradleys in reserve. It became apparent through the first few months that mounted patrols with armored vehicles were paramount. The TF had to use vehicles that could withstand the blast of IEDs as the soft-skinned and Stryker vehicles simply could not hold up against the onslaught on the IEDs. During the same period, 1-2 SCR lost six vehicles. Later during this operation, Hort instructed the armored vehicles to accompany the soft-skinned vehicles in preparation for a complex attack or IED. This mix of firepower also allowed the American forces to attack the enemy without always resorting to the main gun. Bradleys with their 25 mm, Strykers with their remote .50-cal, and tanks with their loaders, gunners, and TCs' machine guns made it possible to kill the enemy without destroying the city.

The tanks were also used in conjunction with the aerial advantage that the TF had during this operation. Although the TF had recon capabilities on the ground, they also had it via drones.[38] The drones that were used had both unarmed and armed capabilities. This "air recon" allowed the ground troops to have a better idea as to what was going on beyond the scope of their mission. Many times, the enemy would be spotted and ground troops would be alerted of their location to engage and kill them. The biggest obstacle to using these drones was the permission needed by the ground forces. For the unmanned, unarmed drones that were simply used for recon and aerial pictures, permission was needed from the brigade leadership.[39] When it came to unmanned armed drones, permission was needed from the division headquarters. This made it difficult to spot the enemy and engage them immediately. This became a common theme throughout the war as the troops on the ground were often fighting what the division commanders wanted to achieve against what they were seeing on the battlefield in front of them. Between 2006 and 2008, Phillip Johndrow was the CSM for MND Baghdad. He had this to say about the struggle between the division and the brigades carrying out their orders:

> We got there and several car bombs went off in Sadr City within the first couple of weeks of being there. Several hundred Iraqi civilians were killed, and I started thinking to myself, "Hold on, here we go." I remember GEN Fil sitting at the end of the table along with GEN Brooks, GEN Campbell, COL Ballantine, and myself, and he said, "Gentlemen, we're going to see this through. We're going to fix this and I can see it." GEN Fil is a very deep, religious man, and he said, "I pray every day that we're going to see this through." His calming effect in that room I think really made a difference. You know, every time I went to Iraq, I thought that the people that I was with were hand-picked by the Chief of Staff

of the Army to put this great team together, and this being my third time there, I realized that the Army has so many great officers, non-commissioned officers (NCOs) and Soldiers that everybody gets on the team, they figure out where they fit, and they rise to the level that they need to rise to. This team was no different; it was a tremendous team that we had there, and each one had a very important part that they had to play. GEN Fil was very good at delegating each one of the deputy commanding generals with their responsibilities, and the chief of staff and what he saw my role was, and we all went about our business.

I'll tell you, with GEN Odierno and GEN Petraeus both coming on board, we started establishing the combat outposts (COPs) and the joint security stations (JSSs), and the combat outpost was a station that just had U.S. soldiers on it. Joint security station was one that we would co-habit with the Iraqi Police (IP) and Iraqi Security Forces (ISF). We had done that first time I was in Iraq as a squadron sergeant major, and then we pulled back and we were giving things back to the ISF and the Iraqi people, and we went back into the big forward operating bases (FOBs). We thought maybe it was too soon, and we went back to doing that but we did so much more. We did a lot more with doing our rounds with the Iraqi people, letting them know, "Hey, we're in this together." I associate it with a cop on a beat. When you're a cop on the beat that you're on and walk or drive that beat and you get to know the people on that beat, and they know you're going to be there for a while, they get more understanding, you get to know each other as you drink tea together. If something's not right, they're going to come and tell you about it. As opposed to having five doors that you might go and kick down looking for the insurgents, they'll say "You know what, instead of kicking down those five doors, if you just get that door over there, that's the person you want, you're just going to upset four other families and turn them against you by doing that." That started bringing things together, and when we looked at moving people around on the battlefield, you would have people in the town that were visually upset about moving any units, because they had become so accustomed to that unit being there. You had captains that were calling the mayor of that town because they became so involved. You had units that didn't want to leave because they had invested so much time, input, and resources in that town that they wanted to see it through.[40]

Controlling the launch sites became the main objective for Hort and the rest of the TF. They started mapping where the JAM forces had access to open spaces and putting tanks and Bradleys in an overwatch position near those areas.[41] The battle up to this point had been hard fought. Normally, the tanks were a great equalizer for any battle, but the issue was simply numbers. The JAM forces had more and they seemed to have an endless supply of mortar rounds and small arms rounds. The American forces found themselves in constant combat with the JAM forces and it could be argued that this enemy was more determined than any that the Americans had faced up to this point.[42] The problem that Hort and his men found in Sadr City was the same issue that 1SG Colella and 1–12 Cavalry had faced in Baqubah: the army only had one brigade in the area where there should have been at least two. And this time no brigade would come to their aid. Hort attempted to ramp up the number of mounted patrols, ordering 1–2 SCR to conduct longer mounted and dismounted patrols and 1–68 to do the same.[43]

These new intensive patrols were meant to attempt to combat the fierce fighting that the JAM forces were presenting. The launch sites continued to be used by the JAM forces and they continued to launch rockets at the coalition patrol bases, which held vital stores of food and ammunition. The attacks were also ramped up on ISF checkpoints; ISF forces were often powerless to stop them. These new patrols were known as "disruption patrols."[44] After many of the new areas that were patrolled had been seized or held for long periods, they were passed down to the ISF. This was an important part of the mission as Hort knew that having the Iraqi man down some of these places could at least buy some time for the TF to attack and destroy JAM forces. The new issue was the aggressiveness of the JAM forces. They were no longer just sending groups of five to ten soldiers to confront the brigade TF. Often, the TF found themselves facing fifty to one hundred enemy fighters, and with the patrols only being conducted by a platoon element, the infantry units often found themselves outnumbered 2:1.[45] Couple that with the continued loss of vehicles and manpower and Hort found himself in a situation like to Dave Sutherland's.

Hort wanted to expand the AO of 1–68 to take advantage of their tanks and truly go on the offensive against JAM. He ordered that the tankers continue their restricted weapons status but permitted the company commanders to allow the tankers to use their main guns as they saw fit to destroy the enemy. This put the tankers in a similar position to the one they were in in Baqubah. The companies could now designate an officer to give permission to fire the main gun in the absence of the commander.[46] Hort also requested more troops from MND-Baghdad. Hammond was quick to act and allowed three company-sized elements to join Hort to fight off the JAM forces. Alpha 1-21 Inf (Stryker, 25th ID), Charlie 1-27 Inf (Stryker, 25th ID), and Team C from 1-64 Armor (two tank platoons and two mechanized infantry platoons, 3rd ID) would join the fight immediately.[47] Team C and C 1-27 joined 1-68 CAB. This tremendously increased their firepower and dismounted capabilities. The offensive portion of this newly formed TF would start on March 29, 2008.

During the operations towards the end of March, a greater emphasis was placed on the launch sites. But now, Hort and the TF attacked the areas that housed suspected JAM forces. The fiercest fighting took place when Hort ordered 1-68 and 1-2 SCR to attack a soccer field and an apartment complex simultaneously.[48] 1-2 SCR attacked the soccer field at 0500. This field was a launch site near route Gold and at that time, over 100 JAM fighters had gathered to launch rockets at the Green Zone and other coalition targets in the area. 1-2 was joined by 1-21. They encircled the field and the assault began. The infantry dismounted and were covered by the remote .50-cals on the infantry Stryker vehicles (ICV). The fighting lasted 13 hours as the JAM forces fought back using mainly small arms and RPGs. This attack was a surprise to the JAM forces as they had to rally their troops and on three separate occasions attempted a counterattack. This fight was the first stage in clearing the JAM forces from the area. Bravo Company led this attack and was credited by Hort for breaking the JAM forces' attempts at a counterattack.[49] By the end of the attack, 77 JAM soldiers had been killed. No U.S. forces were KIA and seven were WIA.

The attack on the apartment was carried out the same day by 1-68. This apartment building was near Habbibiyah. Charlie 1-68 set out at 0600 and were tasked with the outer cordon. They received enemy fire as soon as they arrived. The tankers returned fire using HEAT rounds from the main gun; during the early phase of this operation over 15 main gun rounds were used.[50] Charlie needed to ensure that the heavy machine guns and snipers were neutralized before the infantry forces entered the building. During an anonymous interview with a squad leader from Charlie Company 1-27, he described the attack on the apartment building and the prospect of working with tankers:

> As a SSGT, I had been in 6 years all in light infantry. I had never been attached to tankers. In fact, I had never seen too many tanks before this fight. The apartment attack started early as shit. The tankers surrounded the building and started shredding it. It was main gun after main gun into the building. Captain Uthlaut [company commander] was on the ground with us as we cleared the building. We waited in our Strykers while the tankers kept pounding the building. It was about an hour or so after we arrived when the tankers got on the radio and let the CO know that they did not see any enemy fighters in their sights. The CO ordered us to approach the building with the Strykers and then drop ramp and enter the building. As soon as we entered the building, we started taking fire from the JAM guys. I think they said there were about 40 enemy fighters in that building. We went platoon by platoon clearing the building. There were 4 floors. There was a mech infantry platoon attached to 1-68 so they did the inner cordon. So, we could clear rooms without someone sneaking up on us. It was roasting even in the morning. I think by the time we got done we were well over 100 degrees outside. The floors were pretty long. I took my squad through the second floor. I think we took fire in three of the rooms, the rest were just your average apartment rooms and most of them were empty. It took about 5 hours to finish the building. Once that one was done, we did the other buildings next to it. It took us into the afternoon to finish it. The tankers only fired a few rounds into the other buildings. I think if you are asking about how the tankers affected the fight that day, if they didn't pepper the buildings and get rid of the enemy machine gunners and snipers, more of our guys from Charlie probably wouldn't have made it.[51]

On April 5, 2008, the brigade TF turned over control of the cleared buildings and the apartment to the 42nd Iraqi Army Brigade. This brigade had the manpower and vehicle capabilities to hold both areas until a plan was put in place to forward.[52] The decision was made by Hammond to allow the Iraqi Army to continue to clear launch sites and buildings. Hort and his men became the QRF for the Iraqi Army as they moved forward and cleared areas in and around route Gold. Hort continued to observe what was going on he concluded that he did not want to leave American forces in Sadr City in an overwatch position. He divided the Iraqi Army brigade up and placed them in several overwatch positions to ensure that the JAM forces could not use the sites against coalition forces.[53] The next move had to be to keep JAM forces out of the area that had been cleared. Hammond and Hort met in early April 2008 to discuss what the next steps needed to be and what resources were available to the brigade.[54]

The reality for Hort was that although he and his TF were making strides in terms of reducing the number of enemy forces within the selected area of Sadr City where they were fighting, there was a problem with keeping JAM forces from continuing to come in and provide large amounts of reinforcements. The solution was simple: build a wall.[55] Hort realized that if he were able to construct a barrier between coalition and JAM forces, he could set up an entry control point (ECP) and force all civilians to pass through it and get patted down by coalition forces. This stopped the JAM soldiers from being able to come in with weapons to pass out amongst the enemy soldiers. Hort wanted to use a concrete slab known as a "T-Wall." These large slabs varied in size and could be 3–20 ft long and weigh over 500 lbs.[56] Hort developed a plan that involved the army engineers using a crane and meticulously placing each slab of the

Company Commander Capt. David Uthlaut and Charlie 1-27 INF 2nd SBCT (Stryker), Camp Taji, Iraq 2008. (U.S. Army photo / Staff Sgt. J.B. Jaso III)

wall for two miles to force the enemy into one small area where coalition soldiers were constantly on guard. The wall was also blast resistant. No rocket or small arms fire would destroy it.

The wall was built along route Gold. 1-2 SCR and 1-68 CAB worked in different directions to get the wall built more quickly. 1-2 worked from the eastern edge of Jamiliyah to the middle, while 1-68 worked from the middle moving north.[57] Hort attempted to only work at night to exploit the advantage that the American forces had with their night vision equipment. This proved to be problematic as the JAM used this as an opportunity to ramp up their IED efforts. Hort stated that his vehicles were constantly hitting IEDs at night while they were on their way to the building sites. This forced the TF to conduct breaching and EOD operations nightly which took hours and drastically held up progress.[58] Hort and his TF changed their tactics to build during the daylight hours. The immediate consequence of this action was that the enemy forces were much livelier during the daytime.

Hort placed tanks and Bradleys on each side of the construction sites. While the walls were being placed, the engineers were under constant enemy fire. Once the T-Walls were placed individual soldiers had to climb a ladder and unhook the strap holding them. These soldiers were targeted by sniper and small arms fire by the JAM forces.[59] To counter these attacks on the vulnerable soldiers, tankers were taken off a restricted status and were given permission to fire their main guns at the discretion of the tank commander. Volley after volley of main-gun and machine-gun rounds were fired from the Abrams tanks at JAM forces. Hort states over two hundred main gun rounds were used during the building of the wall.[60] This put pressure on the enemy forces as they knew that if the wall was completed it would be a devastating blow to their bid to control Sadr City. This wall continued in conjunction with operations into Sadr City. American forces continued to aid and assist the Iraqi Army as they attempted to drive out the enemy forces from the city.

This battle continued until May 12, 2008. It was at this time that Muqtada al-Sadr signed a peace treaty with the Iraqi government to usher in a cease-fire between the JAM army and the coalition forces. During this operation, Abrams tanks and their tankers proved once again how valuable they were to the army and their goal of conquering the insurgent forces in Iraq. Tankers were made to leave their tanks behind, serve as infantrymen, and then jump right back on their vehicles and provide armored support for the mission in Sadr City. It was the tankers who led the way and provided protection for the infantry soldiers as they were building the wall in Sadr City. Without the tank's ability to fire at long range and the tankers' mastery of the guns' systems and reflexes to use them, soldiers' lives would have been lost and the mission compromised. Tankers proved that their value lay within their training and their determination to complete the mission regardless of what the mission may be. The entire 3rd Brigade TF are to thank for the success in Sadr City. However, it was the armored forces that provided cover and suppression against the JAM soldiers that made victory and the completion of the wall possible.

Conclusion

The U.S. Army M1A1 tanker has evolved over time. Tankers were able to lead the way time and time again during the battles they fought during Operation *Iraqi Freedom*. It is possible to overlook these accomplishments because of the leaders and the overall notion that tanks are simply there to destroy. Every tanker that fought during this conflict was molded by the culture and training they received at Ft. Knox. It is important to give Ft. Knox the credit it deserves for the quality of tankers and overall soldiers that the fort was able to produce over the years prior to it no longer being the home of the armor training center, since relocated to Ft. Benning, GA. The culture of the armor units was directly tied to the culture of the armor center that tankers enjoyed during garrison.[1]

The culture of the tankers morphed from being just an enlisted aspect and moved even into the officer ranks. The armored corps became a group of men that knew the importance of brotherhood and vehicle maintenance. Maintenance and care of the tank have been the cornerstone of the armored corps from the inception of the tank.[2] The tankers came to view the tank as an extension of themselves. This was evident by the motto of the tankers during this time which was "death before dismount." The love for the tank is something that sets tankers apart from any of their combat brethren. Nowhere else in the military during this time could you find a MOS that had the love and dedication to their weapon as did the tankers of the army. This love is what made tankers stay on their tanks for hours at a time on Mondays after formation. The pride and sense of urgency that was instilled into tankers led them to strive to have the perfect tank that was clean and that properly worked in every facet.

This was something that in garrison was expected. In combat, it is the difference between having a tank in the fight and a tank in the mechanics bay.[3]

There has always been a rivalry between tankers and other combat units in the U.S. Army. One of the main reasons for that is simply that being in an armor unit was different. The culture was different, the leadership was different and the treatment of tankers was different. To see how different the culture was during this time and before, one of the things to examine is the garrison life for the infantry and how different it was from an armor unit. During the early portion of this work, the garrison experience of an armor unit was examined. For the infantry, there was a perception that they focused solely on the physical fitness level of the soldiers.[4] In the infantry during this time, soldiers would run three to six miles three times a week, and there was a constant focus on physically pushing the soldiers. The leaders were all infantry and the vehicles were often an afterthought.[5] When that is how the daily routine goes for one group of people, it is possible to harbor ill will for another group of soldiers that wear the same uniform as you and who perhaps only run 3 miles twice a week; the consensus often becomes that tankers are lazy and they do not work as hard as other combat units. This is a misconception about the experience of garrison life for tankers.

Tankers have a different focus than other combat units. This focus was something that both officers and enlisted men had during this time. That focus is on the men and their vehicles. That is to say that perhaps during this time, tankers were not in the physical condition that infantrymen were, but the discipline and focus of the armor units were not set on how fast or how long someone could run. The goal for tankers has always been to have a well-rounded soldier who has discipline in every aspect of their military life and is also adaptable to any situation. This is exactly the reason that when tankers were asked to leave their tanks and fight as dismounted soldiers in several of the battles that were discussed, they performed those duties admirably. It is hard to imagine any other combat unit switching jobs completely and still having the success tankers had during OIF.[6] During this war, much was asked of tankers. Not only were tankers needed to bring the firepower of an Abrams to the fight, but they also had to be able to be proficient in their duties. Tankers could not simply bring a tank to the battle, they had to be counted on to destroy the enemy and to prove that their presence in an urban environment was needed.

It is difficult to put into words how important the "Golden BDU Era" was for the molding of the armored corps. The entirety of the army was simply different during the BDU era. However, it was the discipline that made this era different. The look and appearance of the soldiers in their pressed uniforms with mirror-shined boots was a sight that would never be duplicated even in today's army.[7] The highlighted period of this era was between 1993 and 2003. This was a period when, arguably, the armored corps was at its peak.[8]

It was during this period that the armored corps started to modernize. They went from the M1A to M1A2 Sep. They also modernized the way the battalion and brigade were structured. For the vast majority of HBCTs or ABCTs during this time period, the leadership at the brigade level were tankers. This allowed the culture to be funneled down to the soldiers without the interruption of different ideologies by other command staff that were not armor. It was important for this time period that armor officers be in charge of the heavy brigades to ensure the training of the armored staff was done in a manner that helped the tankers and mechanized infantry reach the maximum level of proficiency.[9] The fact that tankers were not focusing on COIN operations as much during this time was not a negative as it allowed tankers to learn the ins and outs of their tanks. One of the biggest issues after this golden era was over was the fact that tankers in general stopped being as proficient on their tanks because they had to leave them in training and combat to help beef up the infantry numbers.

The training and culture for tankers had to be different by necessity. Over time that necessity turned into a way of life. Tankers had to learn to focus their effort on the tank and make it a part of them. They needed to know about every aspect of the tank. What button did what, what parts went where, and what were operator-level fixes as opposed to something that the XO or the mechanics needed to be involved in. These nuances of tanking are something that takes years for the soldiers to have fully embedded in them. It was up to the officers and the NCOs to show how important these things were to the younger soldiers and to instill the love for the armor and the pride in doing their job to the incoming soldiers. Soldiers had to see that love and determination from their leaders or they would not have a reason to put that effort in themselves. Pride and passion militarily are hereditary. Passing that fire and desire down to other soldiers is something that tankers took pride in. That is precisely why for years, the armored corps was able to continue to churn out quality 19Ks (and 19As) who loved what they did and were proficient at their job.

If a specific group of people were to be singled out for the success that tankers had prior to and during OIF, it would be the NCOs. The NCOs are the backbone of any combat MOS, but for the tankers, they are perhaps more vital due to their role inside the tank and the close proximity that they have with a smaller number of soldiers.[10] During the BDU era, a pure tank battalion had a CSM that had been tanking for 15-plus years. This was a huge benefit to the battalion to have someone that had experience on the tank and knew exactly what the tank crews were going through. It was also a benefit to the BC who relied on the CSM to be the voice of the enlisted men. The biggest role of the CSM was perhaps the advisory role that he played with the BC. It was vital in order to meet the needs of the soldiers, and sometimes to discipline them, to have a CSM who was in touch with the companies that he oversaw. Often enlisted men assumed that everything that came down from the battalion was from the CSM. That is often why tankers had a skewed view of the CSM and had the assumption that he was a disciplinarian and nothing more.[11]

This, of course, is false as much of the CSM's job is to do what is best for the enlisted men, and sometimes that means completing actions or implementing policies that are not popular with the lower-ranking soldiers. The CSM is an example of what tankers should be at that level, which is disciplined, level-headed and intelligent. The brigade level is where it starts for these senior NCOs to have an effect on the tanker at the company level. It is not that the division or corps CSM does not play a role in the molding of a tanker. But they simply do not have the interaction with the soldiers at the company level. Even in combat, the division or corps CSM would rarely stop by a COP or a JSS to see the soldiers. They simply do not have the time and they have subordinate CSMs for that.[12] The battalion leadership had the most influence over tankers during this period that was discussed. They gave mandates about when the vehicles needed to be looked after and then it was up to the companies to implement those orders. The first sergeant was then and will always be the standard bearer of a company. In the BDU era, they were always the ones with 10-plus years of experience, pressed uniforms, and mirror-shined tanker boots.[13]

In armor units during this time, every single action that took place was supervised by the first sergeant. That included physical fitness, weapons classes, gunnery, map or land navigation training, and anything soldier-level related that the company commander scheduled for the soldiers to complete. The first sergeant was the first standard bearer that soldiers saw when they entered their line units. It was up to him to be the disciplinarian of the company. He had to make sure that every soldier in the company was always in the right uniform, at the right place, doing the right thing, and there at the right time.[14] It was perhaps simpler for the first sergeant to supervise his company in an armor unit due to the fact that the company only has on average 65 soldiers compared to an infantry company that has on average 140. This also provides the first sergeant in an armor unit a chance to foster a closer bond with soldiers that perhaps was absent with other combat units. Tankers often were seen having barbecues after a PT test, gunnery, or a major achievement for the company. This was something that other pure battalions did not do and it was one of the many reasons that a sense of resentment was created towards the armor battalions during this time. There was this notion that tankers were lazy and did not focus on being soldiers which was the furthest thing from the truth; they simply were rewarded differently for their achievements and took every opportunity to have fun and do things that fostered a brotherhood.

Regardless of the battles that tankers were involved in during OIF, the one that will have etched the tankers into military history is "Thunder Run." It is difficult to explain just how important Thunder

Run was for the army and the reputation of the tankers. For many of the army leaders, this fight was supposed to be similar to *Desert Storm*.[15] The war was supposed to be over as soon as the coalition forces took Baghdad. Obviously, this is not what happened. However, the invasion of Baghdad was the brightest or one of the brightest moments for tankers during OIF. Tankers were able to showcase their discipline and military prowess as they moved quickly towards Baghdad, killing hundreds of enemy fighters and enemy tanks along the way. This trek to Baghdad also showed how powerless the enemy tanks were against the Abrams. It could be argued that it was during this invasion of Iraq that the enemy realized that they needed to change their tactics as the notion that they could stand up to the armor of the United States was disproved almost immediately. The tank crews constantly punished the older Soviet tanks as they made their way to their objective. The garrison training was never more evident than during this moment. The armored corps launched hundreds of main-gun rounds at the enemy with almost pinpoint precision.[16]

The platoon-level training was something that was also illuminated during the invasion. The training of the gunners is the sole responsibility of the tank commander. In the case of the officer's tank (PL, CO, BC), that duty falls to the section sergeant. The platoon leader often was a new tanker themselves and did not have the experience to train a gunner to complete the task that was needed for them to be successful. For the new tankers that enter into an armor unit, their gunner is the first leader that they encounter. With the section sergeants being aware of that, it was vital for the section sergeants to not only teach the gunners the vital aspects of tanking which include vehicle parts and maintenance; but to also teach them how to be a leader to younger soldiers. That leadership was vital as gunners, who were often young themselves, were asked to hurl large 120 mm main gun rounds at the enemy, killing those inside the other vehicle. The psychological aspect of that was important for tankers. SFC Williams had this to say about firing the main gun of an Abrams tank: "You have to teach the young gunners that yes tanking is fun, but essentially you are killing another human. Once the round leaves the main gun you can't get it back."[17]

That was one of the important pieces of training that was taught at the platoon level. Although the Abrams were a powerful tool for war, there needed to be some type of restraint and respect for the tank in order to lead one. This also played into the culture of tanking. Tankers as a whole respect the vehicle that they use. Knowing the consequences of firing the wrong type of round, at the wrong time, or killing civilians, were all things that tankers were taught and trained on in garrison. Gunnery evolved over time to be the cornerstone event for the armored corps. This is also an event that can be examined for the differences between combat jobs and, more importantly, the infantry. Gunnery is the non-combat event that all tankers work towards each year. The training and discipline of the tank crew are put on full display during gunnery as they show the battalion leaders their proficiency and accuracy. Tankers take gunnery very seriously. It can often look as though that is not the case because of the fun and entertainment that comes with going to gunnery, but that is merely a side effect of going to training for 30 days straight. Leaders in the armor knew that if they wanted to get the most out of their soldiers, they needed to let them enjoy their craft.[18]

This and the other aspects of the armor that have been talked about during this work were the heart of the armor. Tankers and their culture are different because they were meant to be different. They were meant to live on their tanks and to function as a tank crew. The brotherhood that was made due to that culture is what allowed tank crews, platoons, companies, and armor battalions to achieve the success they did during Operation *Iraqi Freedom*. The Abrams themselves are amongst the world's greatest tanks (if not the best). The sheer firepower and armor that Abrams brought to the battlefield were simply unmatched by the enemy. The Iraqi insurgents throughout this fight could not adequately withstand the might of the Abrams so they had to find a way to slow them down and were able to do that with the use of IEDs and DFPs.[19] Even the notion that tankers were not combat-effective or necessary because of this new tactic by the enemy proved to be false. The siege of Sadr City in 2008 proved how valuable tanks were to the coalition effort. The end result for the entirety of this war was the fact that tanks and tankers were invaluable. There were certainly instances where more

In Loving Memory of Fort Knox, Kentucky: "Death Before Dismount." (U.S. Army)

of an infantry effort was needed and tankers had to take a secondary role in the conflict, but never were they obsolete. The armored corps of the U.S. Army was the tip of the spear during OIF and the tankers performed their duties with courage, honor and military precision.

Endnotes

Introduction

1. U.S. Army War College. *The U.S. Army in the Iraq War: Surge and Withdrawal 2007–2011 Book 4* (Independently Published, 2019).
2. Robert Colella, *Battle for Baqubah: Killing our Way Out* (U.S.: I Universe, 2012).
3. Col. Jonathan Bender, interviewed by Andrew Wright I, Topeka, KS (via Zoom), May 22, 2021. Zoom recording located in personal office, Topeka, KS.
4. CSM Levares Jackson, interviewed by Andrew Wright I, Ft. Riley, KS (via Zoom), June 3, 2021. Zoom recording located in personal office, Topeka, KS.
5. LTC Nathan Davis, interviewed by Andrew Wright I, Topeka, KS (via Zoom), May 4, 2021. Zoom recording located in personal office, Topeka, KS.
6. Garrison is the time soldiers are located on their base in the United States. During this time soldiers train, and complete administration tasks prior to combat deployment.

Chapter 1

1. The United States Army Armor Training and Leader Development Strategy FY21, 17.
2. James Kelly Morningstar, *Patton's Way: A Radical Theory of War* (Annapolis, Maryland: Naval Institute Press, 2017).
3. 1SG Marshall Yuen, interviewed by Andrew Wright I, Topeka, KS (via Zoom), May 1, 2021. Zoom recording located in personal office, Topeka, KS.
4. 1SG Bryan Greenlee, interviewed by Andrew Wright I, Topeka, KS (via Zoom), May 12, 2021. Zoom recording located in personal office, Topeka, KS.
5. David E. Johnson, *Fast Tanks, and Heavy Bombers: Innovation in the U.S. Army, 1917–1945* (NY: Cornell University Press, 2003).
6. United States Army Press, *The History and Role of the Armor: US Army Armor School Ft. Knox, KY* (U.S.: Merriam Press, 1966).
7. Ibid., 32.
8. United States Army Press, *The History and Role of the Armor: US Army Armor School Ft. Knox, KY* (U.S.: Merriam Press, 1966).

9. 1SG Marshall Yuen interview.
10. The United States Army Armor Training and Leader Development Strategy FY21.
11. Ibid., 25.
12. 1SG Bryan Greenlee interview.
13. Jason Conroy and Ron Martz. *Heavy Metal: A Tank Company's Battle to Baghdad* (U.S.: Potomac Books, 2005).
14. CSM Joshua Bittel, interviewed by Andrew Wright I, KS (via Zoom), June 8, 2021. Zoom recording located in personal office, Topeka, KS.
15. Ibid.; 1SG Bryan Greenlee interview.
16. LTC Nathan Davis interview.
17. 1SG Bryan Greenlee interview.
18. Ibid.
19. LTC Nathan Davis interview.
20. 1SG Bryan Greenlee interview.
21. Ibid.
22. 1SG Marshall Yuen interview.
23. "Crawl, walk, run" is the army's way of ensuring that soldiers aren't overwhelmed with information. This idea allows small portions of information or training to be given to soldiers incrementally.
24. "Smoking" is physically correcting mistakes that soldiers make. Physical punishment is administered for misbehavior or disobedience.
25. 1SG Bryan Greenlee interview.
26. 1SG Zolemke, interviewed by Andrew Wright I, KS (via Zoom), June 7, 2021. Zoom recording located in personal office, Topeka, KS.
27. Ibid.
28. Place where armored and light vehicles are staged. Maintenance is also done on these vehicles in this area.
29. CSM Levares Jackson interview.
30. Army TM 9-1200-206-40-2 Maintenance Manual Abrams Tank (Washington, D.C. Headquarters of the Department of the Army, 2007).
31. LTC Nathan Davis interview.
32. Ibid.
33. 1SG Bryan Greenlee interview.
34. Ibid.
35. Ibid.
36. https://generalpatton.org/.
37. LTC Nathan Davis interview.
38. Galen Peterson, *Strike Hard and Expect No Mercy: A Tank Platoon Leader in Iraq* (U.S.: Koehler Books, 2021).
39. ATP 6-02.53 Techniques for Tactical Radio Operations. Washington, D.C. Headquarters, Department of the Army. Updated January 2016.
40. Pat White, "Task Force Iron Dukes Campaign for Najaf," *Armor Magazine* 113, no. 6 (2004): 7.

41. 1SG Bryan Greenlee interview.
42. Ibid.
43. LTC Nathan Davis interview.
44. Ibid.
45. Ibid.
46. Ibid.
47. Amos Fox, "On the Employment of Armor," *Armor Magazine* Winter 2019 Edition.
48. 1SG J. Andrade, interviewed by Andrew Wright I, KS (via Zoom), July 19, 2021. Zoom recording located in personal office, Topeka, KS.
49. 1SG Bryan Greenlee interview.
50. Ibid.
51. Ibid.
52. LTC Nathan Davis interview.
53. 1SG Bryan Greenlee interview.
54. A family of belt-fed, gas-operated medium machine guns that chamber the 7.62 × 51 mm NATO cartridge. The 240 has been used by the United States Armed Forces since the late 1970s.
55. 1SG Marshall Yuen interview.
56. Conroy and Martz, *Heavy Metal*, 23.
57. Ibid., 44.
58. Robert Zucchino, *Thunder Run: The Armored Strike to Capture Baghdad* (U.S.: Atlantic Monthly Press, 2004), 27.
59. Conroy and Martz, *Heavy Metal*, 33.
60. LTC Nathan Davis interview.
61. Zucchino, *Thunder Run*, 17.
62. 1SG Bryan Greenlee interview.
63. Col. Jonathan Bender interview.
64. Ibid.
65. 1SG Bryan Greenlee interview.
66. Ibid.
67. Ibid.
68. Col. Jonathan Bender interview.
69. Colella, *Battle for Baqubah*, 77.
70. 1SG Bryan Greenlee interview.
71. CSM Joshua Bittel interview.
72. 1SG Bryan Greenlee interview.
73. LTC Nathan Davis interview.
74. Ibid.
75. Ibid.
76. 1SG Bryan Greenlee interview.
77. Ibid.
78. Capt. Woodward, interviewed by Andrew Wright I, KS (via Zoom), June 6, 2021. Zoom recording located in personal office, Topeka, KS.

79. Col. Jonathan Bender interview.
80. Ibid.
81. https://www.benning.army.mil/Infantry/199th/2-16/ABOLC/Reporting.html.
82. "Top" is the name given to the company's 1SG.
83. Interview with U.S. Army retired master sergeant (19K) October 2022 via Zoom in Topeka, KS.
84. Ibid.
85. 1SG Bryan Greenlee interview.
86. Ibid.
87. 1SG Marshall Yuen interview.
88. Ibid.
89. Capt. Woodward interview.
90. Interview with U.S. Army retired master sergeant.
91. Peter Maass, "Thunder Run (Military Strategy in the Iraq War)," *The New York Times Magazine* (2003): 97.
92. CSM Joshua Bittel interview.
93. TM 9-1200-206-40 (1-5&P), CSM Joshua Bittel interview.
94. Ibid.
95. 1SG Darryl Bradley, interviewed by Andrew Wright I, Ft. Riley, KS, June 3, 2021. Recording located in personal office, Topeka, KS.
96. Ibid.
97. ATP 3-20.15 Tank Platoon (MCRP 3-10B.1).
98. Promotable indicates that the soldier is eligible to be promoted to the next rank.
99. ATP 3-20.15 Tank Platoon (MCRP 3-10B.1).
100. SFC X. Johann, interviewed by Andrew Wright I, KS (via Zoom), June 3, 2022. Zoom recording located in personal office, Topeka, KS.
101. Ibid.
102. Ibid. PMCIs are pre-mission checks of either military men or equipment.
103. SFC Timothy Williams Sr. interview. The rank of corporal is a lateral movement in rank. A corporal is an NCO while a specialist is not.
104. Ibid.
105. Ibid.
106. Capt. Woodward interview.
107. 1SG Bryan Greenlee interview.
108. ATP 3-90.1-Armor and Mechanized Infantry Company Team (Washington, D.C. Department of the Army).
109. 1SG Marshall Yuen interview.
110. ATP 3-90.1
111. Capt. Woodward interview.
112. Ibid.
113. 1SG Bryan Greenlee interview.
114. ATP 3-90.5 Combined Arms Battalion (Washington, D.C. Headquarters, Department of the Army, July 2021).

115. CSM Joshua Bittel interview.
116. LTC Nathan Davis interview.
117. Ibid.
118. Col. Jonathan Bender interview.
119. CSM Hardy interview.
120. Interview with U.S. Army retired master sergeant.
121. Ibid.
122. Ibid.
123. 1st. Sgt. J. Andrade interview.
124. Brian W. Neil, "Future Military Operations on Urbanized Terrain," *Marine Corps Gazette* 85, no. 7 (2001): 23.
125. SFC Timothy Williams Sr. interview; sensitive items are any equipment that is unique and valuable to military personnel This includes weapons, optics such as night vision, and BII on the vehicles.
126. Col. Jonathan Bender interview.
127. Ibid.
128. Interview with U.S. Army retired master sergeant.
129. "Zeroing" pertains to evaluating all the weapons on the tank and ensuring they can hit targets from short and long distances.
130. FM 3-20.21-Heavy Brigade Combat Team Gunnery (Washington, D.C.: Department of the Army, 2003).
131. Bruce Oliver Newsome and Gregory Watson, *M1 Abrams Main Battle Tank Manual: From 1980 (M1, M1A1 and M1A2 Models)* (UK: Haynes Publishing, 2017).
132. Ibid., 53.
133. FM 3-20.21 HBCT Gunnery.
134. 1SG X. Crandall interview.
135. Peterson, *Strike Hard*, 34.
136. LTC Davis, interview.
137. Ibid.
138. Col. Jonathan Bender, interview.
139. Ibid.
140. SFC Timothy Williams Sr., interview.
141. There is an SOP for nearly every aspect of military life in both garrison and combat.
142. Anthony Rose and Travis Brandon, "Training for Military Operations on Urbanized Terrain," *Armor* 116, no. 3 (2007), 26.
143. 1SG Bryan Greenlee interview.

Chapter 2

1. Headquarters, Department of the Army, TC 3-20.31, Training and Qualification–Crew, 2015.
2. Ibid., 4-1.

3. Conroy and Martz, *Heavy Metal*, 16.
4. Ibid., 17.
5. U.S. Government, *The U.S. Army in the Iraq War Volume 1: Invasion Insurgency Civil War 2003–2006* (Independently Published, 2019).
6. Conroy and Martz, *Heavy Metal*, 20.
7. Zucchino, *Thunder Run*, 13.
8. Conroy and Martz, *Heavy Metal*, 22.
9. CSM Levares Jackson interview.
10. "CSM Otis Smith Thunder Run," interview by Dr. Robert Cameron. A project of the Combat Studies Institute, the Operational Leadership Experiences interview collection archives firsthand, multi-service accounts from military personnel who planned, participated in and supported operations in the Global War on Terrorism August 2007. https://cgsc.contentdm.oclc.org/digital/collection/p4013coll13/id/735/rec/16.
11. Jamie Lowther and Charlie McGrath. "Tactical View: Facing Down the Fedayeen." *Ft.Com* (2003): 1.
12. A. Hills, "Hearts and Minds or Search and Destroy? Controlling Civilians in Urban Operations," *Small Wars & Insurgencies* 13, no. 1 (2002), 1–24.
13. Tim McLaughlin, "The Iraq war diaries of Lt. Tim McLaughlin," The War Diaries. *The Bronx Documentary Center* (March 15, 2013).
14. Michael D. Skaggs, "Tank-Infantry Integration," *Marine Corps Gazette* 89, no. 6 (2005), 41–43.
15. Rose and Brandon, "Training for Military Operations or Urbanized Terrain."
16. Maass, "Thunder Run (Military Strategy in the Iraq War)."
17. CSM Otis Smith interview.
18. "LTG David Perkins on Thunder Run," interview by Dr. Tony Carlson. A project of the Combat Studies Institute, the Operational Leadership Experiences interview collection archives firsthand, multi-service accounts from military personnel who planned, participated in and supported operations in the Global War on Terrorism May 2013. https://cgsc.contentdm.oclc.org/digital/collection/p4013coll13/id/3181/rec/9.
19. Ibid.
20. SFC Timothy Williams Sr. interview.
21. Army University Press, "The Drive to Baghdad," October 8, 2019. Military History Video, 51:28. https://youtu.be/O7pbW1QoPaI.
22. Interview with U.S. Army retired master sergeant.
23. Army University Press, "The Drive to Baghdad," 20:46.
24. Conroy and Martz, *Heavy Metal*, 27.
25. Ibid., 30.
26. James Kinnear and Stephen Sewell, *Soviet T-62 Main Battle Tank* (NY: Osprey Publishing, 2011).
27. Ibid., 22.

28. Kevin Benson, "A War Examined: Operation Iraqi Freedom, 2003," *Parameters* (Carlisle, Pa.) 43, no. 4 (2013): 119–23.
29. Conroy and Martz, *Heavy Metal*, 55.
30. Steven Zaloga and Peter Sarson, *T-72 Main Battle Tank 1974–93* (NY: Osprey Publishing, 1993).
31. Stephen Sewell, "T-72. T-64. T-80?? Why Three Tanks?" *Armor 107*, no. 4 (1998), 21.
32. Gregory Fontenot and E. J. Degen, *On Point: The United States Army in Operation Iraqi Freedom* (U.S.: Create Space Independent Publishing Platform, 2013).
33. LTC Ernest Marcone interview.
34. Ibid.
35. Peterson, *Strike Hard*, 13.
36. Capt. Woodward interview.
37. William R. Hawkins, "Iraq: Heavy Forces and Decisive Warfare." *Parameters* (Carlisle, Pa.) 33, no. 3 (2003): 61–67.
38. Mark Mazzetti, "The Battle for Baghdad Begins: Marine and Army Units Advance through Republican Guard Defenses; Mark Mazzetti, U.S. News Defense Reporter, is Reporting from the Headquarters of the 1st Marine Expeditionary Force, Commanded by Lt. Gen James Conway," *U.S. News & World Report* (2003), 1.
39. Thomas Mockaitis, *The Iraq War Encyclopedia* (U.S.: ABC-CLIO, 2013), 33.
40. "Firefights" are military engagements between the coalition forces and the Iraqi resistance.
41. Malcolm Nance, *The Terrorists of Iraq: Inside the Strategy and Tactics of the Iraq Insurgency 2003–2014* (U.S.: CRC Press, 2014), 23.
42. Conroy and Martz, *Heavy Metal*, 48.
43. Conroy and Martz, *Heavy Metal*, 33.
44. U.S. Army War College, *The U.S. Army in the Iraq War Volume 1*, 67.
45. LTG David Perkins interview.
46. Army University Press. "The Fight for Baghdad." August 2020, 50:12. https://youtu.be/d8uaFZAxzpw.
47. SFC Timothy Williams Sr. interview.
48. CSM Joshua Bittel interview.

Chapter 3

1. Zucchino, *Thunder Run.*
2. U.S. Army War College, *The U.S. Army in the Iraq War Volume 1*, 81.
3. Ibid., 56.
4. Ibid., 87.
5. Fontenot and Degen, *On Point*, 33.

6. Army University Press, "OIF: The Drive to Baghdad," YouTube. October 8, 2019. Military history, 19:52. https://youtu.be/O7pbW1QoPaI?si=hrCFpK9cJzdbAWZO.
7. The U.S. cavalry is composed of "troops" instead of companies, and "squadrons" instead of battalions.
8. Ibid., 36.
9. CSM Hardy interview.
10. Fontenot and Degen, *On Point*, 48.
11. U.S. Army War College, *The U.S. Army in the Iraq War Volume 1*, 89.
12. Jeffrey Noll, "The Battle of Samawah: Fire Support in the Urban Fight," *Infantry* 94, no. 6 (2005), 39.
13. U.S. Army War College, *The U.S. Army in the Iraq War Volume 1*, 97.
14. Ibid.
15. Ibid., 98, 99.
16. Skaggs, "Tank-Infantry Integration."
17. CSM Harding interview.
18. Garrison E. Haning, "Winning the Battle of Perception: How Self-Expression Shapes Warrior Identity," *Army* 64, no. 9 (2014), 26.
19. U.S. Army War College, *The U.S. Army in the Iraq War Volume 1*, 99.
20. Ibid.
21. Zucchino, *Thunder Run*, 17.
22. Ibid., 22.
23. "Col. Eric Schwartz on Thunder Run," interviewed by Robert Cameron. Operational Leadership Experiences Project, Combat Studies Institute, Fort Leavenworth, KS April 2007. https://cgsc.contentdm.oclc.org/digital/collection/p4013coll13/id/822/.
24. Conroy and Martz, *Heavy Metal*, 175.
25. Ibid., 176.
26. Ibid.
27. Army University Press, "The Drive to Baghdad," August 2020, 47:59. https://youtu.be/d8uaFZAxzpw.
28. Capt. Woodward interview.
29. Conroy and Martz, *Heavy Metal*, 176.
30. Ibid., 179.
31. Army University Press, "The Fight for Baghdad," 28:55.
32. Ibid., 28:55.
33. Ibid., 31:02.
34. Ibid., 31:24.
35. Zucchino, *Thunder Run*, 21.
36. Ibid., 57.
37. Army University Press, "The Fight for Baghdad," 32:00.
38. CSM Santiago interview.

39. Conroy and Martz, *Heavy Metal*, 180.
40. LTG David Perkins interview.
41. Army University Press, "The Fight for Baghdad," 31:02.
42. Zucchino, *Thunder Run*, 157.
43. LTG David Perkins interview.
44. Ibid.
45. Zucchino, *Thunder Run*, 122.
46. Army University Press, "The Fight for Baghdad," 30:20.
47. Conroy and Martz, *Heavy Metal*, 196.
48. Ibid.
49. Army University Press, "The Fight for Baghdad," 35:24.
50. Col. David Perkins interview.
51. Conroy and Martz, *Heavy Metal*, 197.
52. Ibid.
53. CSM Otis Smith interview.
54. Benson, "A War Examined: Operation Iraqi Freedom, 2003."
55. Dennis Steele, "Back with the 3-15," *Army* 55, no. 9 (2005), 38.
56. Ibid.
57. Nicolas Fiore, "The 2003 Battle of Baghdad: A Case Study of Urban Battle during Large-Scale Combat Operations," *Military Review 100*, no. 5 (2020), 127–39.
58. Col. David Perkins interview.
59. Conroy and Martz, *Heavy Metal*, 209.

Chapter 4

1. U.S. Army War College, *The U.S. Army in the Iraq War Volume 1*, 345.
2. Ibid., 346.
3. Ibid., 348.
4. U.S. Army War College, *The U.S. Army in the Iraq War Volume 1*, 347.
5. Capt. Peter Glass. Interview by Operational Leadership Experiences Project team with Combat Studies Institute, digital recording, March 29, 2006. Fort Leavenworth, KS. Digital recording stored on CD-ROM at Combined Arms Research Library, Fort Leavenworth, KS.
6. Dick Camp, *Battle for the City of the Dead: In the Shadow of the Golden Dome, Najaf, August 2004* (U.S.: Zenith Press, 2011).
7. Tyler Coley, *Ghosts of Fallujah* (Independently Published, 2018), 11.
8. Ibid., 75; "Task organized" is when a company or companies from one battalion is assigned to another in order to give them different capabilities. This often happens between armor and infantry units.
9. Coley, *Ghosts of Fallujah*, 64.
10. U.S. Army War College, *The U.S. Army in the Iraq War Volume 1*, 350.

11. John F. Sattler and Daniel H. Wilson, "Operation AL Fajr: The Battle of Fallujah-Part II," *Marine Corps Gazette* 89, no. 7 (2005), 12–24.

12. 1SG Marshall Yuen interview.

13. James T. Cobb, Christopher A. LaCour, and William H. Hight, "The Fight for Fallujah," *FA Journal* (2005), 22.

14. LTC John Reynolds, interview by Operational Leadership Experiences Project team with Combat Studies Institute, digital recording, March 14, 2006. Fort Leavenworth, KS. Digital recording stored on CD-ROM at Combined Arms Research Library, Fort Leavenworth, KS.

15. CSM Levares Jackson interview.

16. Sattler and Wilson, "Operation AL Fajr."

17. David Bellavia, *Remember the Ramrods: My Army Brotherhood in War and Peace* (U.S.: Mariner Books, 2022), 33.

18. David Bellavia, *House to House* (U.S.: Free Press, 2008), 67.

19. Ibid., 141.

20. Coley, *Ghosts of Fallujah*, 18

21. LTC Reynolds interview.

22. Maj. Erik Krivda, Interview by Operational Leadership Experiences Project team with Combat Studies Institute, digital recording, February 6, 2006. Fort Leavenworth, KS. Digital recording stored on CD-ROM at Combined Arms Research Library, Fort Leavenworth, KS.

23. SFC X. Johann interview.

24. Capt. Peter Glass interview.

25. Coley, *Ghosts of Fallujah*, 99.

26. LTC Rainey interview.

27. Coley, *Ghosts of Fallujah*, 23.

28. Capt. Peter Glass interview.

29. Ibid.

30. Capt. Peter Glass interview.

31. Amos Fox, "On the Employment of Armor," *Armor Magazine* Winter 2019 Edition.

32. Capt. Peter Glass interview.

33. CSM Hardy interview.

34. Coley, *Ghosts of Fallujah*, 74.

35. Capt. Woodward interview.

36. Maj. Erik Krivda interview.

37. Capt. Peter Glass interview.

38. Coley, *Ghosts of Fallujah*, 77.

39. Capt. Peter Glass interview.

40. Teresa Malcolm, "The Battle for Fallujah," *National Catholic Reporter* 42, no. 36 (2006), 15.

41. Capt. Peter Glass interview.

42. LTC Nathan Davis interview.

43. CSM Joshua Bittel interview.
44. Capt. Peter Glass interview.
45. Ibid.
46. Coley, *Ghosts of Fallujah*, 160.
47. Capt. Peter Glass interview.
48. Capt. Peter Glass interview.
49. Ibid.
50. 1SG Marshall Yuen interview.
51. 1SG Bryan Greenlee interview.
52. Capt. Peter Glass interview.
53. Coley, *Ghosts of Fallujah*, 65.
54. Capt. Peter Glass interview.
55. Ibid.
56. LTC Nathan Davis interview.
57. Ibid.
58. Capt. Peter Glass interview.
59. United States Army Press, *The History and Role of the Armor.*
60. Capt. Peter Glass interview.
61. David Bellavia, *House to House*, 31.
62. Ibid., 95.
63. Capt. Neil Prakash, interview by Operational Leadership Experiences Project team with Combat Studies Institute, digital recording, October 20, 2006. Fort Leavenworth, KS. Digital recording stored on CD-ROM at Combined Arms Research Library, Fort Leavenworth, KS.
64. William S. Nance, "The Armored Reconnaissance Squadron and the Mechanized Cavalry Group," *Armor* 115, no. 1 (2006), 7.
65. Capt. Neil Prakash interview.
66. Ibid.
67. Ibid.
68. Ibid.
69. Ibid.
70. Ibid.
71. Dale Andrade, *Surging South of Baghdad: The 3rd Infantry Division and Task Force Marne in Iraq, 2007–2008* (U.S.: Military Bookshop, 2010), 22.
72. Capt. Neil Prakash interview.
73. Ibid.
74. "Recon by fire" is engaging a building or area with a chosen weapon system to determine if there is an enemy present in the area. This allows for recon without sending in dismounted troops.
75. Capt. Neil Prakash interview.
76. Bellavia, *House to House*, 47.
77. LTC Nathan Davis interview.

78. Capt. Neil Prakash interview.
79. "Route security" is when vehicles or dismounted troops monitor a road for several hours to deter the enemy from planting an IED or setting up an ambush.
80. Capt. Neil Prakash interview.
81. Ibid.
82. Ibid.
83. CSM Timothy L. Mace, interview by Operational Leadership Experiences Project team with Combat Studies Institute, digital recording, April 19, 2006. Fort Leavenworth, KS. Digital recording stored on CD-ROM at Combined Arms Research Library, Fort Leavenworth, KS.
84. CSM Levares Jackson interview.
85. CSM Timothy L. Mace interview.
86. Capt. Woodward interview.
87. CSM Timothy L. Mace interview.
88. Ibid.
89. Nance, "The Armored Reconnaissance Squadron and the Mechanized Cavalry Group."
90. Vincent Foulk, *The Battle of Fallujah: Occupation, Resistance, and Stalemate in The War in Iraq* (U.S.: McFarland & Company Inc. 2007), 101.
91. 1SG Bryan Greenlee interview.
92. CSM Timothy L. Mace interview.
93. Ibid.
94. Ibid.
95. Interview with U.S. Army retired master sergeant.
96. William R. Hawkins, "Iraq: Heavy Forces and Decisive Warfare," *Parameters* (Carlisle, Pa.) 33, no. 3 (2003), 61–67.
97. Foulk, *The Battle of Fallujah*, 117.
98. Bellavia, *House to House*, 58.
99. CSM Timothy L. Mace interview.
100. Ibid.
101. SSG David Bellavia. Interview by Operational Leadership Experiences Project team with Combat Studies Institute, digital recording, July 27, 2006. Fort Leavenworth, KS. Digital recording stored on CD-ROM at Combined Arms Research Library, Fort Leavenworth, KS.
102. Ibid.
103. SSG Bellavia interview.
104. Julian Barnes and Amer Saleh, "This One Could be Really Tough; U.S. Forces Expect to Face House-to-House Fighting and a Real Hard-Core Foe in Fallujah; Baghdad; Baqubah, Iraq," *U.S. News & World Report* 137, no. 17 (2004), 68.
105. Bellavia, *Remember the Ramrods*, 17.
106. SSG David Bellavia interview.
107. Bellavia, *House to House*, 185.

108. SSG David Bellavia interview.
109. Ibid.
110. Bellavia, *House to House*, 102.
111. LTC Ernest Marcone interview.
112. LTC Nathan Davis interview.
113. Capt. Peter Glass interview.

Chapter 5

1. Michael Silverman, *Awakening Victory: How Iraqi Tribes and American Troops Reclaimed Al Anbar and Defeated Al Qaeda in Iraq* (U.S.: Casemate Publishers, 2011), 43.
2. Ibid., 54.
3. Jim Michaels, *A Chance in Hell* (U.S.: St. Martin's Press, 2010), 78.
4. Michaels, *A Chance in Hell*, 57.
5. Ibid., 54.
6. 1SG Marshall Yuen interview.
7. Michaels, *A Chance in Hell*, 42.
8. Ibid.
9. Ibid., 51.
10. Col. Sean MacFarland, interview by Operational Leadership Experiences Project team with Combat Studies Institute, digital recording, January 28, 2008. Fort Leavenworth, KS. Digital recording stored on CD-ROM at Combined Arms Research Library, Fort Leavenworth, KS. https://cgsc.contentdm.oclc.org/digital/collection/p4013coll13/id/2364/rec/1.
11. Michael Fumento, "Return to Ramadi." *The Weekly Standard* (New York, N.Y.) 12, no. 11 (2006), 23.
12. CSM Levares Jackson interview.
13. Col. Sean MacFarland interview.
14. Ibid
15. Ibid.
16. 1SG Darryl Bradley interview.
17. Fumento, "Return to Ramadi."
18. Silverman, *Awakening Victory*, 22.
19. Ibid., 33.
20. "Combat outposts" are reinforced buildings or structures that have been commandeered by the Army. Sniper positions and guard towers are then set up in order to have a base to patrol from. These outposts are generally selected from enemy-controlled portions of the city.
21. Silverman, *Awakening Victory*, 40.
22. Col. Sean MacFarland interview.
23. Ibid.

24. Dick R. Couch, *The Sheriff of Ramadi: Navy SEALs and the Winning of al-Anbar* (Naval Institute Press, 2008), 38.
25. MSG Daniel Hendrex, interview by Operational Leadership Experiences Project team with Combat Studies Institute, digital recording, September 14, 2006. Fort Leavenworth, KS. Digital recording stored on CD-ROM at Combined Arms Research Library, Fort Leavenworth, KS. https://cgsc.contentdm.oclc.org/digital/collection/p4013coll13/id/294/rec/11
26. Ibid.
27. Col. Sean MacFarland interview.
28. Ibid.
29. Michaels, *A Chance in Hell*, 44.
30. The 101st Airborne Division is located in Ft. Campbell, KY. This infantry unit was put under the command of Sean MacFarland for the operations in Ramadi.
31. Col. Sean MacFarland interview.
32. Ibid.
33. Michaels, *A Chance in Hell*, 67.
34. Ibid.
35. Ibid., 67.
36. Ibid.
37. Michaels, *A Chance in Hell*, 74.
38. Ibid., 77.
39. Col. Sean MacFarland interview.
40. Michaels, *A Chance in Hell*, 74
41. Ibid., 73.
42. LTC Nathan Davis interview.
43. Ibid.
44. Michaels, *A Chance in Hell*, 74.
45. A "sit-rep" is a report from the engaged commander that illuminates the number of enemy fighters, the location of both enemy and American forces, and any casualties.
46. "Danger-close" refers to some type of requested incoming aerial bombardment that will land 100 yards or less from friendly troops.
47. Col. Sean MacFarland interview.
48. Silverman, *Awakening Victory*, 43.
49. Michaels, *A Chance in Hell*, 72.
50. Maj. Joseph Albrecht, Interview by Operational Leadership Experiences Project team with Combat Studies Institute, digital recording, April 14, 2010. Fort Leavenworth, KS. Digital recording stored on CD-ROM at Combined Arms Research Library, Fort Leavenworth, KS. https://cgsc.contentdm.oclc.org/digital/collection/p4013coll13/id/1897/rec/3
51. Michaels, *A Chance in Hell*, 72.
52. Interview with anonymous U.S. Army retired master sergeant.
53. Ibid.

54. Michaels, *A Chance in Hell*, 74.
55. Ibid.
56. Ibid., 74.
57. Col. Sean MacFarland interview.
58. Ibid.
59. Ibid.
60. Ibid.
61. Ibid.
62. Ibid.
63. Col. Anthony E. Deane, *Ramadi Declassified: A Roadmap to Peace in the Most Dangerous City in Iraq* (U.S.: Praetorian Books, 2016), 16.
64. Ibid., 30.
65. Interview with anonymous U.S. Army retired master sergeant.
66. Deane, *Ramadi Declassified*, 17.
67. Col. Jonathan Bender interview.
68. Deane, *Ramadi Declassified*, 18.
69. Ibid., 16.
70. Silverman, *Awakening Victory*, 53.
71. Deane, *Ramadi Declassified*, 22.
72. Col. Sean MacFarland interview.
73. Silverman, *Awakening Victory*, 54.
74. Ibid.
75. CSM Garfield interview.
76. Col. Tony Deane, interview by Operational Leadership Experiences Project team with Combat Studies Institute, digital recording, September 3, 2008. Fort Leavenworth, KS. Digital recording stored on CD-ROM at Combined Arms Research Library, Fort Leavenworth, KS. https://cgsc.contentdm.oclc.org/digital/collection/p4013coll13/id/1453/rec/2
77. Ibid.
78 SFC Timothy Williams Sr. interview.
79. 1SG Marshall Yuen interview.
80. Anthony E. Deane, "Providing Security Force Assistance in an Economy of Force Battle," *Military Review* 90, no. 1 (2010): 80–90.
81. U.S. Army War College, *The U.S. Army in the Iraq War Volume 1*, 610.
82. Deane, "Providing Security Force Assistance in an Economy of Force Battle."
83. Tim Dyhouse, "Ramadi: Success Rides on the Marines' Shoulders." *Veterans of Foreign Wars* Magazine 95, no. 1 (2007), 12.
84. Silverman, *Awakening Victory*, 22.
85. Thomas E. Ricks, "Situation Called Dire in West Iraq Anbar Is Lost Politically, Marine Analyst Says." *The Washington Post*, September 11, 2006. https://www.washingtonpost.com/archive/politics/2006/09/11/situation-called-dire-in-west-iraq-span-classbankheadanbar-is-lost-politically-marine-analyst-saysspan/0d815991-c7fe-4aee-97ec-ba95ca9a5c00/

86. Ibid.
87. U.S. Army War College, *The U.S. Army in the Iraq War Volume 1*, 610.
88. Ibid.
89. Ibid.
90. Ibid., 611.
91. Deane, "Providing Security Force Assistance in an Economy of Force Battle."
92. Col. Sean MacFarland interview.
93. Maj. Joseph Albrecht interview.
94. Ibid.
95. In 632 CE, the prophet Muhammed died. After his death, in-fighting led to the division of the Muslim world, and the division brought about two factions, Sunni and Shi'a. The Sunni were the leading and prominent political party under the reign of Saddam Hussein.
96. Maj. Joseph Albrecht interview.
97. U.S. Army War College, *The U.S. Army in the Iraq War Volume 1*, 62.
98. Ibid., 62.
99. Maj. Joseph Albrecht interview.
100. Col. Sean MacFarland interview.
101. Maj. Joseph Albrecht interview.
102. Ibid.
103. Maj. Joseph Albrecht interview.
104. Silverman, *Awakening Victory*, 98.

Chapter 6

1. U.S. Army War College, *The U.S. Army in the Iraq War Volume 2*, 195.
2. Ibid.
3. "Operation Phantom Thunder Hits Iraqi Insurgent Strongholds," *Army* 57, no. 8 (2007), 78.
4. An explosively formed penetrator (EFP), also known as an explosively formed projectile, or a deep forma penetrator (DFP), is a self-forging warhead, or a self-forging fragment: a special type of shaped charge designed to penetrate armor effectively.
5. Colella, *Battle for Baqubah*, 33.
6. U.S. Army War College, *The U.S. Army in the Iraq War Volume 2*, 195.
7. Bruce Van Dusen, "The Surge: The Whole Story," August 2009, Military History. https://youtu.be/rSb5l_Rco24.
8. Ibid.
9. Colella, *Battle for Baqubah*, 35.
10. Ibid.
11. Peterson, *Strike Hard*, 126.
12. Colella, *Battle for Baqubah*, 30.

13. Ibid., 40.
14. Peterson, *Strike Hard*, 69.
15. Colella, *Battle for Baqubah*, 40.
16. Peterson, *Strike Hard*, 75.
17. U.S. Army War College, *The U.S. Army in the Iraq War Volume 2*, 198.
18. Colella, *Battle for Baqubah*, 96.
19. Van Dusen, "The Surge: The Whole Story," 31:15.
20. Ibid., 33:25.
21. Colella, *Battle for Baqubah*, 124.
22. Ibid., 242.
23. Ibid., 236.
24. Ibid., 242.
25. Steve Negus, Iraq Correspondent, "Uphill Struggle to Vanquish 'Icon of Jihad,'" *Ft.Com* (2007), 1.
26. Ibid.
27. Colella, *Battle for Baqubah*, 232.
28. Colella, *Battle for Baqubah*, 237.
29. Negus, "Uphill Struggle to Vanquish 'Icon of Jihad.'"
30. Colella, *Battle for Baqubah*, 220.
31. U.S. Army War College, *The U.S. Army in the Iraq War Volume 2*, 196.
32. Ibid.
33. "Operation Phantom Thunder Hits Iraqi Insurgent Strongholds," 78.
34. Ibid.
35. Maj. Jeffrey Noll, interview by Operational Leadership Experiences Project team with Combat Studies Institute, digital recording, November 25, 2012. Fort Leavenworth, KS. Digital recording stored on CD-ROM at Combined Arms Research Library, Fort Leavenworth, KS. https://cgsc.contentdm.oclc.org/digital/collection/p4013coll13/id/2901/rec/3
36. Ibid.
37. Negus, "Uphill Struggle to Vanquish 'Icon of Jihad.'"
38. LTC Ernest Marcone interview.
39. Colella, *Battle for Baqubah*, 231.
40. Ibid., 231.
41. U.S. Army War College, *The U.S. Army in the Iraq War Volume 2*, 200.
42. Ibid.
43. Ibid.
44. Ibid., 200.
45. Maj. Jeffrey Noll, interview.
46. U.S. Army War College, *The U.S. Army in the Iraq War Volume 2*, 200
47. Colella, *Battle for Baqubah*, 238.
48. SFC Timothy Williams Sr. interview.
49. U.S. Army War College, *The U.S. Army in the Iraq War Volume 2*, 202.

50. Ibid., 199.
51. Colella, *Battle for Baqubah*, 266.
52. Ibid.
53. Maj. Anthony Gore, interview by Operational Leadership Experiences Project team with Combat Studies Institute, digital recording, May 11, 2011. Fort Leavenworth, KS. Digital recording stored on CD-ROM at Combined Arms Research Library, Fort Leavenworth, KS. https://cgsc.contentdm.oclc.org/digital/collection/p4013coll13/id/2338/rec/
54. Maj. Anthony Gore interview.
55. Ibid.
56. U.S. Army War College, *The U.S. Army in the Iraq War Volume 2*, 215.
57. Colella, *Battle for Baqubah*, 250.
58. An army combat brigade consists of five combat battalions and at least two support battalions.
59. Petersen, *Strike Hard*.
60. Deane, *Ramadi Declassified*.
61. Neil Smith and Sean MacFarland, "Anbar awakens: The tipping point." United States Army and Marine Corps Counterinsurgency Center, Ft. Leavenworth, KS, 2008.

Chapter 7

1. Peterson, *Strike Hard*, 75.
2. U.S. Army War College, *The U.S. Army in the Iraq War Volume 2*, 360.
3. Ibid., 368.
4. Peterson, *Strike Hard*, 125.
5. The "green zone" is the area in and around the capital Baghdad. These areas house the leadership of Iraq and the military leadership of the United States.
6. David Enders, "Behind the Wall: Inside Baghdad's Sadr City," *The Virginia Quarterly Review* 85, no. 3 (2009), 120–35.
7. U.S. Army War College, *The U.S. Army in the Iraq War Volume 2*, 369.
8. Ibid.
9. Ibid.
10. Ibid., 370.
11. CSM Phillip Johndrow, interview by Operational Leadership Experiences Project team with Combat Studies Institute, digital recording, July 9, 2009. Fort Leavenworth, KS. Digital recording stored on CD-ROM at Combined Arms Research Library, Fort Leavenworth, KS. https://cgsc.contentdm.oclc.org/digital/collection/p4013coll13/id/1987/rec/20.
12. David E. Johnson, M. Markel, and Brian Shannon, *The 2008 Battle of Sadr City: Reimagining Urban Combat* (U.S.: Rand Publishing, 2013).
13. Ibid., 31.

14. Iraqi citizens are paid to go to NTC to help train the soldiers for their upcoming deployment.
15. Peterson, *Strike Hard*, 125.
16. Ibid., 100.
17. Peterson, *Strike Hard*, 205.
18. Ibid.
19. U.S. Army War College, *The U.S. Army in the Iraq War Volume 2*, 371.
20. Johnson, Markel, and Shannon, *The 2008 Battle of Sadr City*, 33.
21. Ibid., 39.
22. U.S. Army War College, *The U.S. Army in the Iraq War Volume 2*, 372.
23. Johnson, Markel, and Shannon, *The 2008 Battle of Sadr City*, 41.
24. Task & Purpose, "The Final Battle of Iraq: Sadr City." YouTube. October 26, 2001. Military History. https://youtu.be/ZRC29Gm_P0U.13:43.
25. Johnson, Markel, and Shannon, *The 2008 Battle of Sadr City*, 47.
26. Ibid., 48.
27. Peterson, *Strike Hard*, 214.
28. Ibid., 217.
29. Ibid.
30. Maj. Ryan Williams, interview by Angie Slattery Hundley with the Operational Leadership Experiences Project team with Combat Studies Institute, digital recording, November 1, 2012. Fort Leavenworth, KS. Digital recording stored on CD-ROM at Combined Arms Research Library, Fort Leavenworth, KS. https://cgsc.contentdm.oclc.org/digital/collection/p4013coll13/id/2840/rec/41.
31. Peterson, *Strike Hard*, 205.
32. Ibid., 207.
33. Ibid., 219.
34. Peterson, *Strike Hard*, 220.
35. Maj. Ryan Williams interview.
36. Task & Purpose, "The Final Battle of Iraq: Sadr City," 4:03.
37. Peterson, *Strike Hard*, 216.
38. Johnson, Markel, and Shannon, *The 2008 Battle of Sadr City*, 48.
39. Maj. Ryan Williams interview.
40. CSM Phillip Johndrow interview.
41. Johnson, Markel, and Shannon, *The 2008 Battle of Sadr City*, 58.
42. U.S. Army War College, *The U.S. Army in the Iraq War Volume 2*, 372.
43. Johnson, Markel, and Shannon, *The 2008 Battle of Sadr City*, 58.
44. Ibid., 59.
45. Ibid.
46. Peterson, *Strike Hard*, 222.
47. Johnson, Markel, and Shannon, *The 2008 Battle of Sadr City*, 60.
48. Ibid., 63.
49. Ibid.

50. Peterson, *Strike Hard*, 231.
51. Anonymous Army SSG, interviewed by Andrew Wright I, KS (via Zoom), June 3, 2023. Zoom recording located in personal office, Topeka, KS.
52. Johnson, Markel, and Shannon, *The 2008 Battle of Sadr City*, 65.
53. Ibid., 66,
54. U.S. Army War College, *The U.S. Army in the Iraq War Volume 2*, 373.
55. Enders, "Behind the Wall: Inside Baghdad's Sadr City."
56. Ibid.
57. Johnson, Markel, and Shannon, *The 2008 Battle of Sadr City*, 72.
58. Michael Gordan, "The Last Battle," *The New York Times Magazine* (2008), 34.
59. CBS News, "The Battle of Sadr City," November 9, 2010. Military Education, 12:46. https://youtu.be/E4Yhj6CSOkU.
60. Ibid., 4:36.

Conclusion

1. 1SG Marshall Yuen interview.
2. William Donnelly, "From Sergeant Snorkels to Drill Sergeants: Basic Training of Male Soldiers in the U.S. Army, 1953–1964," *The Journal of Military History* 86, no. 2 (2022), 399.
3. CSM Joshua Bittel interview.
4. SFC Timothy Williams Sr. interview.
5. Ibid.
6. Peterson, *Strike Hard*, 161.
7. Interview with anonymous U.S. Army retired master sergeant.
8. Ibid.
9. LTC Ernest Marcone interview.
10. 1SG Marshall Yuen interview.
11. Colella, *Battle for Baqubah*, 12.
12. Bellavia, *House to House*, 82.
13. Interview with anonymous U.S. Army retired master sergeant.
14. 1SG Bryan Greenlee interview.
15. Zucchino, *Thunder Run*, 29.
16. LTC Rick Schwartz interview.
17. SFC Timothy Williams, interview.
18. CSM Levares Jackson interview.
19. Colella, *Battle for Baqubah*, 115.

Bibliography

Primary Archived Sources

Brown, Todd S. 1974-2. Iraq War, 2003—Personal narratives, American. 3. United States Army. Infantry Division (Mechanized), 4th. I. Title. DS79.76. B774 2007 956.7044'342092-dc22.

McLaughlin, Tim. "The Iraq war diaries of Lt. Tim McLaughlin," The War Diaries. The Bronx Documentary Center (March 15, 2013).

Raghavan, Sudarsan. "19 Tense Hours in Sadr City alongside the Mahdi Army." *The Washington Post*, March 29, 2008.

Shaw, David. "First Sergeant in B Company 2nd Battalion, 6th Infantry, 1st Armored Division." *USASMA Digital Library*. September 2008.

Smith, Neil, and MacFarland, Sean. "Anbar Awakens: The tipping point," United States Army and Marine Corps Counterinsurgency Center, FT. Leavenworth, KS, 2008.

Primary Unpublished Sources (Interviews)

1SG J. Andrade, interviewed by Andrew Wright I, KS (via Zoom), July 19, 2021. Zoom recording located in personal office, Topeka, KS.

Col. Jonathan Bender, interviewed by Andrew Wright I, Topeka, KS (via Zoom), May 22, 2021. Zoom recording located in personal office, Topeka, KS.

CSM Joshua Bittel, interviewed by Andrew Wright I, KS (via Zoom), June 8, 2021. Zoom recording located in personal office, Topeka, KS.

1SG Darryl Bradley, interviewed by Andrew Wright I, Ft. Riley, KS, June 3, 2021. Recording located in personal office, Topeka, KS.

1SG X. Crandall, interviewed by Andrew Wright I, Ft. Riley, KS, June 7, 2021. Recording located in personal office, Topeka, KS.

LTC Nathan Davis, interviewed by Andrew Wright I, Topeka, KS (via Zoom), May 4, 2021. Zoom recording located in personal office, Topeka, KS.

1SG Bryan Greenlee, interviewed by Andrew Wright I, Topeka, KS (via Zoom), May 12, 2021. Zoom recording located in personal office, Topeka, KS.

CSM David Hardy, interviewed by Andrew Wright I, Ft. Riley, KS, June 3, 2022. Recording located in personal office, Topeka, KS.

CSM Levares Jackson, interviewed by Andrew Wright I, Ft. Riley, KS (via Zoom), June 3, 2021. Zoom recording located in personal office, Topeka, KS.

SFC X. Johann, interviewed by Andrew Wright I, KS (via Zoom), June 3, 2022. Zoom recording located in personal office, Topeka, KS.

LTC Ernest Marçone, interviewed by Andrew Wright I, KS (via Zoom), March 25, 2022. Zoom recording located in personal office, Topeka, KS.

1SG Schaffer, interviewed by Andrew Wright I, KS (via Zoom), June 3, 2021. Zoom recording located in personal office, Topeka, KS.

SFC M. Williams, interviewed by Andrew Wright I, KS (via Zoom), June 3, 2022. Zoom recording located in personal office, Topeka, KS.

SFC Timothy Williams Sr., interviewed by Andrew Wright I, KS (via Zoom), May 21, 2021. Zoom recording located in personal office, Topeka, KS.

Capt. Woodward, interviewed by Andrew Wright I, KS (via Zoom), June 6, 2021. Zoom recording located in personal office, Topeka, KS.

1SG Marshall Yuen, interviewed by Andrew Wright I, Topeka, KS (via Zoom), May 1, 2021. Zoom recording located in personal office, Topeka, KS.

1SG Zolemke, interviewed by Andrew Wright I, KS (via Zoom), June 7, 2021. Zoom recording located in personal office, Topeka, KS.

Primary Published Sources (Interviews)

Albrecht, Maj. Joseph. Interview by Operational Leadership Experiences Project team with Combat Studies Institute, digital recording, April 14, 2010. Fort Leavenworth, KS. Digital recording stored on CD-ROM at Combined Arms Research Library, Fort Leavenworth, KS. https://cgsc.contentdm.oclc.org/digital/collection/p4013coll13/id/1897/rec/3

Amyett, SSG Jimmy. Interview by Operational Leadership Experiences Project team with Combat Studies Institute, digital recording, July 31, 2006. Fort Leavenworth, KS. Digital recording stored on CD-ROM at Combined Arms Research Library, Fort Leavenworth, KS. https://cgsc.contentdm.oclc.org/digital/collection/p4013coll13/id/234/rec/1

Baker, Capt. Douglas. "Thunder Run." Interview by Robert Cameron. Operational Leadership Experiences Project, Combat Studies Institute, Fort Leavenworth, KS, April 2007. https://cgsc.contentdm.oclc.org/digital/collection/p4013coll13/id/686/rec/60

Barnello Jr., CSM William. "Thunder Run." Interview by Robert Cameron. Operational Leadership Experiences Project, Combat Studies Institute, Fort Leavenworth, KS, August 2007. https://cgsc.contentdm.oclc.org/digital/collection/p4013coll13/id/669/rec/10

Bayer, Col. Peter. "Thunder Run." Interview by Robert Cameron. Operational Leadership Experiences Project, Combat Studies Institute, Fort Leavenworth, KS, August 2007. https://cgsc.contentdm.oclc.org/digital/collection/p4013coll13/id/730/rec/11

Bellavia, SSG David. Interview by Operational Leadership Experiences Project team with Combat Studies Institute, digital recording, July 27, 2006. Fort Leavenworth, KS. Digital recording stored on CD-ROM at Combined Arms Research Library, Fort Leavenworth, KS. https://cgsc.contentdm.oclc.org/digital/collection/p4013coll13/id/264/rec/2

Deane, Col. Tony. Interview by Operational Leadership Experiences Project team with Combat Studies Institute, digital recording, September 3, 2008. Fort Leavenworth, KS. Digital recording stored on CD-ROM at Combined Arms Research Library, Fort Leavenworth, KS. https://cgsc.contentdm.oclc.org/digital/collection/p4013coll13/id/1453/rec/2

Formica, Col. Michael. Interview by Operational Leadership Experiences Project team with Combat Studies Institute, digital recording, April 21, 2006. Fort Leavenworth, KS. Digital recording stored on CD-ROM at Combined Arms Research Library, Fort Leavenworth, KS. https://cgsc.contentdm.oclc.org/digital/collection/p4013coll13/id/134/rec/1

Gaines, SFC Ronald. "Thunder Run." Interview by Robert Cameron. Operational Leadership Experiences Project, Combat Studies Institute, Fort Leavenworth, KS, April 2007. https://cgsc.contentdm.oclc.org/digital/collection/p4013coll13/id/662/rec/15

Glaser, Maj. William. "Thunder Run." Interview by Robert Cameron. Operational Leadership Experiences Project, Combat Studies Institute, Fort Leavenworth, KS, October 2005. https://cgsc.contentdm.oclc.org/digital/collection/p4013coll13/id/170/rec/12

Glass, Capt. Peter. Interview by Operational Leadership Experiences Project team with Combat Studies Institute, digital recording, March 29, 2006. Fort Leavenworth, KS. Digital recording stored on CD-ROM at Combined Arms Research Library, Fort Leavenworth, KS. https://cgsc.contentdm.oclc.org/digital/collection/p4013coll13/id/145/rec/1

Gore, Maj. Anthony. Interview by Operational Leadership Experiences Project team with Combat Studies Institute, digital recording, May 11, 2011. Fort Leavenworth, KS. Digital recording stored on CD-ROM at Combined Arms Research Library, Fort Leavenworth, KS. https://cgsc.contentdm.oclc.org/digital/collection/p4013coll13/id/2338/rec/

Hendrex, MSG Daniel. Interview by Operational Leadership Experiences Project team with Combat Studies Institute, digital recording, September 14, 2006. Fort Leavenworth, KS. Digital recording stored on CD-ROM at Combined Arms Research Library, Fort Leavenworth, KS. https://cgsc.contentdm.oclc.org/digital/collection/p4013coll13/id/294/rec/11

Hibner, Maj. David. "Thunder Run." Interview by Robert Cameron. Operational Leadership Experiences Project, Combat Studies Institute, Fort Leavenworth, KS, April 2007. https://cgsc.contentdm.oclc.org/digital/collection/p4013coll13/id/664/rec/5

Krivda, Maj. Erik. Interview by Operational Leadership Experiences Project team with Combat Studies Institute, digital recording, February 6, 2006. Fort Leavenworth, KS. Digital recording stored on CD-ROM at Combined Arms Research Library, Fort Leavenworth, KS. https://cgsc.contentdm.oclc.org/digital/collection/p4013coll13/id/185/rec/1

Kuo, Capt. Ryan. "Thunder Run." Interview by Robert Cameron. Operational Leadership Experiences Project, Combat Studies Institute, Fort Leavenworth, KS, April 2007. https://cgsc.contentdm.oclc.org/digital/collection/p4013coll13/id/661/rec/14

Laauwe, Maj. Brad. "Thunder Run." Interview by Lawrence Lessard. Operational Leadership Experiences Project, Combat Studies Institute, Fort Leavenworth, KS, February 2009. https://cgsc.contentdm.oclc.org/digital/collection/p4013coll13/id/2225/rec/64

Linn, Capt. Joseph. "Thunder Run." Interview by Robert Cameron. Operational Leadership Experiences Project, Combat Studies Institute, Fort Leavenworth, KS, April 2007. https://cgsc.contentdm.oclc.org/digital/collection/p4013coll13/id/671/rec/19

MacFarland, Col. Sean. Interview by Operational Leadership Experiences Project team with Combat Studies Institute, digital recording, January 28, 2008. Fort Leavenworth, KS. Digital recording stored on CD-ROM at Combined Arms Research Library, Fort Leavenworth, KS. https://cgsc.contentdm.oclc.org/digital/collection/p4013coll13/id/2364/rec/1

Mahaffey, Maj. Christopher. "Thunder Run." Interview by Robert Cameron. Operational Leadership Experiences Project, Combat Studies Institute, Fort Leavenworth, KS, August 2007. https://cgsc.contentdm.oclc.org/digital/collection/p4013coll13/id/729/rec/7

Mazurek, Capt. James. "Thunder Run." Interview by Robert Cameron. Operational Leadership Experiences Project, Combat Studies Institute, Fort Leavenworth, KS, April 2007. https://cgsc.contentdm.oclc.org/digital/collection/p4013coll13/id/676/rec/21

McNew, Maj. Tom. "Thunder Run." Interview by Robert Cameron. Operational Leadership Experiences Project, Combat Studies Institute, Fort Leavenworth, KS, May 2007. https://cgsc.contentdm.oclc.org/digital/collection/p4013coll13/id/962/rec/28.

Noll, Maj. Jeffrey. Interview by Operational Leadership Experiences Project team with Combat Studies Institute, digital recording, November 25, 2012. Fort Leavenworth, KS. Digital recording stored on CD-ROM at Combined Arms Research Library, Fort Leavenworth, KS. https://cgsc.contentdm.oclc.org/digital/collection/p4013coll13/id/2901/rec/3

Nussio, LTC Ricky. "Thunder Run." Interview by Robert Cameron. Operational Leadership Experiences Project, Combat Studies Institute, Fort Leavenworth,

KS, April 2007. https://cgsc.contentdm.oclc.org/digital/collection/p4013coll13/id/650/

Perkins, LTG David. "Thunder Run." Interview by Robert Cameron. Operational Leadership Experiences Project, Combat Studies Institute, Fort Leavenworth, KS, May 2013. https://cgsc.contentdm.oclc.org/digital/collection/p4013coll13/id/3181/rec/9

Prakash, Capt. Neil. Interview by Operational Leadership Experiences Project team with Combat Studies Institute, digital recording, October 20, 2006. Fort Leavenworth, KS. Digital recording stored on CD-ROM at Combined Arms Research Library, Fort Leavenworth, KS. https://cgsc.contentdm.oclc.org/digital/collection/p4013coll13/id/288/rec/1

Rainey, LTC James. Interview by Operational Leadership Experiences Project team with Combat Studies Institute, digital recording, April 19, 2006. Fort Leavenworth, KS. Digital recording stored on CD-ROM at Combined Arms Research Library, Fort Leavenworth, KS. https://cgsc.contentdm.oclc.org/digital/collection/p4013coll13/id/162/rec/1

Reynolds, LTC John. Interview by Operational Leadership Experiences Project team with Combat Studies Institute, digital recording, March 14, 2006. Fort Leavenworth, KS. Digital recording stored on CD-ROM at Combined Arms Research Library, Fort Leavenworth, KS. https://cgsc.contentdm.oclc.org/digital/collection/p4013coll13/id/456/rec/2

Richard, 1SG David. "Thunder Run." Interview by Robert Cameron. Operational Leadership Experiences Project, Combat Studies Institute, Fort Leavenworth, KS, August 2007. https://cgsc.contentdm.oclc.org/digital/collection/p4013coll13/id/724/

Schwartz, Col. Eric. "Thunder Run." Interview by Robert Cameron. Operational Leadership Experiences Project, Combat Studies Institute, Fort Leavenworth, KS, April 2007. https://cgsc.contentdm.oclc.org/digital/collection/p4013coll13/id/822/

Schwimmer, Capt. Evan. "Thunder Run." Interview by Robert Cameron. Operational Leadership Experiences Project, Combat Studies Institute, Fort Leavenworth, KS, April 2007. https://cgsc.contentdm.oclc.org/digital/collection/p4013coll13/id/663/rec/4

Smith, CSM Otis. "Thunder Run." Interview by Robert Cameron. Operational Leadership Experiences Project, Combat Studies Institute, Fort Leavenworth, KS, August 2007. https://cgsc.contentdm.oclc.org/digital/collection/p4013coll13/id/735/rec/16

Walker, SSG Chad. "Thunder Run." Interview by Robert Cameron. Operational Leadership Experiences Project, Combat Studies Institute, Fort Leavenworth, KS, August 2007. https://cgsc.contentdm.oclc.org/digital/collection/p4013coll13/id/728/rec/6

Primary Published Sources (Books)

Axelrod, Alan. *Patton: A Biography*. New York: Palgrave Macmillan, 2006.

Bellavia, David. *House to House*. U.S.: Free Press, 2008.

Bellavia, David. *Remember the Ramrods: My Army Brotherhood in War and Peace*. U.S.: Mariner Books, 2022.

Colella, Robert. *Battle for Baqubah: Killing our Way Out*. U.S.: I Universe, 2012.

Conroy, Jason, and Martz, Ron. *Heavy Metal: A Tank Company's Battle to Baghdad*. U.S.: Potomac Books, 2005.

Farina, Anthony. *Angels in Sadr City: A Soldier's Memoir of the Final Battle for Baghdad*. U.S.: Gold 5 Publishing, 2015.

Fisk, Matthew J. *Black Knights Dark Days: The True Story of Sadr City's Black Sunday*. U.S.: Warriors Publishing Group, 2015.

Kennedy, Kelly. *They Fought for Each Other: The Triumph and Tragedy of the Hardest Hit Unit in Iraq*. U.S.: St. Martin's Griffin, 2011.

Ludwig, Konrad. *Stryker: The Siege of Sadr City*. U.S.: Roland-Kjos Publishing, 2013.

Peterson, Galen. *Strike Hard and Expect No Mercy: A Tank Platoon Leader in Iraq*. U.S.: Koehler Books, 2021.

Tyler, Coley. *Ghosts of Fallujah*. Independently Published, 2018.

Secondary Published Sources (Books)

Andrade, Dale. *Surging South of Baghdad: The 3rd Infantry Division and Task Force Marne in Iraq, 2007–2008*. U.S.: Military Bookshop, 2010.

Bryars, Pepper J. *American Warfighter: Brotherhood, Survival, and Uncommon Valor in Iraq, 2003–2011*. U.S.: Barnhill House, 2016.

Camp, Dick. *Battle for the City of the Dead: In the Shadow of the Golden Dome, Najaf, August 2004*. U.S.: Zenith Press, 2011.

Cottam, Martha L., Joe W. Huseby, and Bruno Baltodano. *Confronting Al Qaeda: The Sunni Awakening and American Strategy in Al Anbar*. Lanham, Maryland: Rowman & Littlefield, 2016.

Couch, Dick. *A Tactical Ethic: Moral Conduct in the Insurgent Battlespace*. Annapolis, Md: Naval Institute Press, 2010.

Couch, Dick. *The Sheriff of Ramadi: Navy SEALs and the Winning of Al-Anbar*. Annapolis, Maryland: Naval Institute Press, 2008; 2013; 2010.

Deane, Anthony. *Ramadi Declassified: A Roadmap to Peace in the Most Dangerous City in Iraq*. U.S.: Praetorian Books, 2016.

Fontenot, Gregory, and Degen, E. J. *On Point: The United States Army in Operation Iraqi Freedom*. U.S.: Create Space Independent Publishing Platform, 2013.

Forty, Simon. The *History of Tanks*. U.S.: Demand Media Limited, 2015.

Forty, Simon. *Tank Warfare, 1939–1945*. PA: Pen and Sword Military, 2020.

Foulk, Vincent. *The Battle for Fallujah: Occupation, Resistance, and Stalemate in the War in Iraq*. NC: McFarland Publishing, 2006.

Green, Daniel R., and William F. Mullen III. *Fallujah Redux: The Anbar Awakening and the Struggle with Al-Qaeda.* Annapolis, Maryland: Naval Institute Press, 2014.

Hoffman, John. *Tip of the Spear: U.S. Army Small-Unit Action in Iraq, 2004–2007.* Independently Published, 2021.

Johnson, David E. Fast *Tanks, and Heavy Bombers: Innovation in the U.S. Army, 1917–1945.* NY: Cornell University Press, 2003.

Johnson, David, Markel, M., and Shannon, Brian. *The 2008 Battle of Sadr City: Reimagining Urban Combat.* U.S.: Rand Publishing, 2013.

Keane, Michael. *Patton: Blood, Guts, and Prayer.* Washington, D.C: Regnery Pub, 2012.

Kinnear, James, and Stephen Sewell. Soviet *T-62 Main Battle Tank.* NY: Osprey Publishing, 2011.

Lewis, Adrian. *The American Culture of War: The History of U.S. Military Force from World War II to Operation Enduring Freedom.* U.S.: Routledge, 2017.

Malkasian, Carter. *Illusions of Victory: The Anbar Awakening and the Rise of the Islamic State.* New York, NY, United States of America: Oxford University Press, 2017.

Michaels, Jim. *A Chance in Hell.* U.S.: St. Martin's Press, 2010.

Millett, Alan. *For the Common Defense: A Military History of the United States from 1607 to 2012.* U.S.: Free Press, 2012.

Mockaitis, Thomas. *The Iraq War Encyclopedia.* U.S.: ABC-CLIO, 2013.

Morningstar, James Kelly. *Patton's Way: A Radical Theory of War.* Annapolis, Maryland: Naval Institute Press, 2017.

Nance, Malcolm. *The Terrorists of Iraq: Inside the Strategy and Tactics of the Iraq Insurgency 2003–2014.* U.S.: CRC Press, 2014.

Newsome, Bruce Oliver, and Watson, Gregory. *M1 Abrams Main Battle Tank Manual: From 1980 (M1, M1A1 and M1A2 Models).* UK: Haynes Publishing, 2017.

Rayburn, Joel, and Sobchak, Frank. *The U.S. Army in the Iraq War—Volume 2: Surge and Withdrawal: 2007–2011.* Independently Published, 2019.

Russell, James A. *Innovation, Transformation, and War: Counterinsurgency Operations in Anbar and Ninewa, Iraq, 2005–2007.* Stanford, California: Stanford Security Studies, 2011; 2010.

Silverman, Michael. *Awakening Victory: How Iraqi Tribes and American Troops Reclaimed Al Anbar and Defeated Al Qaeda in Iraq.* U.S.: Casemate Publishers, 2011.

The United States Army Armor Training and Leader Development Strategy FY21.

United States Army Press. *The History and Role of the Armor: US Army Armor School Ft. Knox, KY.* U.S.: Merriam Press, 1966.

U.S. Army War College. *The U.S. Army in the Iraq War Volume 1: Invasion Insurgency Civil War 2003–2006.* Independently Published, 2019.

U.S. Army War College. *The U.S. Army in the Iraq War: Surge and Withdrawal 2007–2011 Book 3.* Independently Published, 2019.

U.S. Army War College. *The U.S. Army in the Iraq War: Surge and Withdrawal 2007–2011 Book 4.* Independently Published, 2019.

Yeide, Harry. *Fighting Patton: George S. Patton Jr. through the Eyes of His Enemies.* Minneapolis, MN: Zenith Press, 2014.

Zaloga, Steve. *Armored Attack 1944: U.S. Army Tank Combat in the European Theater from D-day to the Battle of the Bulge.* PA: Stackpole Books, 2022.
Zaloga, Steven, and Sarson, Peter. *T-72 Main Battle Tank 1974–93.* NY: Osprey Publishing, 1993.
Zucchino, Robert *Thunder Run. The Armored Strike to Capture Baghdad.* U.S.: Atlantic Monthly Press, 2004.

Secondary Published Sources (Videos)

Army University Press. "The Fight for Baghdad." August 2020. 50:12. https://youtu.be/d8uaFZAxzpw
"Leading a Tank Platoon." https://vimeo.com/441385080/ccb3501040

Secondary Articles

Baker, Douglas F. "Relevance of Armor in Counterinsurgency Operations." Army Command and General Staff Coll, Ft. Leavenworth, KS, 2012.
Barnes, Julian E. "A Thunder Run Up Main Street; Najaf, Iraq." *U.S. News & World Report* (2003): 32.
Barnes, Julian E., and Amer Saleh. "This One could be really tough; U.S. Forces Expect to Face House-to-House Fighting and a Real Hard-Core Foe in Fallujah; Baghdad; Baqubah, Iraq." *U.S. News & World Report* 137, no. 17 (2004): 68.
Benson, Kevin. "A War Examined: Operation Iraqi Freedom, 2003." *Parameters* (Carlisle, Pa.) 43, no. 4 (2013): 119–23.
Burton, Brian, and John Nagl. "Learning as we go: The US Army Adapts to Counterinsurgency in Iraq, July 2004–December 2006." *Small Wars & Insurgencies* 19, no. 3 (2008): 303–27.
Carroll, J. J. "Combined Arms Training for MOUT Operations." *Marine Corps* Gazette 87, no. 9 (2003): 58.
Charlton, John W. "OIF Digital Battle Command: Baptism by Fire." *The Army Communicator* 28, no. 4 (2003): 30.
Clark, Edward, III. "Insurgent Attack in Ramadi: Platoon Leader Recounts Urban Engagement." *Infantry* 98, no. 2 (2009): 33.
Ciccarelli, Daniel J., Charles W. Kean, and Brett G. Sylvia. "BCT Walk and Shoot: Training Tactical Leaders on Setting Conditions to Achieve Combined Arms Maneuver." *Infantry* 105, no. 3 (2016): 42.
Cobb, James T., Christopher A. LaCour, and William H. Hight. "The Fight for Fallujah." *FA Journal* (2005): 22.
Davie, H. G. W. "The Logistics of the Combined-Arms Army–the Rear: High Mobility through Limited Means." *The Journal of Slavic Military Studies* Volume 33, 2020—Issue 4.

Dehghanpisheh, Babak. "'This Ain't Over Yet'; Operation Phantom Fury Lived Up to its Name as American Soldiers Stormed Fallujah. On the Ground with the Marines." *Newsweek* (2004): 40.

Donnelly, William M. "From Sergeant Snorkels to Drill Sergeants: Basic Training of Male Soldiers in the U.S. Army, 1953–1964." *The Journal of Military History* 86, no. 2 (2022): 399.

Dougherty, William J., and Matthew B. Dennis. "Combined Arms Training and New, Emerging Theories on Training." *Infantry* 99, no. 3 (2010): 43.

Durante, Arthur A., Jr. "Soldiering in Sadr City." *Infantry* 93, no. 6 (2004): 41.

Dyhouse, Tim. "Ramadi: A Tale of Two Cities." *VFW. Veterans of Foreign Wars Magazine* 94, no. 11 (2007): 14.

Dyhouse, Tim. "Ramadi: 'Heart of an Insurgent Hotbed'." *VFW. Veterans of Foreign Wars Magazine* 94, no. 6 (2007): 22.

Elliman, Toby D., Molly E. Schwalb, Stephen Krauss, Peter Mikoski, and Amy B. Adler. "US Army Drill Sergeants: Stressors, Behavioral Health, and Mitigating Factors." *Military Medicine* 186, no. 7–8 (2021): 767–76.

Enders, David. "Behind the Wall: Inside Baghdad's Sadr City." *The Virginia Quarterly Review* 85, no. 3 (2009): 120–35.

Eshom, Scott D. "Full-Spectrum Bridging Operations in Iraq." *Engineer* 37, no. 4 (2007): 8.

Faris, John H. "The Impact of Basic Combat Training: The Role of the Drill Sergeant in the all-volunteer army." *Armed Forces and Society* 2, no. 1 (1975): 115–27.

Fiore, Nicolas. "The 2003 Battle of Baghdad: A Case Study of Urban Battle during Large-Scale Combat Operations." *Military Review* 100, no. 5 (2020): 127–39.

Foran, Heather M., and Amy B. Adler. "Trainee Perceptions of Drill Sergeant Qualities during Basic Combat Training." *Military Psychology* 25, no. 6 (2013): 577–87.

Foulis, Stephen A., J. M. Hughes, B. A. Spiering, L. A. Walker, K. I. Guerriere, K. M. Taylor, S. P. Proctor, and K. E. Friedl. "US Army Basic Combat Training Alters the Relationship between Body Mass Index and percent Body Fat." *BMJ Military Health* (2021): by military-2021-001936.

Fox, Amos. "On the Employment of Armor." *Armor Magazine* Winter 2019 Edition.

Fumento, Michael. "Return to Ramadi." *The Weekly Standard* (New York, N.Y.) 12, no. 11 (2006): 23.

Graham, William H., Jason A. Kirk, and Gary D. Calese. "Like no Other: The Battering Rams in Operation Iraqi Freedom." *Engineer* 37, no. 4 (2007): 4.

Grant, Greg. "U.S. Army Reworks FCS Brigade Structure." *Defense News* (Springfield, Va.) 21, no. 17 (2006): 8.

Haning, Garrison E. "Winning the Battle of Perception: How Self-Expression Shapes Warrior Identity." *Army* 64, no. 9 (2014): 26.

Hawkins, William R. "Iraq: Heavy Forces and Decisive Warfare." *Parameters* (Carlisle, Pa.) 33, no. 3 (2003): 61–67.

Head, William. "The Battles of Al-Fallujah: Urban Warfare and the Growth of Air Power." *Air Power History* 60, no. 4 (2013): 32–51.

Headquarters, Department of the Army, TC 3-20.31, *Training and Qualification – Crew*. 2015.

Hills, A. "Hearts and Minds or Search and Destroy? Controlling Civilians in Urban Operations." *Small Wars & Insurgencies* 13, no. 1 (2002): 1–24.

Kagan, Kimberly. "The Real Surge: Preparing for Operation Phantom Thunder." Institute for the Study of War, 2007. http://www.jstor.org/stable/resrep19537

Kitfield, James. "The Battle for Sadr City." *National Journal* (1975) 40, no. 19 (2008): 60.

Knapik, Joseph J., Michelle Canham-Chervak, Edward Hoedebecke, William C. Hewitson, Keith Hauret, Christy Held, and Marilyn A. Sharp. "The Fitness Training Unit in U.S. Army Basic Combat Training: Physical Fitness, Training Outcomes, and Injuries." *Military Medicine* 166, no. 4 (2001): 356–61.

Knapik, Joseph J., Shawn J. Scott, Marilyn A. Sharp, Keith G. Hauret, Salima Darakjy, William R. Rieger, Frank A. Palkoska, Stephen E. VanCamp, and Bruce H. Jones. "The Basis for Prescribed Ability Group Run Speeds and Distances in U.S. Army Basic Combat Training." *Military Medicine* 171, no. 7 (2006): 669–77.

Larew, Karl G. "From Pigeons to Crystals: The Development of Radio Communication in U.S. Army Tanks in World War II." *The Historian* (Kingston) 67, no. 4 (2005): 664–77.

Lowthier, Jamie and Charlie McGrath. "Tactical View: Facing Down the Fedayeen." *Ft.Com* (2003): 1.

Maass, Peter. "Thunder Run (Military Strategy in the Iraq War)." *The New York Times* magazine (2003): 97.

Maddox, Brian. "Checkmate on the Northern Front": The Deployment of Task Force 1-63 Armor in Support of Operation Iraqi Freedom." *Armor* 115, no. 2 (2006): 49.

Malcolm, Teresa. "The Battle for Fallujah." *National Catholic Reporter* 42, no. 36 (2006): 15.

Mazzetti, Mark. "The Battle for Baghdad Begins: Marine and Army Units Advance through Republican Guard Defenses; Mark Mazzetti, *U.S. News Defense Reporter*, is Reporting from the Headquarters of the 1st Marine Expeditionary Force, Commanded by Lt. Gen James Conway." U.S. News & World Report (2003): 1.

McEnery, Kevin. "Improving Professional Relevance in the U.S. Army Armor Basic Officer Leader Course." *Performance Improvement* (International Society for Performance Improvement) 56, no. 6 (2017): 18–27.

McKinney, Chris, Mark Elfendahl, and H. R. McMaster. "Why the US Army Needs Armor: The Case for a Balanced Force." *Foreign Affairs*. 92 (2013): 129.

Moore, John C. "Sadr City: The Armor Pure Assault in Urban Terrain." *Armor* 113, no. 6 (2004): 31.

Nance, William S. "The Armored Reconnaissance Squadron and the Mechanized Cavalry Group." *Armor* 115, no. 1 (2006): 7.

"Nasiriyah: The 'Wild West' of Iraq." *VFW. Veterans of Foreign Wars Magazine* 90, no. 9 (2003): 18.

Negus, Steve. Iraq Correspondent. "Uphill Struggle to Vanquish 'Icon of Jihad'." *Ft.Com* (2007): 1.

Neil, Brian W. "Future Military Operations on Urbanized Terrain." *Marine Corps Gazette* 85, no. 7 (2001): 23.

Noll, Jeffrey. "The Battle of As Samawah: Fire Support in the Urban Fight." *Infantry* 94, no. 6 (2005): 39.

"Operation Phantom Thunder Hits Iraqi Insurgent Strongholds." *Armor Magazine* 57, no. 8 (2007): 78.

Ozernoy, Ilana, and Julian E. Barnes. "Taking Fallujah; U.S. Forces Strike Iraq's Hard-Core Insurgents; Washington; Fallujah, Iraq." *U.S. News & World Report* 137, no. 18 (2004): 16.

Pechacek, Jim, and Reed Webb. "Crewman's Associate (CA) Cognitive Decision Aiding (CDA) Applications for the U.S. Army's Future Main Battle Tanks." *Expert Systems with Applications* 11, no. 2 (1996): 191–206.

Ricks, Thomas E. "A Light in Ramadi." *Army*, vol. 59, no. 3, 2009, 54.

Ripley, Tim. At U.S. Central Command, in Qatar. "Military Briefing: A New Iraqi Army?" *Ft.Com* (2003): 1.

Robinson, Paul. "The Surge that Failed." *American Conservative* (Arlington, Va.) 6, no. 15 (2007): 12.

Sattler, John F. and Daniel H. Wilson. "Operation AL Fajr: The Battle of Fallujah-Part II." *Marine Corps Gazette* 89, no. 7 (2005): 12–24.

Sewell, Stephen. "T-72. T-64. T-80?? Why Three Tanks?" *Armor* 107, no. 4 (1998): 21.

Shea, Neil. "Ramadi Nights." *The Virginia Quarterly Review* 84, no. 1 (2008): 6.

Sheikh, Fawzia. "Analyst: Tight Budgets Will Doom Modernization: NTC Changes Driven by New Heavy Brigade Combat Team." *Inside the Pentagon's Inside the Army* 18, no. 34 (2006): 1–12.

Simons, William. "Advanced Gunnery for the HBCT." *Infantry* 95, no. 6 (2006): 22.

Skaggs, Michael D. "Tank-Infantry Integration." *Marine Corps Gazette* 89, no. 6 (2005): 41–43.

Snakenberg, Mark K. "An Nasiriyah America's First Battle in Operation Iraqi Freedom." Army History, no. 76 (2010): 32–43. http://www.jstor.org/stable/26296788.

"Special Report: War in Iraq." *The Economist* (London) 367, no. 8319 (2003): 22–28.

Steele, Dennis. "Back with the 3-15." *Army* 55, no. 9 (2005): 38.

Svitkova, Katarína. "Cities, Warfare and Civilians Security: Concepts and Practice of Military Operations on Urban Terrain." *Obrana a Strategie* 15, no. 2 (2016): 51–68.

Ricks, Thomas E. "A Light in Ramadi." *Army* (Washington, D.C. 1956) 59, no. 3 (2009): 54.

Roper, Daniel S., and Richard L. Kiper. "The Rediscovery of Doctrine: The US Army and Counterinsurgency." *Security Challenges* 6, no. 1 (2010): 23–42. http://www.jstor.org/stable/26459468.

Rose, Anthony, and Travus Brandon. "Training for Military Operations or Urbanized Terrain." *Armor* 116, no. 3 (2007): 26.

Rosen, Nir. "Muqtada Al-Sadr and the Army of the Mahdi." *The Progressive* (Madison) 68, no. 6 (2004): 29.

Rowland, David B. "New Era of Engagement Requires Infantry Battalions to Adapt." *Army* 65, no. 2 (2015): 40.

Simms, Ben R., and Curtis D. Taylor. "The Battle for Salem Street." Army History, no. 65 (2007): 4–15. http://www.jstor.org/stable/26295268.

Terrell, Paul D. "No, the Honor Belongs to 1-64 Armor." *Armor* 113, no. 2 (2004): 46.

"The Battle of an Nasiriyah." *Marine Corps* Gazette 87, no. 9 (2003): 40.

Ukeiley, Scott E. "Reconnaissance and Surveillance: Combined Arms for the BLT." *Marine Corps Gazette* 80, no. 9 (1996): 35.

"US Forces Battle Insurgents in Ramadi, XINHUA." *WorldSources* Online (2004).

Waldman, Andrew. "Heavy Challenges." National Guard (1978) 64, no. 10 (2010): 30.

Walsh, Todd E. "The Fight for Kufa: Task Force 2-37 Armor Defeats Al-Sadr's Militia." *Armor Magazine* 113, no. 6 (2004): 26.

Ware, Michael. "Into the Hot Zone." *Time Canada* 164, no. 21 (2004): 26.

White, Emmett R. "FCS Ties Training, Rehearsal and Execution into One Package." *Army* (Washington, D.C. 1956) 57, no. 3 (2007): 84.

White, Pat. "Task Force Iron Dukes Campaign for Najaf." *Armor Magazine* 113, no. 6 (2004): 7.

Military Training Manuals

Army TM 9-1200-206-40-2 Maintenance Manual Abrams Tank. Headquarters in the Department of the Army. Revised 2007.

ATP 3-20.15—Tank Platoon (MCRP 3-10B.1).

ATP 3-90.1 Armor and Mechanized Infantry Company Team.

ATP 3-90.5 Combined Arms Battalion.

DA PAM 750-3 Soldier's Guide for Field Maintenance Operations.

FM 3-20.21 Heavy Brigade Combat Team (HBCT) Gunnery (Reprinted W/Basic Incl C1).

FM 3-20.21 Tank Gunnery.

FM 6-27 The Commander's Handbook on the Law of Land Warfare (Washington, D.C.: U.S. GPO, 2019), para. 1–19. The U.S. Army's manual on the law of land warfare specifically constrains commanders' use of military force in urban battles and exhorts the commander to exceed the minimal requirements of military necessity, humanity, honor, distinction, and proportionality when planning to use military force near civilians and non-combatants.

STP 17-19K1-SM Soldier's Manual, MOS 19K, Armor Crewman, Skill Level 1.

TC 3-20 Integrated Weapons Training Strategy (IWTS).

TC 3-20.21-1 Individual and Crew Live-Fire Prerequisite Testing.

TC 3-20.31-1 (Gunnery Skills Test).

TC 3-20.31 (Training and Qualification, Crew).

TC 21-306 Tracked Combat Vehicle Driver Training.

TM 9-1200-206-40 (1-5&P). M1A1/A2 Maintenance.

USARARMS PAM 360-20 Tank Platoon SOP.